MOBILIZING
MINDS

CREATING WEALTH
FROM TALENT
IN THE 21ST-CENTURY
ORGANIZATION

MOBILIZING MINDS

Lowell L. Bryan
Claudia I. Joyce

McGraw-Hill

New York   Chicago   San Francisco
Lisbon   London   Madrid   Mexico City   Milan
New Delhi   San Juan   Seoul   Singapore
Sydney   Toronto

The **McGraw·Hill** Companies

1 2 3 4 5 6 7 8 9 0   DOC/DOC   0 9 8 7

ISBN-13: 978-0-07-149082-5
ISBN-10:   0-07-149082-5

McGraw-Hill books are available at special quantity discounts to use as premiums and sales promotions, or for use in corporate training programs. For more information, please write to the Director of Special Sales, Professional Publishing, McGraw-Hill, Two Penn Plaza, New York, NY 10121-2298. Or contact your local bookstore.

This book is printed on acid-free paper.

CONTENTS

PART IV

IDEAS TO MOTIVATE
BETTER BEHAVIORS

PART V

CONCLUSION

PREFACE AND
ACKNOWLEDGMENTS

At this, the dawning of the 21st century, it is not surprising that the top leadership teams in large companies are having trouble finding their way to a new organizational model that fits the needs of the modern, digital, global economy. Nor is it surprising that frontline workers and midlevel managers are finding their work a hard struggle.

The economic changes that have taken place in the last 15 years have been profound. Adjusting to such changes takes time. New ideas arrive through trial and error. They don't spring up overnight as though from the head of Zeus.

The organizational innovations of the 1920s, which we refer to in this book as the "20th-century organizing model," were created to gain control of the large industrial companies that had emerged during the late 19th century. The innovators of that model—Alfred Sloan at General Motors and his counterparts at Standard Oil, DuPont, and other companies—were inspired by the ideas, propounded 30 years earlier, by Frederick Taylor and others. It took some six decades for those ideas to be refined by such thinkers as Peter Drucker and Marvin Bower and adopted worldwide.

Finding the organizing approaches that meet the needs of the 21st-century economy will undoubtedly come faster. The trial-and-error period of discovery has been underway for over a decade now. The purpose of this book is to help accelerate this process of organizational innovation, to speed it along faster than it otherwise might proceed.

As we undertook our research for this book, we drew upon the work of a wide variety of other thinkers. Our research drew us to reread-ing such classics as Alfred Chandler's *Strategy and Structure* and *Scale and Scope*, Antony Jay's *Management and Machiavelli*, and Charles Handy's *Gods of Management*. We read Peter Drucker's writings exten-sively. We also found *The Company*, written by John Micklethwait and Adrian Woodridge, to be particularly helpful in understanding the his-tory of how the organization of companies evolved over time.

We then turned to a number of recent books by those who are pon-dering the future of corporate organization. These included John Roberts, *The Modern Firm*; Eric Beinhocker, *The Origin of Wealth*; Tom Davenport, *Thinking for a Living*; Harold Leavitt, *Top Down*; and Thomas Malone, *The Future of Work*.

Our approach to organizational design is somewhat different from these other writers. We don't view ourselves as organizational theorists but as organizational strategists. We believe that organizational design should be thought about in terms of developing and implementing a corporate strategy. We believe that you can deliberately design organiza-tions to better fit the economic conditions of the 21st century and that you can take discrete initiatives to put such organizations in place. And, we maintain, companies that do so can create enormous new wealth for their shareholders.

*   *   *

In our years of working on organizational issues, we have been struck by the variety and intensity of the organizational debates between aca-demics, consultants, and HR professionals who work in the organiza-tional field. If you get very far in the field, you find yourself caught up in intellectual debates not just on the issues of trading off hierarchy ver-sus collaboration but also on such related issues as the benefits of cen-tralization versus decentralization, the role of management versus lead-ership, and organization design versus change management.

Harold Leavitt, of Harvard, describes much of this as the debate between "humanizers" and "systemizers" in his book *Top Down*:

> "Humanizers" focus on the people side of organizations, on human needs, attitudes and emotions. They are generally opposed to hierarchies, viewing them as restrictive, spirit draining, even imprisoning. "Systemizers," in contrast, fixate on facts, measurements, and systems. They are generally in favor of hierarchies, treating them as effective structures for doing big jobs. Humanizers tend to stereotype systemizers as insensitive, anal-retentive types who think if they can't measure it, it isn't there. Systemizers tend to caricature humanizers as fuzzy-headed, over-emotional creatures who don't think straight."[1]

In the past, these debates were relevant. After all, in the world economy of the 20th century, where the costs of interacting and transacting business were very high, the many different organizing models had different advantages and disadvantages. But in today's digital, global economy, many of these historic trade-offs lack meaning.

In a low-interaction-cost world, the issue is not whether hierarchy is better than collaboration or vice versa but how we can use *both* hierarchy and collaboration more effectively, enabling the liberation of talented people from dysfunctional organizations. Hierarchy and collaboration are, and will be, essential elements of all large, successful enterprises. The issue isn't centralization versus decentralization but rather *what* should be centralized and *what* should be decentralized. Similarly, modern companies need both better management and better leadership.

In a world where unproductive complexity is the common enemy, the trade-off of humanizers versus systemizers is a false one. Our feeling is that both sides miss the broader point. As we said before, we feel that in today's world, *both* hierarchy and collaboration have major roles to play. Indeed, the overwhelming opportunity is in the freeing of talented people from unproductive complexity, an emancipation that would enable them to use both hierarchy and collaboration more effectively. Yes, hierarchy and collaboration are, and will be, the essential elements of all large, successful enterprises. Simply said, we need ample doses of both of them.

Hierarchy, for instance, is efficient in setting aspirations, for making decisions, for assigning tasks, for allocating resources, for managing people not capable of self-direction, and for holding people accountable. Even in the 21st century, we need hierarchy to put boundaries around individuals and teams. It must be ensured that workers self-direct and self-organize their own work so that it furthers the interests of the shareholders, not just their own personal interests.

Hierarchy, then, is necessary. But it is large-scale collaboration, across the entire enterprise, enabled by digital technology that is the new element that opens the 21st-century corporation to a greater potential to create wealth. In small organizations, such as teams, natural mutual self-interest often drives people to collaborate. But if you want people to collaborate in a large organization, you need to create this mutual self-interest. You do this by holding talented, ambitious people not just individually but also mutually accountable for their performance in helping others in the organization (for the same reason, basketball players are measured on "assists" as well as points scored). Digital technology provides not just the means to enable efficient, effective large-scale collaboration but also the means to measure each person's assists to motivate them to collaborate with one another in a way not possible in the past.

●   ●   ●

In describing these opportunities, we will not be presenting solutions that are as specific as engineering blueprints but rather that are more on the order of pencil rough sketches ("directional strategies"). We are offering starting places in helping organizations redesign for the 21st century. We want to provoke corporate leaders to think deeply about the organizational issues of their company. We do not pretend to have the definitive answers for any particular company, nor do we offer suggestions for every possible situation.

While most of the ideas in this book have been put in practice by some organizations somewhere, no single company operates the way we propose. Rather than a best-practices book, then, this book is a call to action. It is up to each leader to create the "blueprints" for his or her own organization.

Given the sweep of the book, we had to draw boundaries as well. We decided to limit the focus of the book to the internal organization of the company. We do not, for example, explore the new opportunities to create "open system networks" with other entities outside the boundaries of the company.

We also limit our organizational ideas in this book to those workers who are engaged in "thinking-intensive activities." For all of our analyses, we draw on the definitions used by U.S. Bureau of Labor Statistics (BLS). The BLS defines such workers as people whose jobs require subjective judgment and problem solving. We call these workers "professionals and managers" throughout the book. The truth, of course, is that all workers think and that no bright line defines "thinking-intensive" versus "labor-intensive" jobs. But the often-unpleasant truth is that most of the jobs in most companies call for the use of only a fraction of each worker's thinking capacity. Our hope is that if the approaches described in this book become widespread, more and more workers will find themselves in jobs that make far better use of their thinking capacities.

Readers should be aware that there are many choices and variations to all the ideas described in this book and that some of our ideas are controversial. For example, some people think better of matrix structures than we do. In writing this book, we decided the reader would gain more from it if we took a point of view rather than not doing so and taking instead an "on the one hand, on the other hand" approach.

Finally, we want to emphasize that the ideas in the book represent our opinions and do not necessarily reflect the views of our partners at McKinsey & Company or of our Organization and Strategy Practices.

●   ●   ●

At the end of the day, the choices that are right for any given company will depend on its own particular circumstances. The best urban planning for a New York will be different than the best choices for a London. In addition, companies must think about the small things as well as the large (in terms of urban planning, one must not consider just the highways but also the transit lines, power grids, water lines, and sewage systems). And so it is not enough to consider how hierarchical authority will be used to manage the front line but also how corporate governance will work, how strategies will be created, how knowledge and talent will be mobilized, how performance will be measured, and so on. The sequence of which elements to change first will also depend on the company.

The need for these ideas is greatest in what we call "megainstitutions," by which we mean the very large, complex companies that have emerged in our modern global, digital economy. We use a list of the top 150 companies in the world ranked by market capitalization as a proxy for this category of companies. In 2005, each of the top 150 companies, on a weighted-average basis, had a market capitalization of over $80 billion, 116,000 employees, and a net income of over $5 billion. By a simple extrapolation, there will be 400 such companies that will exist by 2014 that will be as big as the 150th company on the list today. In the book we will also use the term "superclass" to represent the biggest and best of these megainstitutions. We use a list of the top 30 ranked by market capitalization as a proxy for this superclass.

●   ●   ●

We have drawn from a diverse range of sources to push our thinking.

In addition to the organizational theorists we've already mentioned, we drew heavily on the thinking of economists Ronald Coase, through his work on interaction costs and the theory of the firm, and David Ricardo on his theory of the source of economic "rents."

We would particularly like to thank our current managing director,

Ian Davis, for encouraging us in the first place to undertake the effort that led to this book. We would also like especially to thank Rajat Gupta, our former managing director, who was leading the Organization Practice when we decided to launch this effort. Further key support was provided by McKinsey's Strategy Practice, especially by Lenny Mendonca and Peter Bisson.

Janamitra Devan and John Horn contributed significantly to our thinking on the source of economic rents from intangibles. We also drew on the thinking of Bill Lewis, former head of the McKinsey Global Institute, and on the thinking of Diana Farrell, who currently heads that institute.

Many of the concepts in this book built upon Lowell Bryan's previous book *Race for the World*, coauthored by Jane Fraser, Jeremy Oppenheim, and Wilhelm Rall.

We also drew on thinking from the Global Forces project led by Ted Hall and Lenny Mendonca of McKinsey & Company in the mid-1990s. This included team members Byron Auguste and James Manyika (among others). This work was published in 1997, and it greatly advanced our thinking on the implications of falling interaction and transaction costs. More recently, we drew on thinking by James Manyika and Scott Beardsley on the economic importance of "tacit interactions" (that is, knowledge work). We also drew on some thinking from our firm's mid-1990s special initiative project led by Michael Patsalos-Fox and Jonathan Day on the Corporation of the Future.

Larry Prusak, who has authored or coauthored many books such as *Working Knowledge* and *In Good Company*, and John Hagel, who has also authored or coauthored several books such as *Net Gain* and *The Only Sustainable Edge: Why Business Strategy Depends on Productive Friction and Dynamic Specialization*, served as advisors to us as we undertook our research and developed our thinking.

We would also like to thank members of the Organization Practice of McKinsey & Company who contributed toward our thinking, including particularly Tsun-yan Hsieh, Mark Loch, Michael Rennie, and Warren Strickland.

We also appreciate the time taken by a variety of McKinsey directors to debate how the issues discussed in the book related to their various clients. In particular, we would like to thank Dominic Barton, Scott Beardsley, Roy Berggren, Peter Bisson, Jungkiu Choi, Toos Daruvala, Clay Deutsch, Bernie Ferrari, Olivier Hamoir, Odd Hansen, Tsun-yan Hsieh, Ari Kellen, Vik Malhotra, Lenny Mendonca, and Joydeep Sengupta. We also want to thank members of our firm who've worked with us in client work on issues related to this book, including Sandy Boss, Marla Capozzi, Saira Chaly-Burgess, Chelsea Clinton, Michael DiBiasio, Alex Edlich, Ben Huneke, Somesh Khanna, John McCormick, Osman Nalbantoglu, Pradip Patiath, Salim Ramji, Yossi Raucher, Ishaan Seth, Angus Sullivan, Rick Ung, Leigh Weiss, and Michele Zanini.

The actual content of the book drew on the work of a large number of McKinsey consultants. Somesh Khanna, Joydeep Sengupta, and Ari Kellen contributed to our early thinking. They produced their own distinctive points of view in their respective areas of interest. Michele Zanini led our team of consultants who worked on the research project itself. He contributed particularly on research into the changed economics of large companies over the last 20 years and on the issues of one-company governance. Kazuhiro Ninomiya was a constant contributor throughout. Other team members who contributed at different times include Alexis Bernard, Brandon Fail, Martin Glesner, Brian Goldman, Tim Kleinman, and Nicholas Ma.

Marla Capozzi worked with us particularly on the subject of dynamic management (Chapter 5); Leigh Weiss and Eric Matson worked with us extensively on the subject of formal networks (Chapter 6). Leigh Weiss also worked with us on talent marketplaces (Chapter 7). Michael Idinopolis contributed to the chapter on knowledge marketplaces (Chapter 8). Regine Slagmulder helped with the chapter on role-specific performance measurement (Chapter 10).

We received significant editorial support, particularly for the portions of the book that also appeared as articles in the *McKinsey Quarterly* or in McKinsey staff papers, from Lang Davison, Bill Javetski, and Saul Rosenberg. We also want to thank Simon London for his help.

We worked closely in writing this book with Erik Calonius, who showed enormous patience as we iterated through what seemed like endless drafts. With help from Tyeshia Cultess, Cornelia Cox bore the brunt of typing these drafts (one of us still insists on writing longhand rather than using a keyboard).

A special thanks goes to Erik Calonius, Brandon Fail, Eric Matson, Laura Habberstad, Leigh Weiss, and Cornelia Cox, who helped us pull the entire book together.

We would also like to thank our families for the support they provided us over the last three years as we worked on this effort.

MOBILIZING
MINDS

INTRODUCTION: MOBILIZING MIND POWER

WE BELIEVE THAT THE CENTERPIECE of corporate strategy for most large companies should become the redesign of their organizations. We believe this for a very simple reason: It's where the money is.

Let me explain: Most companies today were designed for the 20th century. By remaking them to mobilize the mind power of their 21st-century workforces, these companies will be able to tap into the presently underutilized talents, knowledge, relationships, and skills of their employees, which will open up to them not only new opportunities but also vast sources of new wealth.

We didn't come to this conclusion suddenly. In early 1999, we completed a book drawn from our research titled *Race for the World: Strategies to Build a Great Global Firm.*[1] This book was the end product of a major McKinsey-sponsored research effort focused on how companies could capture the opportunities that were evolving thanks to digital technology and the emergence of truly global marketplaces.

When we started the research in 1995, it was hard to make sense of what was happening. But gradually, we realized that a sudden fall in interaction and transaction costs (that is, the costs of people working with one another) was underway—due primarily to advances in digital technology

1

and the relaxation of geographic barriers to competition—and it was causing a fundamental transformation of the global economy. As a result, global markets for goods and services were forming and deepening across industries and geographies. All of a sudden, companies worldwide found they had an overabundance of strategic possibilities in terms of where they could compete, for which customers, in which services, and in which geographies. The simultaneous increase in economies of specialization, scale, and scope also created an abundance of choices in terms of how to compete (that is, as a focused specialist, as a cross-geographic acquirer, and so on). As opportunities opened for everyone, companies suddenly found themselves in a competitive free-for-all, which, in turn, led to an increase in the pace and intensity of competition globally.

Meanwhile, as global markets began to form in both goods and services and for capital and labor, nimble companies found an abundance of cross-geographic and cross-market arbitrage (for example, off-shoring) opportunities. This also began to commoditize the value added of local companies, firms that had previously relied on privileged access to those markets for their competitive advantage. Most important, the fall in interaction costs greatly increased the relative value of intangible assets (for example, talent, knowledge, reputation, and relationships) relative to tangible assets (for example, labor and capital).

When the book was being published, the dot-com boom and stock market frenzy were in full bloom. Stock market valuations were heading into the stratosphere. I have to admit that we, like many others, were a bit enraptured by the possibilities of the "new economy" (or what is now called the "digital age"). Then the stock market suddenly tanked, and the dot-com boom passed by.

When it was over, we were left puzzling about whether it had all been hype or if there had been a fundamental change in the global business environment that demanded companies to operate differently. And if the latter was true, *what* was the change and *how* did the companies cope?

As with most complex puzzles, the answer to this question unfolded at its own pace. One door led to another door, which led to another door.

•   •   •

One of the doors was opened by our clients. As we worked with them to pursue the kinds of strategies we had described in *Race for the World,* we began to realize that most of our clients lacked the organizational capabilities necessary to engage in the pursuit. In particular, they lacked the ability to mobilize the intangibles they needed for success. Moreover, the way most of their companies were being managed—with a focus on delivering next quarter's earnings—made it impossible for line management to find the time to focus on new strategic initiatives (or even to free up sufficient discretionary spending or the talent needed to explore the opportunities seriously). Furthermore, given the pressure to make earnings, most found it difficult to justify making any serious investments in unproven "high-risk" initiatives.

As companies expanded their scale and scope, we found that they were harder and harder to manage. Increasingly, individuals in essential positions found themselves in "undoable" jobs. We began to conclude that the organizing model that companies had been using in the 20th century was not working well in the 21st century.

But we were still left with our puzzle. Had the global economy really changed the business environment so much that it required companies to operate differently now from how they operated in the past? To answer this, in 2004 we decided to do a bit of forensics to gain a better understanding of what had changed economically. In this effort, I worked with a crack team, led by Michele Zanini from McKinsey's Boston office.

We began with the usual suspects, such as changes in returns on capital and growth rates in revenues, company by company. As Michele and I were sifting through the corporate records one afternoon, we saw something unusual: Despite the bursting of the bubble, the total profits and market capitalization of the largest 150 companies (ranked by market value) had grown at an unusually rapid rate even after having been

FIGURE I-1

Total Market Value of Top 150 Companies, 1970 through 2004*

(In billions of dollars)

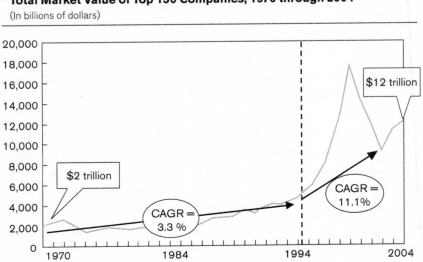

*Only U.S. companies and U.S. ADRs of foreign companies; constant 2004 dollars; 150 largest firms in terms of market capitalization each year (i.e., individual firms enter or exit list based upon their relative market capitalization). *Source: Compustat; McKinsey analysis.*

depressed by the overall market swoon. It clearly could not have all been a bubble, or their earnings and stock prices would have reverted to pre-1995 levels.

Economic theory holds that very large companies should have had difficulty growing profits and market capitalization so rapidly. Increasing complexity, after all, places limits on economies of scale and scope. Indeed, for most of the last decades, very large companies *have* had trouble growing. From 1970 to 1994, the total market capitalization of the largest 150 companies (as ranked by market capitalization) grew at a rate of only about 3 percent annually, or a little more than the GDP growth, and that is what we would have predicted due to the limits on managing increased complexity.[2]

But what was puzzling to us that afternoon was that from 1994 to 2004, the total market capitalization of the very largest 150 companies had grown rapidly for a full decade—11 percent per year (Figure I-1).

Even after the deflation of stock prices in the aftermath of the 1997 to 2001 stock market bubble, the ability of these companies to grow market capitalization was staggering—some $7.5 trillion in a single decade by just 150 companies. This was despite the obvious reality that these companies were dealing with far more *external* complexity in terms of the size and diversity of markets being served in the emerging global marketplace than companies had ever dealt with before.

Even more surprising was that the lion's share of these increases in returns was being driven by just 30 of the very largest companies. They had created some $3.4 trillion of the increased market capitalization! Some of this was from acquisitions and new share issuance, but most of it was from creating greater new wealth. These top 30 companies made up just 2 percent of the top 1,500 public companies, but they equaled 22 percent of the increase in net income and 22 percent of the increase in market capitalization of the 1,500 from 1994.

So what enabled these very large companies to grow their profits and their market capitalization so rapidly?

We knew, of course, that advances in technology had lowered interaction and transaction costs, which was in turn driving fundamental changes in the entire global economy. But what was different about these global economic changes that could have enabled these results?

•   •   •

The breakthrough came when we decided to use the *number of employees* as a proxy for the *internal complexity of the company* and *profit per employee* as a measure of profitability. When we looked at the 150 largest companies by market capitalization in 1984 by these two standards, we found strong linkages between profits and the number of employees, and (just as economists would predict) we found that the more employees (that is, the more internal complexity), the lower the profits per employee. But when we ran the top 150 companies in 2004 through the same analysis, the historic tight linkages disappeared and were replaced by the more scattered image shown in Figure I-2.

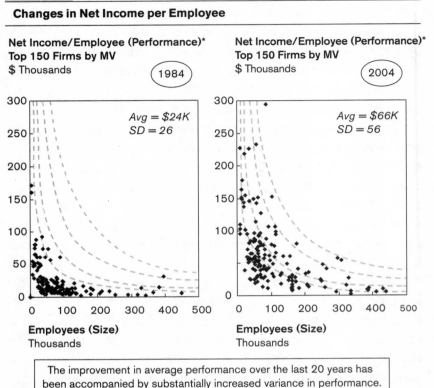

FIGURE I-2

Changes in Net Income per Employee

Net Income/Employee (Performance)*
Top 150 Firms by MV
$ Thousands
1984

Avg = $24K
SD = 26

Net Income/Employee (Performance)*
Top 150 Firms by MV
$ Thousands
2004

Avg = $66K
SD = 56

Employees (Size)
Thousands

Employees (Size)
Thousands

The improvement in average performance over the last 20 years has been accompanied by substantially increased variance in performance.

* Excluding outliers and companies with negative net income; constant 2004 dollars.

Source; Compustat; Global Vantage; McKinsey analysis.

What does Figure I-2 mean? It shows that in the 21st century, some companies have organizing models that are less constricted by internal complexity limits. They can be bigger and more profitable than any of the others. But exactly *which* companies can pull off this trick?

To determine that, we divided the organizations into "thinking-intensive companies" (that is, companies with more than 35 percent of their workers in thinking-intensive jobs that require subjective thinking and problem solving) and "labor-intensive companies" (that is, companies with less than 20 percent of their workers in thinking-intensive

jobs). What we found was that in the case of the labor-intensive companies, the linkage between profit per employee and total employees
really hadn't changed much from 20 years earlier. But, in contrast, the
average profit per employee in companies with heavy mixes (that is,
more than 35 percent) of thinking-intensive workers was higher, and
the dispersion in results was much greater (Figure I-3).

This was one of our eureka moments. Suddenly we could see why
some companies could earn higher profits per employee: The value of
thinking-intensive workers is derived from the value of their minds—
the ideas they develop and the decisions they make—and from the intangible by-products of that work, such as the knowledge, reputations,
and relationships they create.

This, of course, helped confirm our earlier research, which had in-
dicated that intangibles had become more valuable due to the changes
in the global economy. The value of such "mind work" is not highly correlated just to the volume of hours worked but also to quality. The economic conditions of the 21st century are enabling some companies to
create wealth by employing ever larger numbers of thinking-intensive
workers who translate mind work into high-quality, high-return intangibles.

Complexity Frontier

With that understanding in hand, we next began to probe what enabled
some of the companies to outperform the others. Could it be that the
top 30 had been able to use the technology of the digital age to defeat
complexity?

The short answer is no. When we looked at the top 30 by market
value, we saw clearly that an internal complexity limit still existed, even
for these companies. We started to call this a "complexity frontier," a bor-
der that limits how much profit per employee even the best-performing
companies can earn as their number of employees grows (Figure I-4).

But the notion of a complexity frontier helps explain how a company
can grow its market capitalization: If you want market capitalization

FIGURE I-3

Effects of Talent Mix

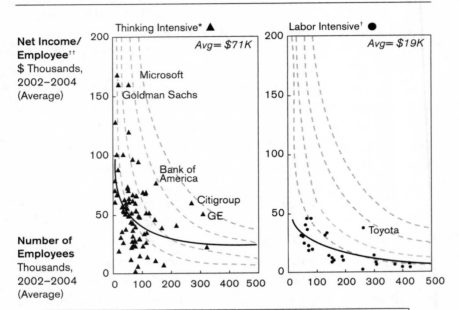

Net Income/ Employee††
$ Thousands, 2002–2004 (Average)

Number of Employees
Thousands, 2002–2004 (Average)

> • Emergence of outperforming companies in thinking-intensive sectors resulted in the recent dispersion of corporate performance.
> • Performance of companies in thinking-intensive sectors was generally better and varied more widely, ranging $10–150K+ per employee vs. $10–50K for companies in labor-intensive sectors.

* Sectors with >35% managers and professionals and substantial value derived from judgment and autonomy of–assets created by–highly specialized workers (e.g., researchers, traders); includes financial services, pharmaceuticals, health-care providers, high tech, media and entertainment, and GE.

† Sectors with <20% managers and professionals and substantial value derived from production or process-oriented labor (e.g., factory workers, cashiers); includes automotive, chemicals, diversified manufacturing (excluding GE), retail and utilities; not pictured, Wal-Mart (1533, 5.9).
Sectors with 20–35% workers on thinking-intensive jobs (not shown) displayed level more similar to talent-intensive names than labor-intensive names but to a lesser degree.

†† Constant 2004 dollars; includes companies only with positive average net income per employee, excluding extreme outliers.

Source: Global Vantage; McKinsey analysis.

FIGURE I-4

Employee Profitability Frontier*

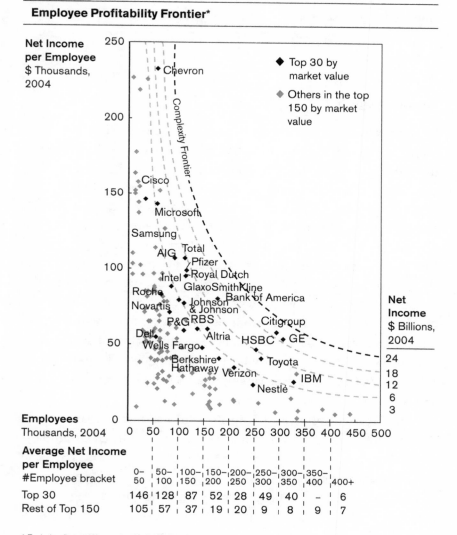

		0–	50–	100–	150–	200–	250–	300–	350–	
Average Net Income per Employee #Employee bracket		50	100	150	200	250	300	350	400	400+
Top 30		146	128	87	52	28	49	40	–	6
Rest of Top 150		105	57	37	19	20	9	8	9	7

* Excludes firms with negative net income in 2004.
Not pictured: Wal-Mart (1700, 6) and ExxonMobil (86, 295).

Source: Global Vantage; McKinsey analysis.

growth, either push back the internal complexity limits (which will enable you to increase profits per employee) or grow the number of people you employ (without diminishing the returns per person). Better yet, do both!

The Smoking Gun

Now that we had passed through that door, another one confronted us. Were the differences we were observing between the top 30 and the rest due to the particular industries these 30 firms were in? Or were they due to something about the companies themselves? To find out, we next compared the top 30 companies by market value to the next 30 largest in their same industries. Those results were startling. The top 30 employed an average of 198,000 workers (168,000 if you exclude Wal-Mart) while the next 30 employed only 117,000.

Now if you know nothing about the companies other than the number of their employees, you would expect a company with 100,000 employees to earn more per employee than a company with 200,000 employees because 100,000 should be less complex to manage. Indeed, the average top-150 company with 100,000 employees in 2004 earned about $50,000 per employee versus about $30,000 for an average top-150 company with 200,000 employees.

But when we compared the top 30 to the next 30 in the same industries, the top 30 actually earned *much more* per person despite employing far larger numbers of people—$83,000 per person versus $53,000 for the next 30 (Figure I-5).

As Michele Zanini said, "This is the smoking gun." Indeed, we realized the success of these companies (relative to others in their industries) was directly linked to their ability to generate "disproportionate rents" (that is, excess returns after paying for all costs including the costs of capital) from their thinking-intensive workforces.

It is significant that the differences in profitability are not based on industry differences. It means that the ability to create high profits per employee and to push back the complexity frontier lies within the

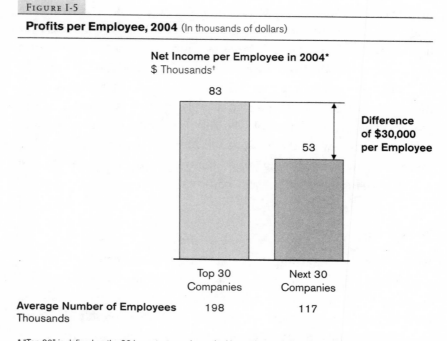

FIGURE I-5

Profits per Employee, 2004 (In thousands of dollars)

companies themselves—their organizational structures, their talents, their business models, and their intangibles—rather than in the industries in which they compete. Thus, the opportunities of the 21st century are internal to companies and, in particular, to how individual companies are organized. If you are effective in your internal organization, in other words, you can become far better at capturing profitable opportunities external to your company.

Does this mean that all you need to do is emulate the top 30 companies that have done so well over the last decade?

No. In the past few years, even the top 30 (excluding the oil companies as special cases) have been slowing down. From 2002 to 2005, their market capitalization has grown by only 6 percent compounded, much slower than the 11 percent they had marked for the decade before and much slower than the growth rates of other large well-run companies (Figure I-6). Also, their earnings grew at a rate of "only" 8 percent over these years. From 1992 to 2001, these well-managed, top 30 companies had benefited greatly from the emergence of a more digital, more globally integrated economy to monetize intangibles and thereby push back the classic limits between internal complexity (that is, number of employees) and profits per employee. But in recent years, they seem to have run into new limits. Now, as the 21st century continues and as these companies are getting larger and more diverse, they are facing new growth limits due to internal complexity.

The Core Problem

Why do even the best companies still face complexity constraints in the digital age? Why can't they capture the opportunities of today's global economy? Because even the best of today's companies were designed for another time. Although many of the top 30 are incredibly well managed, they are still employing an organizing model designed for an earlier era. They were built according to what we call the "20th-century model." They need to find new organizational approaches if they want to resume rapid growth in their earnings and market values.

Smaller, well-managed companies will soon be facing similar internal complexity constraints as they continue to get bigger and more diverse. Meanwhile, the great majority of other companies that are not nearly so well managed continue to operate far below the limits of the complexity frontier. Most companies still earn profits per employee at close to the same low levels earned in the 20th century because they have not become very adept at mobilizing the mind power of their workforces.

The truth is that almost all of today's companies, from the mediocre to the "superclass," were built primarily to mobilize their labor and capital assets—not the intangible assets that enable profits per employee to rise to levels never seen before. Trying to run a company in the 21st century with an organizing model designed for the 20th century places

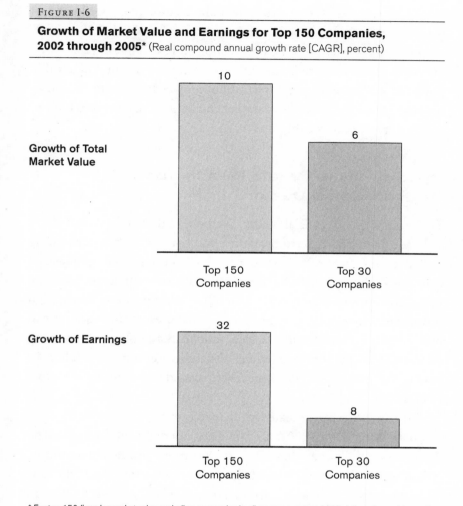

FIGURE I-6

Growth of Market Value and Earnings for Top 150 Companies, 2002 through 2005* (Real compound annual growth rate [CAGR], percent)

Growth of Total
Market Value

| | 10 | 6 |
| Top 150 Companies | Top 30 Companies |

Growth of Earnings

| | 32 | 8 |
| Top 150 Companies | Top 30 Companies |

* For top 150 firms by market value excluding companies in oil sector; constant 2005 dollars; the rapid growth in earnings of the top 150 is partly due to a number of large companies that experienced losses in 2002.

Source: Global Vantage; McKinsey analysis.

limits on how well a company performs. It also creates massive, unnecessary, unproductive complexity—a condition that frustrates workers and wastes money. The plagues of the modern company are hard-to-manage workforce structures, thick silo walls, confusing matrix structures, e-mail overload, and "undoable jobs."

As we will describe in this book, today's companies need to be re-designed to remove unproductive complexity while simultaneously stimulating the effective, efficient creation and exchange of valuable intangibles. They need to be designed so that they can mobilize mind power as well as labor and capital. In other words, we believe companies can overcome the organizational challenges they face and thereby create extraordinary wealth.

Opportunity to Create Wealth from Organizational Design

That's what this book is all about: We believe that all companies can increase their returns from talent and create wealth by designing organizations that fit the 21st century. We believe that companies can consciously design and build organizational interventions that can dramatically improve their ability to mobilize mind power to create high profits per employee. We believe further that these improvements can be derived from the companies' own, unique intangible assets enabling creation of "disproportionate rents" and thereby enormous wealth. We believe this applies not just to poorly managed companies but to well-managed companies too.

The opportunity to create wealth is massive.

If a company with 100,000 employees can make internal organizational design changes that add $30,000 more profit per employee (about the profit per employee difference from the top 30 and the next 30 in their same industries), for instance, it would add $3.0 billion in profits. Given that these profits would be what economists call "rents" (that is, additional earnings requiring no additional, marginal investment of capital or labor), at a 10 percent capitalization rate such increased profits would create $30 billion in new wealth.

If the company could also grow the number of employees earning such high levels of profit per employee by making such organizational design changes, the wealth creation potential would be much higher.

These numbers are not absurd. Remember that the average top-30 company added some $110 billion of market capitalization over the decade between 1994 and 2004 and that the great majority of that growth was new wealth creation, not new share issuance.

The opportunity is to build on each company's unique intangible assets. As David Ricardo famously observed, rents are created by having assets that are better in quality and unique in supply.[3] Today's unique assets are intangibles, which are specific to each company. The lesson to be taken from the impressive performance of the top 30 companies is not to try to imitate them. Companies, like people, have unique talents, organizational capabilities, and intangibles that have arisen from their own particular corporate histories. Trying to imitate a superclass company is like trying to imitate LeBron James's ability to play basketball or Yo-Yo Ma's ability to play the cello. Diversity of intangibles from company to company is good, not bad, for wealth creation. Each company needs to find its own place in the external marketplace by better designing how it operates internally so that it can better mobilize, deploy, and monetize the value from its own unique intangible assets that its talented people produce.

Think how big these opportunities can be. Every large company, even the most labor and capital intensive, has tens of thousands of workers in thinking-intensive jobs, not to mention tens of thousands of workers in other types of jobs who are producing only a fraction of the intangible value they could produce. We believe the target should be to improve profits per employee by 30 to 60 percent or more. As a comparison, the average top-30 company increased profits per employee 70 percent from 1995 to 2004 (from $39,000 to $67,000). The opportunities to improve the performance of workers just from increased *efficiency* alone are huge: Surveys show that a majority of workers in thinking-intensive jobs in large companies feel they waste from half a day to two days out of every workweek on unproductive e-mails, voice-mails, and meetings. For a worker paid $150,000 per year, this translates into wasting from $15,000 to $50,000 of what they are paid per year.

Meanwhile, the opportunities to improve the *effectiveness* of such workers are even larger. The opportunities to mobilize the latent intangible assets (that is, knowledge, skills, relationships, and reputations) of a company's workforce to improve performance are vast. How much business is lost simply because companies can't mobilize the knowledge and relationships within them to provide superior service to customers? How many of the average workers don't leverage the knowledge of the best workers? How many great business ideas are never realized because they never reach the right ears or because they are sunk by corporate politics or because no one has the time or spending capacity to pursue them? How many acquisitions deliver less than expected because the newly formed organization is dysfunctional and can't mobilize the mind power of the resulting merged company?

Organization Design as Corporate Strategy

For any large company, the value of better organizational design is literally in the tens of billions of dollars of increased market value. We believe the opportunity justifies the CEO and the top management team's devoting a large fraction of their total capacity to the internal task of designing and building the needed organizational capabilities. We believe organizational design is the key to unlocking the opportunities of the 21st century.

Relative to nearly any other equivalent investment of time or money a CEO and top management team can make, the potential returns from investing in improving the organization are truly remarkable. But redesigning the organization does not require enormous financial input. It is hard to conceive of how a company of 100,000 employees could spend more than a billion dollars on designing and building the strategic organizational capabilities described in this book. The decision to make such an investment is a no-brainer, especially if the opportunity is to improve profit per employee by $30,000 or more for 100,000 employees and to thereby create tens of billions of dollars of new wealth.

Moreover, unlike the external risks that accompany most strategic initiatives such as unpredictable competitors, the managing risks of organizational change lie largely within the control of the CEO and the top leadership team.

Strategic Imperative

We believe the time has come for corporate leaders to view organizational design as a strategic imperative and a high-return, low-risk opportunity for investment. The classic definition of "strategy" is a plan for actions to be taken with which to gain competitive advantage. Using this definition, we believe corporate leaders need to invest more energy than they have invested in the past in taking actions needed to create the strategic organizational capabilities that will enable their companies to thrive no matter what conditions they meet.

These strategic organizational capabilities will often take years of sustained effort to put in place, but they will pay off in terms of enduring competitive advantage. We believe furthermore that most CEOs will find that they will gain more leverage from focusing on organizational design than they will gain from nearly anything else they can do. Under this theory, you can't control the weather, but you can design a ship and equip it with a crew that can navigate the ocean under all weather conditions.

This is not to say putting a new organizational model in place is easy. Many top leaders are more comfortable making a major acquisition than attempting a major organizational change. The organizational inertia in a large company is often considerable. Organizational design work is hard and time-consuming, and organizational change usually requires dealing with difficult personality issues and corporate politics. Many CEOs would much rather make "big" strategic decisions than make "small" decisions as to where and how to compete or how to resolve internal organizational issues.

Yet, we argue, organizational design is where the money is in the

21st century. Only the corporate leaders can address enterprisewide organizational issues. If they want to create wealth, leaders need to focus their energy and their minds on making their organizations work better.

The Road Forward

So what do we propose?

Most of this book is about the nuts and bolts of designing an organization to capture the opportunities of the 21st century. The first chapter focuses on understanding the complexity facing large companies that are still using an organizing model designed for the 20th century instead of adapting their organizations to the new digital age. The second chapter describes how to think about organizational design within the context of the history of organizational development, and it describes nine ideas to better capture opportunities in the 21st century.

We then devote a chapter to each idea. Which ideas are the most important will vary with the company.

The first ideas are about how to manage better given the requirements of the 21st century. In Chapter 3, we describe opportunities for already well managed companies to remove complexity from their management structures by improving how they use hierarchical authority to drive performance. Specifically, we offer some ideas about how to create a backbone line hierarchy and "frontline field commanders" to improve the ability of managers to mobilize not just labor and capital but also mind power. This set of ideas is most helpful for companies that are finding that their internal complexity is making them hard to manage.

In Chapter 4, we offer ideas about how to move to a "partnership at the top" that combines approaches to one-company governance drawn from best-practice public companies and large private partnerships to create the conditions needed to enable large-scale, enterprisewide collaboration. This set of ideas is most helpful to companies afflicted with thick silo walls, which cause them to have trouble operating as single, integrated firms.

We offer some new ideas in Chapter 5 on how to manage companies dynamically so that they can balance their need to deliver operating earnings with their need to discover, simultaneously, new strategies to create wealth in a rapidly changing world. In particular, we focus on how a portfolio-of-initiatives approach to strategy, using staged gate investment practices, can help companies navigate the confusion, complexity, and uncertainty of today's rapidly changing digital economy to find intangible-based and high-return, low-risk opportunities. These ideas are most helpful for companies that are finding it difficult to grow earnings and to balance short-term versus long-term trade-offs.

We then offer some new ideas in Chapters 6, 7, and 8 for how to enable intangibles to flow better through large companies. As the digital age comes into its own, these ideas, which include formal networks, talent marketplaces, and knowledge marketplaces, are only now becoming possible.

Within companies, formal networks provide the organizational structures to harness the power of the natural communities of mutual interest that have emerged spontaneously in the digital age. A talent marketplace enables managers to "pull" the best talent, given their needs, from large pools of talent, while simultaneously giving that talent a greater choice over assignments to find the job that best fits their skills and development needs. A knowledge marketplace enables companies to motivate knowledge creators and knowledge seekers to exchange knowledge out of mutual self-interest. Each of these approaches enables the removal of unproductive complexity while stimulating the efficient, effective mobilization of mind power. These ideas have relevance to nearly every company, although poorly managed companies will find that before they can pursue them, they first need to address their management challenges.

The final set of ideas is aimed at modifying internal financial performance metrics and the evaluation of individuals in order to change the behaviors of all of a company's professionals and managers. We believe almost all companies are far too focused on producing accounting earnings and accounting returns on capital when they should be focused instead on creating increasing economic returns from intangibles. Furthermore, they rely too heavily on measures of individual accounta- bility and not enough on measures of mutual accountability, thereby promoting dysfunctional behaviors. In Chapters 9 and 10 we will be offering some far-reaching—some would even say radical—ideas that involve fundamentally redesigning a firm's internal financial perform- ance measurement and performance evaluation systems so that they will motivate and drive better, more economic, wealth-creating behaviors.

The last chapter explains how to pursue organizational design as a corporate strategy. It lays out an approach to converting rough-sketch organizational ideas, such as those described in this book, into actual practice without taking excessive risk. This chapter also describes how companies need to put the same energy and focus into designing their own organizations that they have historically devoted to their design of new production processes or new products or to their entry into new markets.

●　●　●

If you are intrigued by our premise, let us explain in the following chap- ters how it really could be done.

Lowell L. Bryan
November 1, 2006

PART I

A NEW
MODEL

1

OPPORTUNITY FOR
BETTER DESIGN

IN THE CLASSIC 1936 FILM *Modern Times,* Charlie Chaplin
was found struggling to cope with the industrial age's idea
of work: Reporting to an assembly line with the task of tight-
ening the bolts on an endless stream of machine parts, the
Little Tramp finds himself unable to keep up, and he is eventually sucked into the cogs and wheels and devoured by the
industrial machine.

Today, we see ourselves falling into a similar fate through
the eyes of Dilbert, only in his case it is a sentence of eternal
frustration, spent doing endless hours of pointless work
within the fluorescent-lit cubicles of the modern white-collar
work-pen.

Having passed through the organizational angst of the
industrial age, we now find ourselves in the digital age, facing a new set of problems.

Ask any midlevel professional or manager at almost any
large company—even a very successful one—and he or she
will tell you that the growing complexity of work is becoming a greater and greater problem.

Surveys confirm the symptoms of the disease, which include e-mail and voice-mail overload, task forces that go nowhere, pointless meetings, delays in making decisions because of scheduling conflicts, too much raw data and not enough information, and challenges in getting the knowledge one needs because of organizational silos. The result is long hours, gobbled lunches at one's desk, and strained personal relationships—with too little progress or productivity to show for it (Figure 1-1).

One survey by the research firm Net Future Institute (NFI) showed that nearly 75 percent of senior managers consider the workload of people in their department to be too heavy. Another survey by the same firm found that most people do their best business thinking not while at work but while commuting to work or in their home. Why? Because that's when they finally get some time to think![1]

The increasing frustration of the workforce is symptomatic of an even more fundamental issue: the organization of most companies today—and how it limits the ability of talented people to perform and take full advantage of the opportunities of the 21st century. The modern, "thinking" company should be a fluid and fast-moving creature, in which its workers discover knowledge and exchange it with their peers, collaborating with others to create value.

The problem, however, is that most of today's large companies fall well short of creating conditions that maximize the productivity of their thinking, problem-solving, self-directed people. Too bad this thinking machine isn't working nearly as well as it should be.

Unproductive Complexity

For a while in the 1990s, we thought that digital technology would enable us to overcome our communication challenges. Interaction costs, indeed, have been falling toward zero. This fall in interaction costs has enabled well-managed companies to leverage their management capabilities. It has greatly helped managers and subordinates to interact with one another. It has enabled workers to collaborate with one another as well and to access public knowledge from the outside world.

FIGURE 1-1

Struggling with Complexity (Percent)

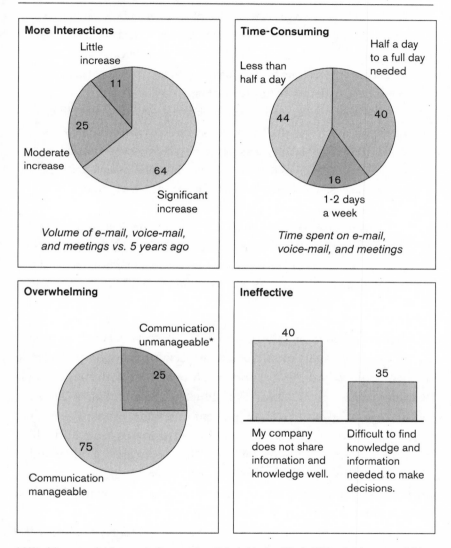

More Interactions

Little increase — 11

Moderate increase — 25

Significant increase — 64

Volume of e-mail, voice-mail, and meetings vs. 5 years ago

Time-Consuming

Less than half a day — 44

Half a day to a full day needed — 40

1-2 days a week — 16

Time spent on e-mail, voice-mail, and meetings

Overwhelming

Communication unmanageable* — 25

Communication manageable — 75

Ineffective

40 — My company does not share information and knowledge well.

35 — Difficult to find knowledge and information needed to make decisions.

* 80% of those reporting "communication unmanageable" admit having difficulty fulfilling their key responsibilities.
Source: Electronic survey of 7,800 global executives who are McKinsey Quarterly *readers in July 2005, excluding results from small companies. Survey may be biased by underestimating problem since many executives who are truly overwhelmed are unlikely to take the time to complete surveys.*

INTERACTION COSTS

Interaction costs involve searching for information and knowledge, co-ordinating activities and exchanges, and monitoring and controlling the performance of others within the same firm. Ronald Coase is widely credited with identifying the economic importance of interaction costs in his 1937 paper The Natu re of the Firm."

We do not usually spend much time thinking about interaction costs. Rather, when we think about the costs of production within a firm, we tend to think about the costs of the tangible inputs to production—such things as the costs of labor, raw materials, land, energy, and capital. Yet the interaction costs, which are embedded in our processes of transforming inputs to outputs, are enormous.

Interaction costs pervade all organizations, particularly those of developed nations. Research undertaken by McKinsey & Company, for example, concluded that interaction costs account for over half (that is, 51 percent) of all labor costs in the United States.[2]

But the fall in interaction costs has not necessarily enabled professionals and managers to collaborate, especially through the thick silo walls of many of today's corporations. Much of the communication is worthless noise: In a 2005 survey conducted by the *McKinsey Quarterly*, of senior and top executives, 60 percent said their company's size and complexity have made it somewhat difficult, or much more difficult, to capture opportunities than it was just five years ago.[3] Little wonder, then, that ineffective bureaucracies develop within large companies, that the head office seems remote from the field, and that the "left hand doesn't know what the right hand is doing."

A symptom of the problem companies face today is simply the amount of energy they waste. We're familiar with one plant manager in one talent-intensive, megainstitution who receives 200 e-mail messages a day. We know of another staff person in a different megainstitution who receives 300 a day. The problem is that as interaction costs head

FIGURE 1-2

Marginal Interaction Costs Falling Sharply in Contrast to Skyrocketing Numbers of Interactions

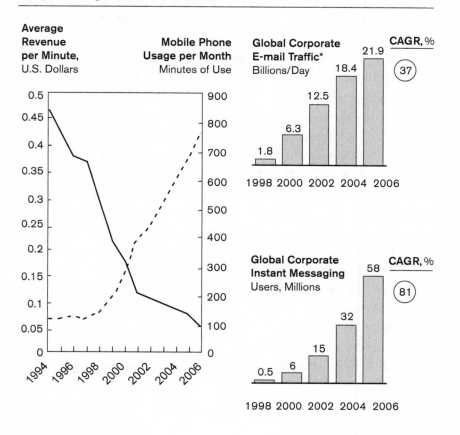

* Excludes unsolicited bulk e-mail.

Source: IDC; Federal Communications Commission (FCC); Pyramid Research.

toward zero, the volume of interactions is headed toward infinity (Figure 1-2).

The problem is that today companies rely on a model designed for the 20th century, one that depends on vertical, top-down hierarchical authority. The problem is that in the 21st century, the key to creating value is not just in providing top-down direction, vertically, but also in

enabling and motivating self-directed, thinking-intensive professionals and managers to work with one another horizontally across the
firm. Leveraging hierarchical leadership is still important, but it has become equally important to enable large-scale collaboration across the
enterprise.

A major barrier to doing so is that the 20th-century model relies on
the self-containment of businesses, a practice that puts boundaries
around this vertical authority. Unfortunately, the great majority of companies using the model have allowed these boundaries to harden into
thick silo walls, impediments that block collaboration across the boundaries. A related complication is that since each manager is usually
allowed to organize his or her business as he or she likes, the organizations are frequently incompatible. This lack of standardization makes it
difficult for a person whose job is defined one way to have much in
common with someone in another silo whose job is defined very differently.

Facilitating the collaboration of well-motivated people with one another across an organization that was not designed to accommodate
much collaboration is enormously challenging. It is analogous to pushing automobile and truck traffic through the heart of European cities
whose streets were designed for the horse and buggy. In cities, the
problem is congestion. In companies, the problem is unproductive
complexity.

Today's vertically oriented organizational structures, retrofitted
with ad hoc and matrix overlays, nearly always make professional work
more complex and inefficient. These vertical structures—relics of the
industrial age—are singularly ill suited to the professional work process.
Professionals need to collaborate horizontally with one another throughout a company, yet vertical structures force such men and women to
search across poorly connected organizational silos to find knowledge
and collaborators and to gain their cooperation once they have been
found.

One could argue that this continued rise in internal complexity is
an inevitable by-product of our times, that unproductive internal com-

plexity is simply the price one pays for operating a big company. Under this rationale, you simply let your people deal with it, day by day, however they can. Unfortunately, this response is the equivalent of addressing the lack of urban planning by permitting urban sprawl.

Another approach is the creation of patchwork solutions—like matrix structures, internal joint ventures, and units—headed by more than one person. These relieve the pressure on one issue but create pressure on others. It is the equivalent of reducing traffic congestion on the expressway by blocking its access roads (which alleviates expressway traffic but makes getting on the expressway difficult or impossible). The problem in such approaches, for companies and cities alike, is that they result in unintended and often negative outcomes. In fact, most companies now suffer from their previously constructed patchwork of expedient, one-off decisions, which, in combination, have greatly confused hierarchical relationships.

Confusion over Hierarchical Authority

The organization of most companies today bears limited resemblance to the original intended design. While there are plenty of well-managed companies that are exceptions, most are struggling: Their hierarchical relationships have become so confused that the power of hierarchy to drive performance is compromised. This dysfunction is usually felt most severely at the front line, where the brainpower and the energy of frontline workers are significantly consumed in the struggle against the internal complexity of their organizations.

The fact is that even the most self-directed, brilliant people can't create wealth by working alone. They need help mobilizing the talents of other thinking-intensive people and securing crucial capital and labor. They need to be able to convert their thinking into moneymaking activities.

When a talented person has a clear hierarchical leader, someone who has the clout to get the needed resources and the authority to make decisions—in other words, someone who can commit the entire organization he or she commands to supporting implementation—it is often amazing how much can be accomplished, and how quickly.

But more frequently, the fate of thinking, creative people, stuck in the traditional hierarchy, is quite similar to that of Charlie Chaplin caught in the wheels of the industrial machine. Only their agony isn't found between the wheels but rather in e-mail overload, meaningless meetings, and the realization that a matrix is just a fancy word for a prison that they can't escape.

The problem is that matrix structures, designed to accommodate the secondary-level management axes that cut across vertical silos, frequently burden professionals with two bosses—one responsible for the sales force, say, and another for a product line. Professionals seeking to collaborate thus need to go *up* the organization before they can go *across* it. Effective collaboration takes place only when would-be collaborators enlist hierarchical line managers to resolve conflicts between competing organizational silos. Much time is lost reconciling divergent agendas and finding common solutions.

Consider, for example, two MBAs at a wine bar, comparing war stories from the front lines of corporate life:

> "We have a terrific opportunity to sell telecommunications equipment in China, but the customer wants a lot of on-the-ground support from our IT area," confides one of the MBAs. "She also wants a Mandarin-speaking engineer to help her manage the project. The problem is that IT won't return my phone calls or even my e-mails. My buddy in Engineering says that I'm being stonewalled because his boss is allocating all the engineers with the necessary language skills to a project that is credited to Engineering—even though my project offers far better profits for the company as a whole."
>
> "Did you go to your boss for help?" asks the other.
>
> "I did. But he said he was powerless to get IT or Engi-

neering to cooperate unless he goes to his boss—which he's reluctant to do."

"Well," the other replies, setting down her glass, "at least you have one boss. I have two. I've been trying to develop a marketing program for the 'working mothers' segment across our product line for four months now. It's got great potential, but my product boss has little interest in this segment, while my sales boss doesn't have access to the product knowledge and the information I need."

"Can't you get your sales boss to call your product boss?"

"He won't. So now I'm trying to get them together. It took me a month to schedule a meeting—and it just got scratched. The CEO called a meeting to discuss our lack of growth. I'm at my wit's end."

A New Problem

To be sure, corporate bellyaching has been around ever since the invention of the corporation. But today the dysfunction is far greater than ever before. Why? For one thing, there are far more thinking workers under the corporate roof. Their need to interact is greater than ever. The digital technology of today has given them a great opportunity to do so—but it has also increased to an unbearable degree the complexity of these interactions.

For another, the matrix structures that were created in the 1960s to use authority to force managers to collaborate with one another were never meant for extensive use. Originally, matrix structures were always to be used sparingly. But today, matrices have blossomed everywhere. The problem is that because companies have now realized how important it is to gain collaboration, they have started to use more and more authority-based matrix structures to force collaboration everywhere. But true collaboration is based on mutual self-interest, not authority. Self-directed people should be motivated to work together, not forced to do so. As matrix structures proliferate, reporting relationships become confused, and the effectiveness of hierarchy erodes. Meanwhile, opportunities to collaborate are lost.

Where does the greatest dysfunction exist? We find it most often in the intermediate structures of the organization. Here we find the organizational silos that create impenetrable walls—walls that block collaboration and the flows of information, knowledge, and talent across the firm. It is here that we find matrix structures that try to bridge the silos with horizontal-vertical hybrids that endlessly convolute reporting relationships. And it is here that we find communications gridlocks—the confluence of different initiatives, by different managers, with different agendas, that often create the organizational equivalent of traffic jams.

Often the underlying source of the dysfunction lies at the very top of the company, especially when corporate politics are rampant. Much of the dysfunction is also created by people focused on making budget—even if it means taking uneconomic actions that make their reported results look better but negatively affect enterprisewide returns.

What causes all these problems? For one thing, the reporting relationships in these intermediate organizing structures are rarely defined. Senior managers are often left to interpret their own roles. They may feel empowered to issue directives to frontline units without feeling the need to coordinate with the managers to whom the frontline units report, thus creating multiple, overlapping initiatives. These can overload the line's capacities to do its job.

In addition, there are often so many intermediate levels of the organization that the top loses touch with the front line, and the front line doesn't really understand what the top is trying to do. Finally, in the intermediate levels, there is a tendency, if things go badly, to elevate decisions to avoid accountability. This tendency forces a large volume of small decisions up to very busy senior and top managers, who serve as tiebreakers. As a consequence, many such jobs become "undoable" from the point of view of the incumbent, or they create "bottlenecks" from the point of view of everyone else.

Much of the underlying problem is the use of internal financial reports that do not reflect the underlying economic relationship of intangibles to profit making. Managers can look good on reported results, even as they take actions that hurt the enterprise. These issues are compounded by performance measurement approaches that reward selfish, divisive behavior at the expense of collaborative behaviors for the common good.

Even strong leaders at the top can get frustrated, especially as they find top-down pressure ineffective in generating better performance. Organizational complexity can sap the power of even the strongest hierarchical leader. Or, as one leader said to us in despair, "I pressed the red button, but the rockets didn't launch."

Mobilizing Mind Power

The work that needs to be done in the 21st century, of course, is different from that which was required in the 20th century. Back then the organizing model was designed to mobilize labor and capital, but today you need to mobilize mind power as well. By "mind power" we mean the intangible output of thinking employees, those who use subjective thinking and problem solving to do their jobs.

If your organization can harness this mind power—if you can boost the profits from each thinking employee—then your organization will be on the path to great success and competitive advantage in the 21st-century world.

Today's corporations have vastly greater numbers of these thinking workers than ever before. GE and Citigroup, for instance, have over 150,000 workers in such thinking jobs. Even such a labor-intensive company as Wal-Mart, with 1.7 million workers, has over 120,000 workers in thinking-intensive jobs (largely in managerial and supervisory positions). We estimate that there are some 20 million such thinking-intensive workers in the largest 1,500 companies in the world.

There are two fundamentally different ways such workers, exercising subjective judgment and problem solving, add value. The first is in using mind power through hierarchical authority to manage other people's work. The second is in self-directing work, collaborating with others, and using one's own, unique skills, knowledge, and thinking capacities.

Throughout this book we will refer to people using their minds primarily to exercise authority as "managers" and to people primarily self-directing their thinking-intensive work as "professionals." Of course, many people in organizations both self-direct their work and manage that of others. In particular, leaders of other professionals often play the role of "player-coach."

Most companies are tapping into only a small fraction of the potential to create wealth from the mind power of all the managers and professionals they employ. During the 20th century, the costs of coordinating work across large companies were so large that mind power was trapped in small pockets of people scattered throughout each company. But nowadays this is no longer true. As a result, today there is an opportunity to earn large "rents" (that is, profits disproportionate to the amounts of labor and/or capital that are invested).

Where the Money Is

It would be reason enough to develop better organizing approaches if all that was accomplished was to make the jobs of talented employees more rewarding. All business leaders know how important talent is to their current success. Furthermore, it could be argued, actions taken that will enable companies to attract, develop, and reward talent bring their own reward. Still, we believe developing a better organizing model is more than that. In the 21st century, it's where the money is.

As we described in the Introduction, many large companies have already shown an ability in the digital age to create rents. Such rents are possible today because these companies have been able to mobilize labor, capital, and mind power into monetizable institutional skills, intellectual property, networks, and brands (Figure 1-3).

The returns from doing so are extremely attractive simply because

FIGURE 1-3

Intangibles as Owned by Either Individuals or Firms

Individual Intangibles	Firm Intangibles
Knowledge can be owned as a private good by individuals.	• Knowledge can become a public good within a firm or can be retained as a private good by the firm when the firm transacts with other parties.* • Firm can combine private knowledge of multiple individuals to provide unique value through **intellectual property.**
Relationships can be interpersonal and owned as a private good by the individuals.	• Relationships can become a public good within the firm. • Firm can mobilize multiple interpersonal relationships and form unique institutional relationships. • Firm can create unique value through building and leveraging **networks.**
Reputation can be attributed to individuals and owned as a private good by individuals.	• Reputation can become a public good within the firm and owned uniquely by the firm as a private good through a **trademark or brand.**
People can use their own skills and own them as a private good.	• Firms can mobilize individual's **talent** by organizing work that he or she could not otherwise self-organize (e.g., client service teams).

Captured by Individuals in the Form of Compensation	Captured by Firms in the Form of Higher Returns to Capital and Labor

* This assumes a Coasian rationale for firms: The firm boundary is located to overcome market interaction costs.

intangibles enjoy potentially enormous scale and scope advantages. Furthermore, because they represent assets that are unique to the individual company (that is, are in unique supply), they can enable creating "natural monopolies" that are difficult for other companies to compete away.

ECONOMIES OF SCALE AND SCOPE

Economies of scale decrease the average cost of production as firms produce more output. The average cost is the total cost of production—including both fixed and variable costs—divided by number of units of output. With economies of scale, each additional output adds less to the total costs than the average of the preceding units.

Economies of scale have historically been limited by the increasing diseconomies of scale including particularly the complexity of coordinating the service of more and more customers, more and more employees, and more and more suppliers, as volume grows. In other words, if firms become "excessively large" relative to minimum efficient size (the volume of production that minimizes unit costs), the marginal costs of increased volume of production will grow faster than the marginal scale effects, and the average unit costs will rise rather than fall.

Economies of scope occur when companies produce multiple goods with shared factor inputs, thereby saving the need to pay for those factors twice. For example, if investments in a brand can be shared across multiple products, then it provides economies of scope. Again, as with economies of scale, economies of scope have also been historically limited by the diseconomies of complexity that arise as the firm's scope expands due to serving more diverse customer bases, with more diverse services and products, over more diverse geographies.

Because of the development of globalization and advances in technology, scale and scope effects have increased across the board—particularly in those effects related to intangibles. By "intangibles" we mean such assets as the brands, intellectual property, and proprietary networks that are unique to individual firms.

Economies of scale can be extremely large for intangible-rich offerings. Indeed, some intangible-based offerings display continual economies of scale no matter how much output is produced. While the fixed costs of producing a distinctive new drug, computer chip, software product, or movie may be very large, for example, the marginal costs of production can be close to zero, thereby creating enormous scale effects.

Intangibles, in fact, can even demonstrate increasing returns to scale. Increasing returns to scale are a corollary to economies of scale: An addition of a factor of production leads to an increase in total productivity (more output per unit of input).[4] Networks, in particular, have this potential, as has been demonstrated through research: One person connected to a network adds no value. Two people connected to a network can interact with each other, so each individual can accomplish more. Ten people connected to a network can interact with nine others, so the number of possible productive interactions is greatly increased, with the result that the productivity of each individual connected to the network is greater.

Globalization and advances in technology have also greatly increased scope effects. Intangible economies of scope are even more special than intangible scale effects simply because large companies tend to be quite different from one another. Each large firm, out of its history, usually competes in very different geographies, products, and customer markets than any other large firm. This creates the opportunity for each firm to find different, and potentially unique, intangible scope advantages that cannot by enjoyed by competitors—*if* the company can create a unique set of product and service offerings that draw upon these differences.

GE, for example, can leverage its distinctive knowledge and capabilities in different aspects of the aircraft market by providing aircraft engines, the leasing or sales financing of the aircraft, the maintenance of the engines and the planes, and the brokerage of used aircraft and parts among customers—all this to offer these goods and services in varying combinations. And since it can benefit from economies of scope, it can do so at better prices. Since GE is essentially the only company that has this particular combination of capabilities and can offer these particular products and services, it is a unique provider in the market for comprehensive aircraft service.

Intangibles can capture economies of scope wherever multiple production processes, businesses, or products can share the asset. A firm can use its "insider" relationships in China, for example, to gain privileged distribution of multiple products to the Chinese market.

Economies of scope can generate rents if the cost and value advantages from them are not shared equally across all competitors. A financial services firm with a privileged relationship with a large client, which thereby acquires superior knowledge of the client's needs, for example, can enable the tailored bundling of services to that specific client (providing both greater value to the client and a cost advantage to the producer by spreading coverage costs across more products).

The ability to create rents, as David Ricardo pointed out over 150 years ago, requires a provider to enjoy unique ownership (that is, unique supply) of an asset that is superior in quality. Valuable intangibles meet the test. Ricardo, though, had a third condition for creating rents: The asset needed also to be limited in supply. But today's owner of intangibles can choose to supply whatever quantity of intangibles it chooses, since the marginal costs of producing any given intangible is often virtually "zero." This ability to control supply of whatever quantity the market demands enables a firm that owns valuable intangibles to enjoy natural monopoly effects (that is, the company is a unique provider).

A natural monopoly, such as an electric utility, occurs when one firm has economies of scale and scope over the range of production needed to supply the entire market, and it is less costly (socially) to have one producer supply the entire market than to have two firms compete. The common structural element of most natural monopolies is large fixed costs and negligible variable costs (or virtually unlimited economies of scale and scope). This enables a natural monopoly to be a "social good" simply because it lowers rather than raises the costs of production. It is cheaper, for example, to have one electric distribution grid supply an entire city than to have two distributors each supplying a portion of the market demand.

Many intangible-rich products have this cost structure. They are the source of much of the rents we've observed that some firms now enjoy. When the intangibles owned by a firm are distinctive (that is, there are no effective substitutes), the firm becomes a sole provider, and therefore has very significant price discretion. But firms can't assume that picking a high price point maximizes profits. With intangible-based natural monopolies (unlike tangible-based monopolies), picking a *low, rather than high, price point* may enable the maximum capture of rents. Because of the extreme economies of scale and scope of many intangible-rich offerings, a lower price point (one that captures all available demand) can often create higher total returns than a high price point that captures only a fraction of potential demand. A lower price point also makes a natural monopoly less vulnerable to competition from close substitutes.

Natural monopolies based on intangibles such as intellectual property (or branding) are usually temporary. They are subject to erosion over time through continuing advances in technology and by the competition's investing in near substitutes. Pharmaceutical companies, for example, must routinely compete by seeking new patents that are targeted at the same health issues addressed by their competitors' patents. Software companies routinely find alternative software solutions to customer needs, and so on. However, while a natural monopoly exists, the returns can be very substantial.

New Opportunities

The ability to capture such rents is not new. For example, throughout most of the entire 20th century, many consumer package goods companies created rents through branding, and many pharmaceutical companies created rents through patent protection. Indeed, the classic way that companies created rents was to develop value propositions based on intellectual property or brands.

What is new is that in the digital age, as intangible scale and scope effects have increased, opportunities to create rents are becoming ubiquitous. Substantial rents are now not just being earned from brands (for example, iPod) and intellectual property (for example, Windows) but also from networks (for example, Google) and institutional skills (for example, Toyota).

Well-managed firms today often combine these categories of intangibles. For example, intellectual property, networks, institutional skills, and brands combine to create production processes and business models (for example, the supply chains of Dell and Wal-Mart). Or networks and institutional skills enable some companies to develop and launch successful products continuously (for example, Apple and Samsung).

The opportunities to create rents in the 21st century are robust. Huge opportunities exist for companies to mobilize mind power in order to help discover and build new, winning value propositions in all of the marketplaces in which they choose to compete. Similarly, there are enormous opportunities to bring intangibles created by the mind power of an acquirer's employees to improve the performance of newly acquired companies (and to bring to bear the mind power of the acquisition to the acquirer). In other words, in the 21st century, mobilizing mind power is the key to getting better results from traditional strategic decisions concerning where and how to compete.

That said, we believe many of the best opportunities in the 21st century are not just from getting better results from traditional strategic decisions. Increasingly, the great new opportunity is for a large company to liberate the latent mind power of its tens of thousands of workers to capture rents in their day-to-day jobs.

The "raw materials" for such rents occur as a by-product of thinking-intensive workers simply doing their jobs. As employees exchange knowledge, debate issues, and solve problems with one another, new knowledge is continuously produced. Reputations emerge as people continually produce valuable work products. Relationships are created as multiple people interact with customers, suppliers, regulators, and so on. Individuals, as they work together, build new, deep personal competencies. Any large company, simply to exist, must employ literally thousands of talented thinking-intensive people, producing such intangibles. The opportunity is to bring the entire firm's mind power and the related intangibles to every job, to increase the value of every person's work, every day. The related opportunity is to simultaneously reduce the cost of unproductive complexity arising from the unnecessary or unproductive search for access to this mind power, or to the unnecessary costs in coordinating work with others. Said differently, the opportunity is to enable all people in the firm to be able to perform better in their roles. You want to enable average workers to perform much closer to the level of your very best employees.

A product marketing executive who can efficiently and effectively mobilize the unique talent, knowledge, relationships, and reputations of the entire firm to develop a winning, differentiated marketing campaign, for instance, can generate more rents than an executive who designs a "me-too" campaign. A manager of a plant who can mobilize enterprisewide mind power to produce output that is superior in quality and lower in cost can also create rents. As an aside, Toyota is a good example of a company already skilled in capturing rents routinely through its "lean manufacturing" institutional skills, skills that are delivered through literally thousands of experienced managers.

It is the opportunity to convert these kinds of "routine opportunities"—opportunities from the latent mind power that already exists in its workforce—that makes us quite comfortable believing that even the average large company, in nearly any industry or headquartered in nearly any geography, should be able to target an increase in profit per employee of 30 to 60 percent or more simply by investing in designing and building the strategic organizational capabilities needed to mobilize mind power.

The good news is that the same investments in building these organizational capabilities (to make all employees better at their jobs) will also improve a company's ability to get better results from the traditional strategic decisions over where and how to compete.

In the past, companies thought about the opportunities to create rents from intangibles in terms of making large investments in research and development to create intellectual property or in advertising to create brand value. We believe the opportunity in the 21st century is much bigger than that.

We are arguing that companies need to view investing in designing and building strategic organizational capabilities as means to capturing rents from everything they do. Companies are being constrained, unnecessarily, by the unproductive complexity of working in their organizations. We believe that investing in capabilities to relax these constraints, thus enabling a company to mobilize not just labor and capital but also the company's unique mind power, is the key to creating wealth in the 21st century.

These strategic organizational capabilities, once created, will enable firms to harness the enormous latent scale and scope effects already inherent in employing tens of thousands of thinking workers serving different customers, operating in different geographies, and producing different goods and services.

Furthermore, we truly believe that companies have only begun to tap the opportunities to create wealth in the 21st century. Why? Because they are still using an organizing model designed for the industrial age rather than for the digital age. To create greater wealth in the future, we believe that all companies should make organizational design the centerpiece of their corporate strategies.

2

DESIGNING ORGANIZATIONS FOR THE 21ST CENTURY

IT TAKES MORE than a little hubris to think that you can successfully design and complete major organizational change initiatives in a modern megainstitution.

Today's megainstitutions are massive, complex, dynamic ecosystems that are continuously adapting to external and internal stimuli.

Externally, the corporation is continuously adapting to changing customer demands, technology, competitor actions, social norms, and regulatory conditions. Internally, there are often myriad competing strategies and conflicting personal agendas, usually played out through organizational politics, as individuals vie with one another for power. The result is one change in leadership after another, a continuous motion that distracts talent from the more pressing issues at hand. Overhanging every action taken is the constant pressure from the capital market to deliver the next quarter's earnings.

The modern public company lives in a fishbowl, as well, which not only makes a shortfall in earnings (against expectations) a cataclysmic event but also gives business executives the attention formerly reserved for actors, sports stars, and royalty. Changing the trajectory of the company through major organizational design changes is hard. To use an old saw, making a major organizational design change in a company is like trying to change a tire on a car that never stops.

Rather than attempting major organizational design changes, many top leaders are more comfortable making limited organizational interventions. The organizational inertia in a large company is considerable as it evolves to its future. Large companies usually operate through a legacy of organizational behaviors, driven by managing approaches established by long-departed former leaders. Unfortunately, most of these organizational behaviors were designed to work for the industrial age, not the digital age; so it is not surprising that they are not always effective today. Nevertheless, they represent "the way we do things around here." Changing organizational mindsets and behaviors is hard and time-consuming. Why distract people from the day-to-day challenge of producing operating earnings, after all?

It is not surprising, therefore, that most leaders opt for tweaking their organizations rather than transforming them. They seem to believe that what organization is all about is picking people. To be sure, as people such as Jim Collins have noted in *Built to Last*, picking the right people is critical. The problem is that it is often done with the mindset that all you need to do is pick the right people, hold them accountable, and let them figure out the rest. Indeed, many of the people you pick may take umbrage at being given any direction over how they should organize their reports. But when different managers, with different responsibilities, make separate, uncoordinated organizing decisions, they usually wind up making it more difficult for people in their respective organizational units to work together. When you multiply this tendency across an entire company, it is no wonder that unproductive complexity is the result.

If top leaders do make structural changes, the changes often amount to little more than quick fixes and "bolt-ons," such as adding a new role to put focus on a particular issue or making an ad hoc change such as having a person report to two people rather than one or putting co-heads in charge of a unit. These changes often serve only to make the entire organization more complex to operate within.

The problem is that large companies desperately need to become less complex rather than more complex. Complexity is the common enemy that limits the performance of all large enterprises. The opportunity, therefore, is to relieve complexity constraints on better performance rather than add to them.

Internal and External Complexity Limits

Economists have long recognized that internal complexity, as it rises, creates increasing limits on economies of scale and scope. The underlying question is not the absolute scale or scope of the company but whether it is "excessively" complex and therefore unable to realize the full economic potential of managing that scale and scope. A 100-person "job shop" producing several versions of a manufactured good would have been excessively complex in the 18th century. But a well-organized, 100-person factory producing very superior manufactured goods need not be excessively complex today, even with a far greater scale and scope of production than its 18th-century counterpart.

The organizational challenge today is in eliminating unproductive (that is, not value-added) complexity while increasing the value earned from managing productive complexity—this to increase economies of scale and scope. A great amount of thinking has gone into determining how to increase the productivity of tangibles (for example, lean manufacturing). Our focus instead is on managing complexity to increase the productivity of intangible assets. This is where we feel the greatest untapped value exists. In terms of employees, this means that you want to increase the number of productive interactions among your workers (those that create or exchange intangibles) while reducing the number of unproductive interactions. To be sure, unproductive interactions are necessary costs of doing business (like searching for information or coordinating work). The trick is to reduce these unproductive interactions to a minimum, thereby pushing back the limits of complexity. As we described earlier, the benefits of doing so get very large, very quickly.

If a company with 300,000 employees can add $13,333 of "rents" per employee (that is, earnings requiring *no* additional employment of capital or labor) by reducing unproductive complexity, it can add $4 billion in additional earnings—which, if valued at a capitalization rate of 10 percent, would be worth approximately $40 billion in market capitalization.

Or if a much smaller company with "only" 10,000 employees can add $50,000 per employee (the potential is greater because the complexity constraints are less), it would add $500 million in profits, or $5 billion in market capitalization (which likely would be an even greater improvement in market value relative to the larger company).

Companies cannot control much of the complexity they face. Much of the complexity of companies that needs to be managed is driven by the continuously changing external world. As Eric Beinhocker and others have observed, companies exhibit complex, adaptive behaviors, which means that to survive, a company, like a species, must continuously adapt and evolve to maintain a "fit" with the ever-changing complexities of the world.[1] Companies have no alternative but to adapt to the changing external world. They must learn to deal with that kind of complexity. The complexity that is avoidable, however, is the internal complexity that results from unnecessarily complex organizations.

The challenge of managing the internal complexity of organizing work is not new; it has been around as long as humans have worked together in organizations.

Role of Hierarchy and Collaboration

There are only two real ways that humans have found for organizing work: hierarchy, which organizes work through authority, and collaboration, which organizes work through mutual self-interest.

In a hierarchy, interactions among workers are primarily top down and bottom up. Hierarchy works because it lowers interaction costs. In a hierarchy, interactions are simple. It is efficient to tell people what to do. And if the person at the top of the organizational pyramid knows more, is smarter, or is a better leader than the other workers, then hierarchy leverages that person's abilities. If the person at the top is not particularly knowledgeable or smart or effective, however, the organization will be worse off.

Collaboration organizes work through mutual self-interest. In collaboration, workers are free to interact with everyone else, and they choose their associations based on the nature of the work that needs to be done. Collaboration enables better use of the specialized skills and the knowledge of different individuals, and it increases total thinking capacity for problem solving. Collaboration, however, usually requires a greater volume of transactions and more complex interactions than hierarchy to organize work.

It is only with the advent of today's networked digital technology that large-scale collaboration among large numbers of workers has become possible. Even with today's technology, however, achieving large-scale collaboration among many people can be very inefficient—not just because the interaction costs to achieve extensive collaboration can be very high but also because human psychology and behavior, combined with different individual self-interests, can make it difficult to get decisions made by relying on collaboration alone (for example, who should play what role?).

The art in organizational design is to find both the right mix of hierarchy and collaboration as well as the right mix of individual and mutual accountability to best achieve the work that needs to be done. This is an age-old challenge. Let's explain what we mean by this.

A (Very Short) History of the Firm

The 20th-century model evolved from the long history of human beings searching for a better way to organize themselves to get work done.

Early on, humans discovered that specialization allows individuals to undertake work that best uses their personal talents. The more experience that people get, the better they get at their work. They develop the intangible assets needed to do the work (that is, knowledge, relationships, reputations, and so on). Once people specialize, they become mutually dependent (because no one produces everything he or she needs). Therefore, people need to trade their own specialized work for the work of others. Markets enable people to do this. But markets often fail to deliver exactly what the customer wants, or they simply don't exist for the particular need. This is where private organizations have come into play. Firms innovate to organize work to produce output otherwise not available in the marketplace (at an equivalent price). In doing so, they combine what can be bought from the market with that which has to be provided uniquely by the firm.[2]

From Roman times to the end of the Middle Ages, the job shop represented the state of the art in organizing firms. Think of such medieval crafts as blacksmithing or weaving, for which the master craftsmen used journeymen and apprentices to expand output. As successful sole proprietors learned to leverage their own talents by organizing people to work for them, these job shops evolved and grew larger. But at the same time as they were adding more workers, they also became more complex, since they now had added to the interaction costs of the people working together under their roofs the costs of searching for information, exchanging knowledge and information, and coordinating work activities.[3]

Despite this, job shops succeeded by creating more output, through the effective organizing of workers, than could have been had through the efforts of a talented worker alone. Job shops were usually limited to about 7 to 10 people, since the level of complexity often became unmanageable after that. A few job shops had 20 or more. The largest firm in Roman times had about 100 employees.[4] These limitations were imposed both by the size of the market available to them and by their capacity to produce output before they reached maximum efficient scale and scope. (Maximum efficient scale or scope is reached when

INTERACTION AND TRANSACTION COSTS

When you read the economic literature, you realize there is no consistent definition of "transaction costs" or "interaction costs." To help the reader understand our ideas, we are providing definitions of "transaction costs" and "interaction costs" as we use the terms.

Transaction costs, as we define them, are the costs associated with getting parties with independent interests to trade items of value. Transaction costs include the interaction costs of making an exchange, including all the costs involved in searching to find trading parties (for example, hiring an agent), making the exchange itself (for example, writing a contract), and the after-trade costs (for example, ensuring compliance with the terms of the contract). In addition, when the parties are not in the same location, the costs of travel and transportation are transaction costs. While transaction costs were originally the costs associated with bartering, today almost all transactions involve one party paying the other party in money.

In contrast, when workers within the same economic entity (for example, a company) work together, they do not usually interact with one another by explicitly trading items of value. Therefore, no money usually exchanges hands when employees interact with one another. Instead, they are paid by their employer to work together. Throughout this book, although transaction costs are actually a subcategory of interaction costs, for simplicity's sake,

- "Transaction costs" will mean the costs of parties with *independent* economic interests trading with one another.

- "Interaction costs" will mean the costs of parties with *dependent* economic interests working together *within* the same economic entity (that is, the costs of organizing people working together within a firm).

incremental production diminishes returns and when incremental returns begin to be offset by rapidly increasing marginal costs of production.) Marginal costs include, particularly, the increasing internal costs
of complexity arising from increased volume of production, managing
more people, serving more clients, offering new products, and serving
wider geographies.

Starting in the early 18th century, however, a dramatic innovation
in organizing work developed. It radically transformed the economies
of specialization, scale, and scope of manufacturing. We call it the factory. The phenomenon it inspired is called "the Industrial Revolution."

Factories enabled the design of work flows and continuous processes
that combined newly available technology (for example, steam engines)
with the efficient mobilization of the factors of production (for example, labor, capital, energy, and raw materials). These work-flow designs
increased dramatically the number of productive interactions among
workers and decreased dramatically the number of unproductive interactions. Factories converted complex interaction, labor-intensive job
shop work to simple, low-interaction-cost, routine work. Given the importance of the costs of physical labor in manufacturing, the factories
enabled stunning increases in the output worked per hour.

The objective of a factory was to lower interaction costs by minimizing the need for workers to search for and exchange knowledge and information. It did this by making the work routine, and, through standardized process and supervision, by making coordination and control
easier. In other words, factories were designed to overcome the costs of
complexity as the scale and scope of the work escalates.

This enabled the work to be performed without much, if any, subjective thinking or problem solving on the part of its workers. It made
them, individually, far more fungible with one another. In turn, high
volumes (available to suppliers) and lower prices (available to customers) provided opportunities to lower transaction and transportation
costs either directly (by spreading fixed costs, like the costs of building
a large cargo ship, over more volume) or indirectly, by providing the incentives to innovators to lower these costs further.

THE THEORY OF THE FIRM

One of the questions of economics is why, once the markets formed, didn't the now more specialized employees simply then eliminate the owners of the firm by organizing the work among themselves through a market? Had they done so, they would have been able to split the owner's share among themselves.

The answer is that it would have happened, all other things being equal, if the transaction costs the workers would have incurred as private counterparties were less than the interaction costs they would have incurred by working within the same firm. Of course, not all things are equal, because the proprietor-owner may have had proprietary intangible assets (for example, knowledge about how to organize the work and a reputation earned from delivering quality output to customers over time). Proprietary knowledge could have enabled the owner to organize the workers to produce more, better output, at lower costs than the employees could have produced by themselves if they had worked separately, and the reputation of the owner could have enabled the firm to attract new customers at lower costs than the employees would have been able to attract if they had worked separately.

In fact, it is the ability to freely share and exchange valuable intangibles within a firm that, as Roland Coase described, is the reason the firm exists. In short, employees of the same firm interact with one another more freely and with lower interaction costs than they would incur if they worked separately.

Another answer to this question is provided by Ken Arrow, author of *The Limits of Organization,* who notes that firms also exist to overcome market failures; that is, firms fill in the gaps wherever markets fail to satisfy economic needs.

In the 21st century, these ideas remain important, particularly since, as today's global markets grow in scale and scope, they continuously take over work that previously was undertaken by firms.

At first, most factories were still relatively small (very few firms employed more than 100 people even as recently as the late 19th century), as were the markets within which they competed. It was the principle of competition among these relatively small firms, including the competition between job shops and "factories," that Adam Smith described in his book *The Wealth of Nations*. In fact, it was the interaction between competitive suppliers and customers within markets served by these small firms that led to his famous "invisible hand" observations about the ability of markets to allocate resources to the highest social good.

Creation of Large Integrated Firms

With the innovation of the factory, the stage was set for the emergence of the large integrated corporation. As Alfred Chandler famously observed in *Scale and Scope,* the "modern business enterprise" came into existence "only when the visible hand of management became more efficient than the invisible hand of market forces."[5] To make this leap, all the company had to do was find the means of overcoming the existing limits to the scale and scope in a particular business. The winning model was usually a joint stock company. Such an organization was able to mobilize the capital and other tangible factors of production (such as raw materials and labor) needed to operate an integrated value chain of production (from the acquisition of raw materials to the distribution to the customer).

The driving force behind the development of most large firms in the late 19th century and early 20th century was usually an individual owner-entrepreneur, a person who saw an opportunity to integrate a value chain of production around a particular kind of economic activity. Thus there was Richard Sears in retailing, John D. Rockefeller in petroleum, Andrew Carnegie in steel, Cornelius Vanderbilt in railroads and shipping, and many others.[6] The organizing approach was both patriarchal and hierarchical. The equivalent, in social organization, was the tribe. As in a tribe, the patriarchal entrepreneur articulated the group's strategic vision, then used the hierarchy (and individual and mutual accountability) to make the organization perform in accordance with that vision. Henry Ford was the epitome of the founding owner-entrepreneur: He was determined to control everything himself. His success in inventing the assembly line enabled him to create one of the most successful industrial firms in the world.

But Ford had a fatal flaw. Even when modern management practices began to appear, he still insisted on controlling everything himself. He held everyone both individually and mutually accountable for "doing it his way." Even as his organization expanded in scale and scope and as its complexity mounted, he let it be known that any employee found with an organizational chart would be fired. That attitude was his undoing. Although Ford survived as a carmaker, he lost what was once a dominating market share to Alfred Sloan's General Motors.

Development of the 20th-Century Model

It was Alfred Sloan, in fact, who (along with Pierre DuPont and drawing on the ideas of other thinkers such as Frederick Taylor) created a new way to organize and manage firms. His model, designed in the 1920s, relied heavily on hierarchy, individual accountability, and divisions to organize firms. General Electric, U.S. Steel, Standard Oil, and many others soon adopted this model. John Micklethwait and Adrian Wooldridge's book *The Company* provides a concise description of how this model, which we call the "20th-century model," came into being.[7] The big idea of this model was the use of the multibusiness (that is, multidivisional organization) that migrated the functional model of production to a multibusiness model usually organized around geography or product. Importantly, this model put the control under a CEO who was an agent for the owners rather than an owner himself. The age of the professional manager had arrived.

This innovation created general managers, each of whom had functional reports, who in turn were delegated with much of the authority of the CEO (subject to the CEO's control, of course) within the business they ran. It expanded from one to a dozen or more "thinking minds" driving the company. This organization of the company into businesses greatly expanded the organization's capacity to mobilize, manage, and control resources beyond the CEO's personal capacity. In turn, this capacity enabled each business to devote its energy to more specialized work (for example, the responsibility for a geographic region), which in turn enabled expansion of the company's overall scale or scope. Expansion was relatively easy. If you needed to add a new product or a new geography, you simply added a new division.

Sloan wrote, "I do not regard size as a barrier. To me it is only a problem of management."

Business schools, consulting firms (including McKinsey & Company), and early management gurus (such as Peter Drucker) promoted this model. By the late 1960s it had spread globally to become the dominant managing model in the developed world.

In the 1960s, 1970s, and early 1980s, the leaders of large companies often put extraordinary energy into designing how these organizations would work. Since complexity is the enemy of economies of scale and scope (especially in a world where the costs of interacting were very high), it was important to eliminate unproductive complexity. Great attention was focused on clarifying the structure of the organization to eliminate confusion over details. Reporting relationships, roles, and processes were carefully defined and communicated. Rules of thumb, such as "Spans of control should not exceed seven people," were applied to designing organizational structures. Axioms of management, such as "Accountabilities should match responsibilities" or "Every person should have one clearly defined boss," were also abundant in the 1960s, 1970s, and early 1980s.

The model itself had many variants. Some single-business companies were structured to be managed by function, others by geography, others by product, and still others by customer group. Some companies were centralized. Others were decentralized. But what they all had in common was a reliance on hierarchical structures that split work up among the individual managers—who themselves were allowed to organize their units as they saw fit. In the process, authority passed down a chain of command. With that came accountability: The individual was expected to perform in accordance with the directions and expectations of the superior officer.

The number of layers in the chain of command in this model varied with the span control of each manager, which, in turn, varied with the nature of the work and how much control was being exercised by each link in the chain, and with the total size of the organization. Some organizations found it necessary to set up a dozen or more layers of hierarchy—until, finally, one reached the front line, where the real work of the company was done.

Widespread Adoption of the Model

The 20th-century model was a wild success, not only in manufacturing but eventually also in firms ranging from commercial banks and retailers to telecommunications companies. Even as the scale and scope of a firm increased, it enabled the enterprises to deliver earnings. The key to its success was that negotiations could progress smoothly down the chain of command concerning expected earnings (that is, the annual budget) and the accountability of each individual to make that budget. This process cascaded down the chain of command until it reached the front line—where the budget expectations were expected to be achieved. This "operating performance pressure" motivated the down-the-line employees to make budgets "at all costs." In turn, that meant selling hard and cutting expenses wherever they could be cut.

For most of the 20th century, and particularly from the end of World War II into the 1980s, it was reasonable for top management to set annual financial targets and to develop long-range plans and "visions" to reach them. These usually meant leveraging core competencies across ever-widening geography. Given the opaqueness of the information provided to shareholders at this time and the strength and profitability of core businesses (much due to weak competition and the pricing umbrellas put in place by companies propped up by regulation), the apparent successes often masked real weaknesses within.

Finally, as powerful global market forces began to be unleashed at the end of the 1980s, the free ride ended. Fewer and fewer weak competitors were left to exploit (most of them in the developed world had already been acquired or had failed). And so we entered the 1990s.

Then, without much warning, the world abruptly changed again.

The Digital Age

Over the last 15 years, driven by falling interaction and transaction costs, the global economy has witnessed a fundamental transition. Interaction and transaction costs have fallen continuously throughout human history, but in the early 1990s—largely due to digital technology but also to changes in regulations, capital mobility, and the development of global standards (such as English as the language of business)—these costs began a sharp descent, one that continues today. In a few short years, working with any other workers, anywhere in the world, in any line of business, became easier than any one of us could ever have imagined.

Moreover, just as lowered interaction and transaction costs increased economies of scale and scope, they also increased economies of specialization. Low interaction and transaction costs allow companies to focus on only those activities they do best. More and more, they are able to obtain from others, at manageable costs, all the pieces of the value chain for which they lack comparative advantage. As the complication and cost of accessing supply through outsourcing decreases, the logic of a world filled only with world-class producers in every piece of the value chain becomes compelling.

This enables companies rich in intangible assets, for example, to capture economies of scale and scope related to those assets while simultaneously divesting activities for which they lacked such intangible advantages. This has made it possible for the best-managed firms, with the most valuable intangible assets, to find prosperity in the digital age.

General Electric is one of them. Over the last 20 years, GE has made a profound shift in its business mix—from being a heavy-

industries-dominated firm to becoming much more of a financial services, energy, and health-care firm. Another way of saying this is that
GE has shifted from labor-intensive activities to thinking-intensive
activities.

In 1984, GE employed 330,000 people. About 20 percent of them
were either managers or professionals. By 2004, GE had reduced its
workforce to 307,000, but its percentage of employees who were professionals or managers had increased to roughly 55 percent. In the
process, as GE added some 100,000 professional and managerial employees, its *profit per employee* per year quadrupled, from $12,500 per
employee in 1984 to $54,000 per employee in 2004. Its market capital-
ization increased from $47 billion to $386 billion—or 825 percent—
while its book equity increased only 482 percent.

GE is representative of a new superclass of firms—which includes
names such as ExxonMobil, IBM, Microsoft, Johnson & Johnson, Toyota, and British Petroleum. These firms are not only very large; they
also have an incredibly rich mix of thinking, talented people. These
companies organize these workers well (even though by 20th-century
principles) and thereby are able to earn outstanding returns, as measured by profit per employee, relative to companies of equivalent size,
as measured by number of employees.

What distinguishes such companies is not only their size but also
their ability to manage. Most are adept at the use of hierarchy, but they
are also able to operate as "one company." Rather than being overcome
by the complexity of operating such large, diverse firms, these thinking, talent-intensive megainstitutions have managed to shift their bases
of competition from tangibles to intangibles, and they are thereby creating extraordinary profits and market capitalization.

Intangibles are critical to such high performance in all industries.
Even very labor-intensive firms (such as Toyota) mobilize world-class
intangibles in "lean manufacturing," which translates into fundamental labor productivity advantages. Even very capital intensive companies
(like ExxonMobil) translate world-class intangibles in exploration and
production into fundamental capital productivity advantages over rivals.

Because the names of these companies are so familiar to all of us, there is a tendency for even close observers to miss the economic significance of their ability to create wealth. During the 1990s, something changed in the economy, something that released the complexity constraints that had been limiting the ability of large companies to create wealth rapidly.

That "something," as we described in Chapter 1, was the ability of some large companies to generate profits based on increased economies of scale and scope from intangibles (in unique supply) that enabled increases in returns without commensurate investments in labor and capital. It is not that these companies adopted fundamentally new managing models to obtain this high performance. It is rather that these companies already had superior intangibles and organizing approaches. The old economy was constraining the scale and scope effects these companies could enjoy. When the economy changed, these latent advantages were released and, in terms of wealth creation, the result was spectacular.

Problem of Large Numbers

But most of even these superclass companies have not entirely captured the full potential of the scale and scope effects latent in their employment of ever-larger numbers of thinking-intensive workers. Even these companies do not deploy organizing models designed for the 21st century. This is good news for these companies. Why? Because if they can overcome this challenge, they will have spectacular opportunities to create wealth.

Not just superclass companies but almost all large companies everywhere are struggling with overcoming the complexity challenges of gaining effective collaboration among the very large numbers of people they employ.

While modern technology offers the potential to enable very large numbers of people to work with others across an organization, complexity constraints today limit the ability to take full advantage of this potential.

Here's the dilemma: Most of the thinking-intensive work, even in superclass companies, is still done by individuals working alone, or at best, within small teams. But many of the great, untapped opportunities of the digital age are elsewhere—in the ability of individuals to communicate across the entire enterprise, to collaborate on work with people they might not even know, to match talents and job opportunities. Because of the sheer number of possibilities, making the right connections is difficult. It is a problem of large numbers. As large numbers of people reach out to each other for information and knowledge, the unwanted by-product is increased complexity.

The number of potential opportunities to collaborate, for instance, rises rapidly as the number of people working together increases. If there are 10 people in an organization, there are 45 potential bilateral collaborative relationships among them. If you have 100 people, there are about 5,000. If you have 100,000, as the largest companies do, there are 5 billion potential bilateral relationships.[8]

Not everyone, of course, needs to interact with everyone else, but even the subgroups in megainstitutions are very large. The client relationship management (CRM) practice of IBM, for example, has 4,000 consultants, which generates some 8 million potential bilateral relationships among them. The challenge in such large populations is to find the one or two people among the larger populations who possess the unique, distinctive knowledge one needs at a particular moment. The problem is exacerbated because, as the numbers grow, the ability to have personal relationships with even a small fraction of the entire population and to be able to interact intensively with each of them diminishes rapidly.

If you were to spend half your time interacting with 1,000 people, for example, you would have about one minute a week to spend with each of them. This means that even within a relatively "small" 1,000-person organization, you are unlikely to know much about your coworkers, nor are you likely to interact very much with many of them. How can you know which of them may have the particular, distinctive knowledge you require? How do you match the best job opportunity within an enterprise to a particular person's unique talents?

But the problem of large numbers is not just an issue of lowering search and coordination costs. The problem of large numbers is exacerbated by the difficulties in maintaining sufficient social cohesion and trust among people who don't know each other—to get them to willingly share information and knowledge or work opportunities.

The greater the number of people, of course, the more difficult the challenge. This is why anthropologists and others have observed that tribal groups tend to split in two when they reach 250 to 500 people. When the group reaches that size, it is difficult for any member of the tribe, even the patriarchal leader, to know everyone. Some, such as Malcolm Gladwell in *The Tipping Point,* have estimated the number for effective connectivity is closer to 150.[9] Yet now we have firms with over 100,000 professionals and managers. It was the tyranny of large numbers, in fact, that caused companies to subdivide their workforces into self-contained businesses in the first place. The problem is that in the digital era, siloed businesses put up barriers that serve to exacerbate the challenges of enabling large numbers of people to collaborate across the enterprise.

Organizational Design Opportunities for All

We believe there are opportunities to improve the organizational design of nearly all companies, even the superclass companies, and thereby to address the challenge of large numbers. However, the organizational design challenges most companies face are great. Most large companies today have organizations that were not so much designed as that merely evolved according to a set of rules (that is, the 20th-century model). While many of the organizations of these large companies may once have had the semblance of a design, as the years have passed, most have evolved into organizations that bear little resemblance to that original design. With some notable exceptions, such as ExxonMobil, GE, IBM, Microsoft, and Toyota, most of these companies rarely operate effectively as one company. The result is widely differing organizational approaches across the company, with those differences being driven not so much by external complexities or by innate differences among businesses as by such vagaries as the personalities of different managers and by the history of how the organization evolved.

One presumption behind the 20th-century model is that individual businesses are independent and self-contained. But, in the digital age, large-scale collaboration across business boundaries is now required. Given the widely differing approaches to organizing roles and evaluating the people who fill them in different organizational units, however, it is not surprising that these differences drive communication challenges and conflicting, rather than complementary, behaviors. At best, these differences require extensive, complex interactions to coordinate work across organizational boundaries. At worst, organizational boundaries have hardened into silo walls, leaving people to behave selfishly.

Trying to overcome these issues through the use of matrix structures and "double counting" of financial results gains some benefits in terms of collaboration, but at great costs in terms of efficiency and effectiveness. The enormous upsurge in the volume of electronic interactions enabled by the digital age combined with the expanded number of thinking-intensive workers results in the unproductive complexity challenges described in Chapter 1.

We believe that the time has come for corporate leaders to take control of their organizations. They need not merely react to the challenges of the digital age. Rather, just as Alfred Sloan and others did in the 1920s, they can design a better way to work—and with it they can launch major strategic organizational change initiatives that can move their corporations along different paths. As we said in the Preface, we believe you can develop a set of carefully designed initiatives, each of which can reduce unproductive internal complexity (that is, unnecessary search and coordination costs) while stimulating the creation and productive flow of valuable intangibles (for example, talent, knowledge), and thereby relax complexity limits. If so, you can enable the better capture of rents and create far greater wealth, not to mention far better working conditions for your employees.

Ideas for Organizing in the Digital Age

In the remainder of this book we will describe a set of ideas to suggest how one can better organize companies to create wealth in the 21st century. The ideas build on one another. Which ideas should be adopted and in what order will depend on the individual company and its particular circumstances.

Ideas to Manage Better

The first three ideas are on how to manage better in the 21st century. While these ideas are not truly new—in that they represent best practices drawn from superclass companies, professional services firms, the military, and staged gate investors—they are combined in ways that are innovative and different and in ways that make them more relevant to designing organizations that can produce higher "profits per employee."

- **Idea 1. Backbone Line Structure.** This idea is for companies that are struggling with the complexity of managing their own organization. Creating a backbone line structure involves streamlining management by increasing the authority of line management to drive earnings performance while creating enterprisewide standards and protocols to bound that authority. A backbone line hierarchy provides frontline managers with clear authority to mobilize the mind power, capital, and labor needed to perform. The idea is to put the tactical control of the complexity of dealing with the external marketplace under backbone frontline managers, or "field commanders." To simplify and focus frontline management, this approach takes accountabilities for developing major new strategies out of the front line and places that accountability with senior and top management. It also takes from the front line the responsibility for the complexity of managing shared support requiring specialized, professional skills, and it places that responsibility under shared central utilities, which are held accountable for their abilities to support the line effectively and efficiently.

- **Idea 2. One-Company Governance and Culture through a Partnership at the Top.** This idea is for companies that have organizations hamstrung by organizational silos, those that make it very difficult to mobilize mind power, labor, and capital on an enterprisewide basis. There are a number of approaches to moving to a one-company governance model, but the one we advocate is based on a "partnership at the top." Such a partnership is built on having a powerful CEO who has sufficient clout from the board to be able to hold top people both individually and mutually accountable and to be able to exit any executive not willing to act as a "partner." This approach involves creating a parent governance committee and a number of subcommittees (for example, IT, HR, technology), each of which takes ownership for exercising one-company governance in its field of focus. Such a committee-based structure requires a disciplined use of time, and therefore this approach demands operating through a unified, integrated corporate calendar. This approach would also normally involve creating an extended partnership that would comprise the several hundred most senior people in the company.

One-company governance also involves moving to a one-company culture that, in turn, establishes and enforces one-company standards, protocols, and values.

In concert with a strong line management structure, one-company governance provides the essential foundation needed to enable a company to be "well managed" and thereby able to use hierarchy to mobilize mind power, labor, and capital.

- **Idea 3. Dynamic Management.** Dynamic management is an idea that is aimed at enabling companies to mobilize the intangibles needed to discover new, wealth-creating strategies and business models as they navigate the external complexity, confusion, and uncertainty of today's world. It provides a way to do so without disrupting the ability or focus of frontline management on day-to-day operating performance. Dynamic management uses a pursuit of a "portfolio of initiatives" to discover wealth-creating opportunities by managing the related investment risks through the use of staged gate investment processes. With this approach, you navigate external complexity and uncertainty rather than make "leaps of faith" that assume away that complexity and uncertainty.

Ideas to Improve the Flow of Intangibles

The next three ideas involve improving the flow of intangibles through the company by using the energy of individuals who are self-directing their own work, thereby overcoming the problems of gaining collaboration among large numbers of employees who don't know each other. These ideas are all relatively new. This is largely because they have become practically possible only in the last decade with the advent of ubiquitous networked digital technology. These ideas are significantly dependent as well upon a company being well managed and operating as one company, and therefore they are less relevant to poorly managed companies.

- **Idea 4. Formal Networks.** A formal network is an organizing capability that uses the natural self-interest of individuals with a common interest to form a structured community that enables them to collaborate with one another easily, particularly through digital technology. It overcomes the problem of large numbers by creating subgroups with hundreds, rather than with tens of thousands, of people interacting with one another. Versions of formal networks, called "communities of practice," have long existed in professional firms; the idea is to bring such practices inside large companies to organize their professionals into networked communities so that they can exchange intangibles with a minimum of search or coordination costs. Formal networks mobilize mind power by enabling communities to build and exchange both personal and collective knowledge in defined areas of mutual interest.

- **Idea 5. Talent Marketplaces.** A talent marketplace is an enterprise-wide organizational capability that takes advantage of the natural self-interest of managers seeking talent and the natural self-interest of job seekers in order to find each other through market mechanisms. While HR professionals still serve as "brokers," this approach puts greater responsibility for personal development on the individual relative to the corporation. The intent is to make it easier for individuals to find jobs that they find exciting and that meet their personal development needs. It also puts a greater burden on managers to make jobs more appealing to job seekers if they want to compete for the best talent. Making talent markets work requires putting in place capabilities and processes to handle searching, competition, pricing, contracting the terms of employment, and so on. Talent marketplaces mobilize mind power by getting the right talent to the right jobs.

- **Idea 6. Knowledge Marketplaces.** A knowledge marketplace is an enterprisewide organizational capability that enables those workers with a natural self-interest in seeking particular types of knowledge to find those author-workers with a self-interest in building a personal reputation. Knowledge marketplaces include such approaches as providing a market exchange for high-quality documents, expertise systems, internal "wikipedias," and internal "blogs." They also include specific processes for ensuring effective searching, competition, and the quality of knowledge being traded, and they provide rewards for knowledge producers. Knowledge marketplaces mobilize mind power by getting the right knowledge to the right minds.

Ideas to Motivate Better Behaviors

The next two ideas are perhaps the most far-reaching, some might even say radical, of those proposed in the book. They involve rewiring the financial reporting systems and the performance evaluation systems of companies to motivate better economic behaviors by individuals. Doing so can enable companies to rely less on supervision and more on motivation to drive constructive behavior, and that, in turn, can make every one of the other ideas described in this book work better.

- **Idea 7. Motivating Economic Behaviors.** This idea requires revamping the financial reporting systems of companies to motivate better economic behaviors in the digital age. Most of today's financial reporting is based on "generally accepted accounting principles" (GAAP) that were designed to report earnings *externally* but that are used by most companies for reporting earnings *internally* as well.

  We are *not* advocating any changes to external reporting conventions. Rather, we are recommending a new approach to internal reporting. We propose that companies put greater weight on returns on talent (and returns to intangibles) than they place on returns on capital. Indeed, we advocate that profit per employee become the primary metric of profitability. We believe that returns on capital should be looked at just to ensure that they are sufficient to cover the costs of capital.

  This chapter also lays out an approach to financial performance measurement that is intended to motivate economic behaviors from managers while preserving and enhancing top management's abilities to deliver the current earnings expected by the market. It also involves shifting to enterprisewide financial performance measures more in tune with the 21st century. Better financial metrics enable the mobilization of mind power by motivating the economic behaviors to do so.

- **Idea 8. Role-Specific Performance Measurement.** Role-specific performance measurement involves defining the behavior expected for each of the roles in a company and then institutionalizing the performance measures of people in these roles to motivate collaborative, economic behaviors. This approach recognizes the importance of role modeling, of the definition of skills required, and of the setting of expectations for performance to enable people to develop a good mental model of behavior, particularly in relation to people occupying similar roles. It then uses role-specific performance measurement to reinforce those desired behaviors.

The intent is to motivate the right behaviors from largely self-directed, thinking-intensive people who require significant autonomy to undertake their work. Under this approach, you hold people not just individually accountable for their performance but also mutually accountable for how well they help others succeed. This approach also enables the creation of compliance processes to provide appropriate consequences to individuals who behave badly.

The biggest change this approach requires is moving from having individual managers be primarily responsible for evaluating performance to institutionalizing performance measurement and career development through personnel committees. Role-specific performance measurement enables mobilizing mind power by motivating better behaviors from people who need to collaborate with one another.

Ideas to Implement an Organizational Strategy

The final idea is to make organizational design for the 21st century the centerpiece of corporate strategy.

- **Idea 9. Organizational Design as Strategy.** Wealth in the 21st century will come from becoming better at mobilizing the mind power latent in each company's workforce of talented employees. Hoping that the existing organizing model will through serendipity evolve to a better design is an inadequate response to the economic changes brought about by our transition to the digital age. Organizational design can no longer be an afterthought. Rather, corporate leaders need to invest an amount of design energy that is sufficient to the task of creating an organization that can thrive no matter what conditions it meets as the 21st century unfolds.

The approach we recommend is to develop a "master plan" of how you want the organization to operate in the future, say, some five years from now, and then to deliberately put it in place through a multiyear portfolio-of-initiatives program that uses stage gating discipline to navigate the execution of organizational change.

Designing and successfully completing major organizational change initiatives will be hard. It will require enormous commitment, focus, and patience from top leadership. But doing so is the key to having a working environment that enables the company's professionals and managers to perform up to their full potential, thereby making it possible for the company to prosper.

Now let's begin exploring these ideas, one at a time.

PART II

IDEAS TO MANAGE BETTER

3

CREATING A BACKBONE LINE STRUCTURE

SOME READERS MAY WONDER why the first ideas we offer up are for making hierarchy work better. Didn't we just get through arguing that collaboration is the great new opportunity of the 21st century?

We focus on hierarchy first because fixing it is essential to reducing unproductive complexity and for creating the conditions that enable enterprisewide collaboration. In this chapter, then, we will focus on how to use a "backbone line structure" to reduce unproductive complexity at the "front line." And in the next, we will explain how to use hierarchy to enable effective enterprisewide collaboration through one-company governance.

From the time of the Pharaohs, all large organizations have relied on hierarchical structures to mobilize their large numbers of people to work together. Despite the advent of technology, hierarchical authority is the most efficient, effective means for organizations to set aspirations, make decisions among competing alternatives, assign tasks, allocate and commit scarce resources, manage people (not capable of self-direction), and hold people accountable. Hierarchy works because it is efficient: It is based on simple, top-down and bottom-up communications. The problem today is not hierarchical authority but rather how that authority is misused. Many companies misuse hierarchical authority and wind up creating very "siloed" structures that block collaboration. We will address that issue in the next chapter.

There is another problem often experienced: Many companies misuse hierarchy to accomplish work activities that could be better accomplished through collaboration. Because leaders find it difficult to inspire the mutual self-interest among their reports to get them to collaborate naturally with one another, they instead complicate their hierarchical structures to force collaboration. The use of such techniques as matrix structures, co-heads of units, and internal joint ventures has added unnecessary unproductive complexity to the frontline work environment in many companies. Furthermore, it has robbed hierarchy of its efficiency and clarity. The natural and correct instinct, when faced with overwhelming complexity and an ineffective management structure, is to simplify. If your hierarchical structure has become too complex and is becoming ineffective, you need to streamline it so that your company can once again become manageable.

In matrix management language this is sometimes expressed as picking a "dominant" or "primary axis of management." The danger in simplifying, of course, is that you will "throw the baby out with the bathwater." You risk getting rid not just of unproductive complexity but of productive collaboration as well.

There are a variety of design alternatives that will help streamline an organization and improve and simplify how it uses hierarchical authority. In this chapter, we will describe our preferred way of streamlining a hierarchy. We call this creating "a backbone line structure." We prefer this approach because it enables use of a strong management hierarchy and, in combination with the one-firm governance approaches we will describe in the next chapter, enables large-scale collaboration as well.

We have a number of core beliefs about how hierarchy should be used:

Our first core belief is that you must have a strong backbone hierarchy.

Our second is that there should be three primary layers of leadership—frontline, senior, and top.

Our third core belief is that we have a bias toward centralizing support functions.

The fourth is that we believe that similar roles should be standardized enterprisewide. For example, a comptroller should have the same description across the company. Divisions should not be allowed to establish their roles and titles independently. A related belief is that organizing structures should parallel one another across the enterprise (to the extent possible).

Finally, our fifth belief is that there should be a basic and simple, well-understood chain of command in decision making.

A Strong Backbone

Nearly all organizations are replete with opportunities to streamline and simplify the use of hierarchical authorities to remove unproductive complexities—while simultaneously increasing that authority's effectiveness. The approach we advocate involves redesigning a company's hierarchical order, thereby improving management's ability to use hierarchical authority to power a company's performance. The effort centers on defining a central management structure, or "backbone," and a general line management structure, tasked with clear decision authority and accountability for operating performance. By a "backbone line structure" we mean a chain of command that puts authority to make tactical decisions close to the front lines. By "frontline manager," we mean someone with the authority to set aspirations, define tasks and roles, assign people and hold them accountable, mobilize resources, and make decisions for frontline workers. The "backbone line structure" can be defined on geographic, client, product, or functional lines (or some combination of them all).

Think of the backbone line structure in the sense of the classic military organization: The frontline commanders are put in full charge, in the fog and confusion of combat, to devise the tactics that take the hill. We want the same effect in organizations: "field commanders" who are fully responsible and who are given the full backing of the organization to pursue tactical opportunities and to address tactical issues.

In this model, backbone leaders would be held accountable for integrating perspectives and making decisions on operating issues within their defined areas of accountability. These operating accountabilities would often include making decisions that involve people who are the leaders' peers, not just people who report up to those leaders.

If it seems familiar, it is: We see the backbone line structure as being a return to the notion of general management, in which frontline managers are expected to be integrative leaders and decision makers, combining client, product, geographic, and functional perspectives as necessary to make tactical decisions. It is also an alternative to matrix management, which we believe leaves employees struggling to determine which of their bosses is primary and which is secondary—and which boss should win a given debate.

Of course, a backbone line structure does more than define authorities. It defines the work being performed as either being "line" (that is, creating earnings from mobilizing the enterprise's resources) or "support" (helping others in their efforts to produce earnings). For example, in a consumer package company, software design engineers might be support. But in a software company, they might be line. Likewise, many critical activities of the enterprise would not necessarily be under the direct authority of the backbone line structure; examples of such activities are managing shared functional support utilities, managing "formal networks" of people across the enterprise, or managing pools of talented workers available for mobilization across the firm. Such activities would be managed by other leaders.

Moreover, certain units may be line for one set of activities while being support for others (particularly when units are responsible for managing shared costs). For example, the credit card division of a bank is considered line when that division is directly acquiring credit customers. But it is considered support when it distributes cards to the bank's retail branch–based customers managed by a separate division. The backbone line structures would be responsible for managing existing capabilities and for determining what services and resources need to be "pulled" from utilities, networks, and talent pools to win in the marketplace. All backbone leaders would be, by definition, powerful decision makers who would have little need to push decisions up the chain of command.

Finally, it is critical that boundaries are established for the authority of line managers, particularly to ensure that the authority is used to make frontline tactical decisions that drive earnings rather than used to make broader strategic or cross-organizational decisions that may come into conflict with other decision makers. The object, in other words, is to define useful personal boundaries to exercising authority but not barriers that discourage people from working together.

Global Bank

To understand how a backbone line structure might work, let's take a look at Global Bank. As we said in the Preface, while most of the ideas in this book have been put into practice, no single company operates the way we propose. Therefore, we have created Global Bank, a hypothetical institution, with almost $1 trillion in assets, headquartered on the East Coast of the United States (Figure 3-1). With 200,000 employees, it makes $10 billion in profits annually (that is, $50,000 per employee). Its largest single business, Global Consumer, is serving retail customers, an activity that represents about 45 percent of Global Bank's earnings.

The Global Wealth Management business accounts for 15 percent of Global Bank's earnings, and the Global Securities Services business accounts for 10 percent of its earnings. The Global Capital Markets & Investment Banking business represents the remaining 30 percent of Global Bank's earnings. The CEO of Global Bank has chosen not to have a president or chief operating officer; instead, the CEO has four

FIGURE 3-1

Global Bank

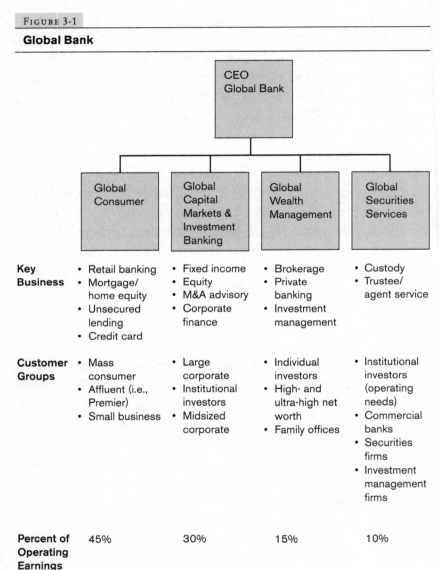

	Global Consumer	Global Capital Markets & Investment Banking	Global Wealth Management	Global Securities Services
Key Business	• Retail banking • Mortgage/ home equity • Unsecured lending • Credit card	• Fixed income • Equity • M&A advisory • Corporate finance	• Brokerage • Private banking • Investment management	• Custody • Trustee/ agent service
Customer Groups	• Mass consumer • Affluent (i.e., Premier) • Small business	• Large corporate • Institutional investors • Midsized corporate	• Individual investors • High- and ultra-high net worth • Family offices	• Institutional investors (operating needs) • Commercial banks • Securities firms • Investment management firms
Percent of Operating Earnings	45%	30%	15%	10%

direct reports, each of whom is responsible for one of the business areas.

Global Consumer, which is Global Bank's single largest business, has some 125,000 employees. The U.S. Banking Division, with 50,000 employees and 2,500 branches, is the largest unit within Global Consumer (Figure 3-2).

The U.S. Banking Division, like Global Bank as a whole, is struggling with complexity. The organization is too sprawling to show on a single chart, so we show only the East Coast region in detail. The East Coast region, with 12,000 employees and 600 branches, is one of four regions within U.S. Banking, which together make up the 50,000-employee, 2,500-branch U.S. Banking Division. The East Coast contributes about $500 million to Global Bank's total profits.

The East Coast region, which was formerly the branch system of one of the five large banks that merged to form Global Bank, is typical of the U.S. Banking Division's four regions. The intermediate structures of the U.S. Banking Division's organization are heavily "matrixed." In fact, 9 of the 12 direct reports to the East Coast banking executive also report to someone else. For this reason, the East Coast IT executive also reports to Corporate IT. The East Coast HR executive also reports to the U.S. Banking Division's HR function. The East Coast Small Business executive also reports to the U.S. Banking Small Business Division executive. And so on. It is a very complex organization.

Now consider the plight of frontline managers reporting up to the New York Metro executive: Every time they have an issue with IT or HR or Mortgages or Consumer Credit, they either have to go "back channel" to personal friends in these units to get the issue resolved, or they need to get their boss, the head of New York Metro, involved in the discussions. Getting Operations to fix an operating issue that is adversely affecting customer service could involve several voice-mails and e-mails. If a face-to-face meeting is required, it could take weeks for everyone involved to find the time to accomplish that. Even if the meeting is scheduled, one of the parties may cancel out at the last minute.

FIGURE 3-2

The Current Organizational Structure of the Global Bank Consumer Business Unit

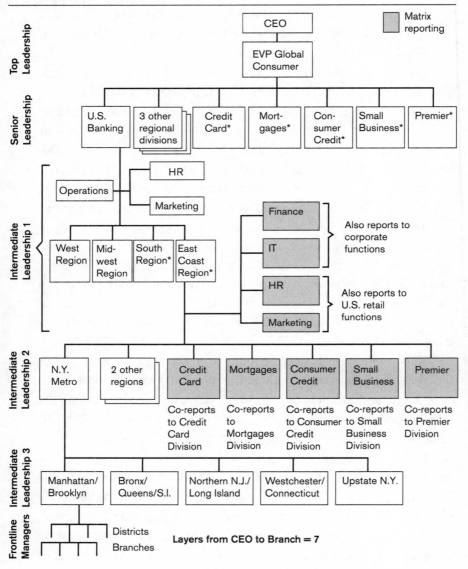

Layers from CEO to Branch = 7

* Not shown are subordinate backbone line managers for leaders in these organizations; each of these divisions/organizations would have several direct reports who would help backbone line managers in fulfilling their day-to-day responsibilities (averaging 9–10 per divisional leader).

To be sure, similar issues have plagued the organizations of large companies for decades. But before the digital age, the pace was slower, the difficulties of communication limited the number of potential people whose work needed to be coordinated with one another, and decision-making roles were clearer (that is, it was always easy to see who was the line manager).

In the digital age, the pace is faster, everyone can communicate with everyone, and numerous powerful senior executives have emerged (that is, leaders of IT, Operations, Marketing, and Finance, not to mention leaders of product versus geography versus customer segments) who act in ways that confuse down-the-line managers as to whose authority to recognize.

In the case of the U.S. Banking Division, much of the challenge is in trying to run the business day to day across a broad range of products, customer groups, and geographies with an enormous array of executives in intermediate positions with competing and conflicting agendas. Leading the day-to-day management of a retail branch system is at its heart a blocking and tackling problem. You win through operational excellence, effective customer service, and proactive marketing in which the objectives are to continually deepen existing customer relationships and to add new customers. But trying to do so when most of your energy is devoted to grappling with internal organizational complexity limits your ability to perform.

How, then, should the U.S. Banking Division cope with these day-to-day operating problems? We believe the answer is in radical revision and simplification of the hierarchical structure.

Paring Down to Three Layers of Backbone Leadership

In the model we are proposing, all the intermediate layers in the organization and all the matrixed roles are eliminated from the backbone leadership structure itself. In this model, most of the layers of hierarchy, and most of the capabilities needed to manage large numbers of frontline people, are put under a beefed-up frontline general manager. Where do these people who were in the middle go? They are moved, either to a shared functional support utility or underneath a frontline manager. By completely eliminating the intermediate organizing structures, the organization is left with only two layers of hierarchy above the backbone frontline manager—a senior leadership layer and a top leadership layer.

How big can a company get with only three primary layers of backbone hierarchy, including frontline managers as one of the layers? A reasonable span of leadership on the part of senior and top leaders could be 10 to 15. Taking 10 top managers, with 10 senior leaders reporting to them (who, in turn, had 10 frontline managers reporting to them) would yield 1,000 frontline units. If each frontline unit represented $100 million in profits, you could have, in theory, a company with $100 billion in profits (which is more than twice as much as the most profitable company today) with just three layers of hierarchy above the front line. Through careful design, three (or at most four) layers of hierarchy above the front line should be sufficient for even the largest megainstitution.

Let's return to the Global Consumer Bank to see how the backbone line structure could streamline and simplify the use of hierarchical authority. In this example, the executive oversees 60 percent (that is, 125,000) of the entire enterprise's employees and accounts for 45 percent of the bank's earnings. However 40 percent (that is, 50,000) of those employees in the Global Consumer Bank report to a single one of his reports—the head of the U.S. Banking Division.

In the new structure, the Global Consumer executive would have 7 senior backbone line managers reporting to him, 4 network leaders, and 2 staff reports (Figure 3-3). The position of the U.S. Banking Division leader would be eliminated, and it would be replaced by four equally sized new divisions (that is, East, South, Midwest, and West) to go alongside the Credit Card, Mortgage, Consumer Credit, Small Business, and Premier (that is, Affluent Consumer) Divisions.

On average, each of these 7 senior backbone leaders would have 7

FIGURE 3-3

The New Organizational Structure of the Global Bank Consumer Business Unit

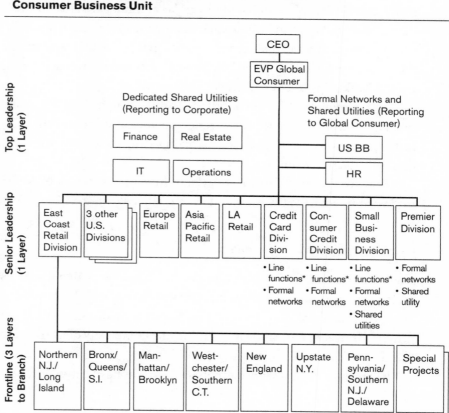

Total Layers from CEO to Branch = 5

*Serves as backbone management for all sales and service activities related to non-branch-based delivery (i.e., dedicated channels and private label distribution to outside distribution channels).

backbone frontline managers reporting to him or her, creating some 50-odd frontline units and a total backbone leadership structure, including all three layers, of fewer than 75. Each of these 50-odd frontline units would contribute, on average, some $90 million to profits, although the range from unit to unit would be wide.

If similar approaches were used in the other three arenas (Global

Wealth Management, Global Capital Markets & Investment Banking, and Global Securities Services), Global Bank would have fewer than 200 backbone frontline units run by general managers and no more than 300 or so backbone line managers for the entire enterprise (including senior and top management). As a group, these 300 backbone line managers would be the executives responsible for delivering Global Bank's day-to-day earnings.

In this model, while the backbone frontline organizational units themselves would be very diverse, reflecting the complexity of the marketplace, we would envision the organizing structures above the front line to be relatively simple.

How would these three layers (front line, senior, and top) work? And what happens to the roles that were previously matrixed?

Frontline Management

As we have said before, most of the work in a company that drives its performance occurs at the front line—at the place where the firm stops and the outside world starts. It is therefore at the front line where the firm needs to adapt its capabilities to "fit" the complexity of the outside world.

In our approach, frontline managers would have three different profiles:

1. Backbone frontline managers

2. Shared utility frontline managers

3. Frontline formal project managers

Backbone Frontline Managers

In our model, the backbone frontline managers are general managers who combine backbone structure with frontline management. This is the critical position needed to clarify all the ambiguity usually associated with the intermediate structure of the organization. They are the field commanders, the integration point of all the geographic, product, customer group, and functional capabilities required to deliver day-to-day operating performance. They run "contribution centers" and are responsible both for revenues and for the costs directly related to creating those revenues. They are high enough in the organization to have real clout and independence of decision making but close enough to the front line to be tuned in to the marketplace.

To be able to do this, backbone frontline managers should have within their direct reports the essential capabilities necessary to deliver results, and if they do not have them, they should be able to draw on shared support utilities, networks, and talent pools as needed without having to ask from higher up in the hierarchy. This frontline general management point would enable the backbone leader to integrate the firm's capabilities to fit whatever particular complexities and circumstances exist. Depending on the work, the backbone frontline manager could be a manager of a professional sales team responsible for a particular market segment or the manager of a group of investment bankers or perhaps the manager of a group of petroleum engineers focused on discovering oil.

To illustrate this, let's return to the East Coast Division of the Global Consumer Bank, which involves the management of large amounts of labor-intensive, as well as "thinking-intensive," work. Applying the notion of backbone line management to the retail arena could lead to the establishment of, for example, some 25 subregional geographic managers within the United States (each responsible for about 100 retail branches), which would be designated as the point of frontline backbone general management in their respective territories. Each of these managers would report respectively either to the East Coast, South, Midwest, or West Retail Banking Divisions.

Figure 3-4 shows the structure of the New Jersey/Long Island branch organization under a backbone frontline manager (who would serve as the general management point for the frontline units reporting to her). As shown in that figure, the New Jersey/Long Island backbone frontline

FIGURE 3-4

New Backbone Frontline Management Structure of the Global Bank New Jersey/Long Island Branch

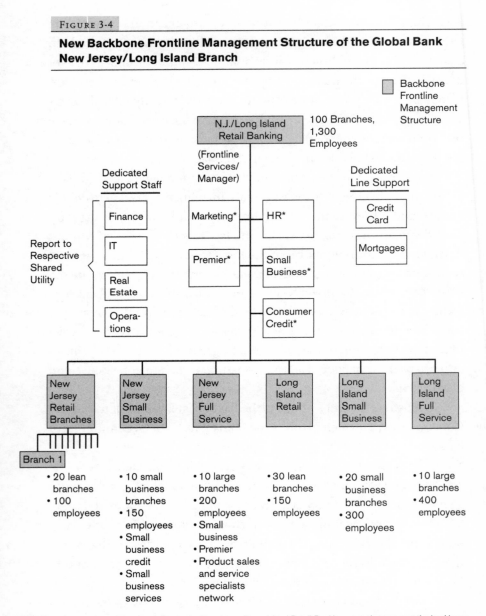

* Distributed support executives, reporting to the New Jersey/Long Island Retail Banking executive, not past the backbone frontline structure, who are networked to respective areas.

manager would be responsible for providing direct leadership to some 6 frontline unit managers, each composed of 10 to 20 branches and 5 distributed staff executives (for example, Marketing, HR, Premier, Small Business, and Consumer Credit).[1] A "distributed staff executive" is a person who reports directly to a line manager, who in turn is responsible for working with shared utilities and support functions to pull whatever support is needed. Some of this support would not be just from functional units but also from other line units (for example, Credit Card).

If the "backbone general manager" for this geography wanted to create a "marketing" campaign and product bundle aimed at the personal banking needs of the affluent small business owner in her territory, for instance, she could pull the needed talent through the talent marketplace for the Small Business, Premier (that is, Affluent), and Marketing units to put that campaign together. In doing so, she would assign a staff direct report (for example, Small Business) who would have responsibility for working with those other units to ensure the right support was received.

She would also have four other dedicated executives for functions like Finance, IT, Real Estate, and Operations.[2] These dedicated executives would not report to her but rather to their respective functional frontline general managers. Nevertheless, they would be responsible for providing support to her unit. In this case, though, these dedicated executives would be, in effect, responsible for marketing their services to her and would be held accountable for their success (through using such techniques as "service-level agreements").

We will describe later the role functions should play in safeguarding the company (for example, ensuring compliance with regulations or standards).

The entire organization under this backbone general manager would have some 100 branch managers and 1,300 total employees, plus any temporarily "borrowed" talent from other units. A "table of organization" would define this unit's target organization (what number of people in what roles and with what skills.[3] Such frontline units would constitute Global Bank's essential "fighting formation" for generating earnings from the branch system.

Under this structure, the capabilities and complexities of managing, mobilizing, and integrating capabilities from the intermediate structures of the organization are moved to the front line. This, in turn, allows them to be tailored to the particular circumstances facing each unit (without complicating the work of other units) and doing so without having those backbone frontline managers spend much time on support activities (that support is managed separately in shared utilities).

A very lean management structure is another characteristic of this particular organization. Only 125 of the employees, 110 of them in branch manager roles, would be in thinking-intensive jobs. In the New Jersey/Long Island branch structure, then, only about 10 percent of the 1,300 people would have thinking-intensive jobs. All but the support executives in these thinking-intensive jobs would be in management roles. Yet the frontline manager would be able to pull all the additional mind power she needed through talent marketplaces and knowledge marketplaces.

Shared Utility Frontline Managers

In the model we are proposing, there will also be shared utility frontline managers who are involved in a wide variety of roles that are critical to the operating performance of the company. Shared utilities are generally cost centers rather than contribution centers. As economies of scale have increased, and as many support functions have become more specialized, the importance of managing shared utilities in enabling the capture of scale and specialization economies has also increased.

Many of these frontline shared utility roles (such as fleet, data center, call center, and plant managers) oversee production work requiring consistent, cost-effective management of labor forces. A very large percentage of all the employees of most firms reside in these units (that is, many of the some 75 percent in most companies who are not in thinking-intensive jobs). Frontline management of production work often will require the use of extensive supervision of multiple layers of hierarchy below the frontline manager, this to control the work of very large numbers of workers. But frontline management of shared utilities also involves the management of thinking-intensive, professional support functions—where the frontline manager may be called a "general counsel," a "comptroller," or a "chief scientist." Another variety of frontline shared utility manager would be a "formal network" manager (described in a later chapter) whose role is to support a specific community of thinking-intensive workers.

The point is that all of these roles need frontline managers with very specific, specialized skills and abilities for the particular kind of frontline work they manage. Furthermore, all of them require managing complexity. Many of these roles, in fact, require finding a fit not only with the complexities of the outside world (for example, call centers with customers or general counsels with regulators and litigators) but also a fit with the internal organization (by providing tailored, cost-effective support to backbone frontline managers and to other frontline units).

The natural desire of line managers at all levels in a hierarchy is to control the support functions on which they depend for their own operations. The problem is that even the best of line managers are no more than "gifted amateurs" in most of the various different professional activities they use (for example, risk, IT, or legal), and furthermore, they do not have the time, the mindsets, or the skills to build or manage the support capabilities they need. Given the desire of all line managers to control their own support units, often the compromise is to use matrix reporting in conjunction with subscale support units. But such compromises are not the answer.

The better answer is to set up scale-effective shared utilities and to have them report directly to senior frontline support managers—and adopt a client service mentality toward the units they support. In other words, these support utilities should be held accountable to serve cost-effectively the internal marketplace of managers and professionals requiring support (just as line units are held accountable for serving an external marketplace). Creating such enterprisewide centers of excellence (with a client service mentality) enables companies to capture the full benefits of the scale, scope, and specialization advantages made possible by today's technology, the formation of global markets, and the opportunities of off-shoring and outsourcing. To enable such shared utilities to work well with line units, companies must incubate cadres of skilled professionals in different disciplines. These people should be assigned to support line managers (throughout the firm) as they are needed.

In the Global Consumer Bank example, the elimination of the U.S. Division would mean that the shared utilities that are supporting the branch system would report to either the EVP Global Consumer or the CEO rather than to a senior backbone manager. But this is the point of this structure: You want the senior backbone line manager overseeing the frontline units focused on strategy and on winning in the marketplace, not on running a support function. The shared support utilities would be accountable for serving the internal marketplace of all the individual frontline backbone units systemwide, not accountable for how well they pleased a particular senior backbone leader. *Whom* they report to is less relevant than *how* they are being held accountable. In the model we are proposing, they would be held accountable for cost-effectiveness and the quality of their support to frontline units.

Ideally, each shared utility manager would report up either to a senior or top manager, someone with deep professional knowledge in the relevant field. In the case of the Global Consumer Bank, for example, a market research shared utility manager would report to the Global Consumer Bank's senior marketing manager.

There are clearly trade-offs involved in how far to take the shared support utility concept. While we have a clear bias toward centralization to capture scale and specialization effects, we also know that the best answer will depend on the specific function and the specific circumstances. In general, the more intensive the interactions required between the front line and the support activity, the greater the need to distribute the activity to the line.

Generally, when the need for cross-corporation standardization is high, we believe the function should report to the corporate center. On the other hand, the function should report to the line when a rapid response is critical or the function is of particularly strategic importance to the line's core mission.

At one extreme, for example, the provision of administrative support to Global Bank's investment bankers would require such intensive interactions with individual bankers that such support would need to be co-located with the line. At the other extreme, data centers should either be managed in an enterprisewide utility or even outsourced. In all cases, defining these relationships carefully is critical. You want to avoid the dysfunction and unproductive complexity that arises when there is ambiguity over who is responsible for what.

Frontline Formal Project Managers

In addition to backbone and shared utility frontline managers, we are also proposing a special kind of frontline manager, one whose responsibilities are not the delivery of day-to-day operating performance using existing capabilities. Rather, this person would be responsible for leading the longer-term tasks of building new capabilities, adapting existing capabilities, or adding or shedding capabilities through acquisition or divestment. Creating these special-project roles enables backbone frontline managers and shared utility managers to focus on operating the business day to day with existing capabilities—without being diverted by the far different challenge of creating new capabilities.

We will explain how these projects should be managed in Chapter 5 on dynamic management. For purposes of the discussion in this chapter, the point to keep in mind is that these roles are also important frontline management roles. Just as in the case of the backbone line manager and the shared utility manager, these projects should also be overseen by a senior leader. But before we get to the next layer of hierarchy—the senior leadership role—we need to look at how frontline management of thinking-intensive work is different from frontline management of more labor intensive work.

Frontline Management of
Thinking-Intensive Work

In the example we used earlier in this chapter (the New Jersey/Long Island backbone frontline manager), most of the reports to that executive consisted of other managers who supervise labor-intensive activities. But there is an increasingly important special category of frontline management that can be found in backbone line roles, in support roles, and in roles that include the management of formal projects. In these cases, the role is not to manage other managers but rather to provide direction to professional, thinking-intensive workers.

These are roles that require the "hands-on management" of people with deep professional skills, roles that require the use of subjective judgment and engagement in problem solving. Some organizational units undertaking professional work (in areas like product design, research, or investment banking) may require some 40 to 70 percent of all the roles in those units to be thinking intensive.

In the digital age, this professional work is often what produces the most wealth. It is also often the work that is the most difficult to manage well. And indeed, by its nature, it is more "craft" work than production work. As such, the frontline manager of such work need not be only a good manager but also actually a "master craftsperson." Scientists need to be led by chief scientists, investment bankers need to be led by master bankers, and lawyers need to be led by a general counsel, and so on.

At their best, these master craftspersons use their hierarchical roles to mobilize the internal and external talent and knowledge needed to achieve the unit's objectives. They also use their roles to hold talented people within the unit both individually and mutually accountable for results. But they do more than that. They serve to develop people's talents in their discipline, through what professional firms call the "apprenticeship model" of management. In this role, they are at the very heart of a firm's ability to create valuable intangible assets.

In the apprenticeship model, the roles of the managers are played by people who have enough skill in the craft to improve upon the work of the others. Their hierarchical power, then, comes not from authority alone but also from the respect they earn from the "apprentices." Without such deep skills, an otherwise talented general manager is powerless to determine how to supervise the work. It is not just the hours put in that counts (in thinking-intensive, professional work), after all, but the creative and intangible result of that work.

The power of the apprenticeship model starts with its ability to leverage the skills of the master craftspersons (that is, the frontline managers with distinctive professional skills) to those with less skill. It often takes 10 years or more to grow a master craftsperson. The model works by having the master craftsperson manage more-junior managers (that is, team leaders) who, in turn, oversee experienced workers (that is, journeymen), who, in turn, supervise inexperienced workers (that is, apprentices). Through the apprenticeship model, work products turn out better, and everyone involved learns more quickly.

At every hierarchical layer, the more-experienced workers gain leverage and the less-experienced workers are able to grow their skills and knowledge. The master craftspersons are, by their nature, micromanagers who pay great attention to detail. In doing so, they touch nearly every person in their group. Whatever work is produced by the group, in fact, will bear the personal stamp of that master craftsperson.

These frontline master craftspersons realize that their real job is not only in the delivery of a valuable work product but also in the growth of their people. They are responsible for defining the roles and responsibilities of the frontline thinking-intensive workers they lead, and they are often personally involved in defining and assigning tasks to individuals and teams. They decide whom to develop and whom to separate out.

The degree to which frontline thinking-intensive people in a particular discipline are successful is significantly dependent on these frontline master craftspersons. They shape the work environment, and in the chain of command they are usually the closest to the workers and know them as individuals.

While frontline professional work is by nature messy, it still offers many opportunities for streamlining the layers of hierarchy above a master craftsperson. For example, in general, the three-layer rule should be followed so that the master craftspersons report to senior leaders who, in turn, report to top management.

In this model, a frontline unit engaged in professional work may sometimes have no more than 20 to 50 thinking-intensive people in it (although we know of communities of upward of several hundred people under frontline managers in some large professional firms).

There are, of course, considerable opportunities to improve the productivity of this work, through the approaches we will describe later in this book. We just want to make the point here that these opportunities do not include reducing the amount of apprenticeship that thinking people receive at the frontline.

Senior Backbone Line Leadership

Once individuals step away from the front line, they quickly lose the very specific knowledge and information that the frontline workers possess—knowledge that allows the front line to deal well with marketplaces, customers, local regulators, and the other complexities of the business world. One danger of this, of course, is that individuals who have been promoted up the chain of command to senior roles may continue to believe that they know best about the front line even though the market will continue to evolve in their absence, rapidly antiquating their frontline knowledge.

Besides this, there are far more important roles for senior backbone leadership to play than that of micromanaging skilled managers reporting up to them. We define "senior leaders" as those who report to top leaders. From their particular vantage point, with a proximity to both the details of the front line and the wider view required of the corporate center, senior managers (who are sitting just above frontline managers) are situated perfectly for leadership. In these roles, they are ideally positioned to mobilize the power of minds and the resources of the entire company and to pursue strategic opportunities while leaving the tactical opportunities to the frontline managers. (We will describe the specific role of senior managers driving strategic initiatives in Chapter 5 on dynamic management.)

Moreover, they are best positioned to inspire the front line, to establish aspirations for frontline managers, to hold the front line accountable for results, and to ensure compliance to standards, protocols, and values. While earlier in their careers most of these executives would have played the frontline management role, in these senior-level jobs they play a different role. They are more leaders of frontline managers than frontline managers themselves. Finally, they are senior enough to focus top management on the needs of the front line, particularly when the front line is not getting enough support from other units. In the Global Bank example, the Global Consumer Division would have 11 members of senior leadership (for example, East Coast Retail, Europe Retail, and Small Business).

In their particular position, senior leaders can act either as leaders or hands-on managers, depending on the circumstances. Senior leaders, for example, may need at times to act as managers rather than as leaders to serve as a temporary backstop, particularly if a frontline leader fails or departs suddenly.

But these senior leaders need to do far more than lead the people who report up to them. It is also imperative that the people in these roles act as corporate citizens—that is, individuals who define their personal success not just in terms of the results of the units that report to them but also in terms of the value they add in helping the entire enterprise prosper. People in these senior leadership roles need to function as pivot points—as parts of the vertical hierarchical structure but also as partners who can collaborate with other senior leaders horizontally across the enterprise.

If they can function in both vertical and horizontal capacities simultaneously, they can become the critical linchpins—enabling a company to gain the benefits of hierarchy in driving down-the-line performance while simultaneously enabling large-scale collaboration across the enterprise. They become the locus of exercising subjective judgment, balancing the desire to maximize the results of the units reporting to them against the needs of the entire enterprise.

The combined use of a backbone hierarchy, shared support utilities, formal networks, and so forth will enable the frontline general manager to deal tactically with the complexities of serving the marketplace, without going up a chain of command. This ability to make tactical decisions without having to go up the chain of command should apply equally to the frontline managers, to the shared utilities, and to formal project managers.

In turn, this can enable the simplification of the reporting relationships between frontline managers and their senior leaders. It should be possible to design a structure where each frontline manager has one, and only one, hierarchical boss. While people under the frontline manager may have to relate to others outside their unit (through a network structure), or may need to draw on shared utilities for service, the design of this model allows the frontline manager to have only one clear hierarchical leader—the senior leader to whom he or she reports.

The same holds true for senior managers. The model is designed to give senior leaders a clear reporting relationship to only one top leader.

This proposed redefinition of "frontline management" and "senior backbone line management" can greatly streamline the hierarchical structure. It also keeps the complexity of the outside world from unnecessarily complicating the internal organization.

But where does top management fit into this structure?

Top Management

At the top of the backbone line structure in this model is a CEO. This leader's role is not only to communicate with clients, the board, and others but also to provide clear leadership to the entire backbone line structure and the critical support functions supporting the line as well. While frontline management will generally drive performance, and senior leadership will drive strategic initiatives and cross-firm collaboration, it is top management that will determine the long-term health of the enterprise.[4]

In the Global Bank example, there would be four top management backbone leaders (Global Consumer, Global Wealth Management, Global Securities Services, and Global Capital Markets & Investment Banking) who would be responsible for producing current earnings through the backbone line structure. But, as we will describe in the next chapter, they would also have responsibilities for enterprisewide leadership, a task they would share with other members of top management.

In addition to the backbone line managers and CEO, the top positions may often include a president (chief operating officer) and a chief financial officer. Other very senior members of management may include the managers of key shared support services (for example, technology, operations, and networks), functions (for example, distribution, manufacturing, and research and development), or professional corporate center services (for example, legal, marketing, strategic planning, and corporate development). Increasingly, these members of management are included in top management, with titles that include the word "chief" (such as "chief technology officer," "chief talent officer," "chief marketing officer," "chief science officer," "chief legal officer," "chief risk officer," "chief knowledge officer," and "chief client officer").

This group of top managers is frequently referred to as the "C level." Usually, these C-level executives would have senior professional staff and frontline managers of shared utilities reporting up to them, but they would generally *not* have any backbone line managers as direct reports.

Need for Definition of Top Structure

Today's largest corporations have truly become "megainstitutions." In our experience, much of the enterprisewide organizational dysfunction of these megainstitutions comes from the lack of definition of the reporting relationships—the roles, responsibilities, and authority of the top 10 to 30 people with each other. We believe that moving to a backbone line structure can help enormously by clarifying the roles of line versus support. A good portion of this dysfunctional complexity can also be addressed by creating the one-company governance structures and one-company culture described in the next chapter.

Much of the rest of the dysfunction can be addressed by clearly defining individual roles and responsibilities and providing boundaries around each person's authorities. Such structures and definitions can enable the people at the top to become, in effect, a single layer of leadership rather than operating through multiple layers of hierarchical management with conflicting objectives, all jockeying for power and influence.

A great deal of the jockeying for power at the top is between line management with support staff. Part of this conflict today is for good reason: Most line managers in many support areas lack any real knowledge, and often they may lack the abilities to make good decisions in the absence of sound advice from high-talent staff professionals. Moreover, much of the role of support functions is to keep the organization under control—and compliant with both external regulations and the company's own standards and protocols.

Up until now in this chapter, we've assumed that the backbone line hierarchy has unquestioned authority to operate the business day to day. But we've been silent on how support functions relate to this backbone line structure. Let's examine this relationship now.

Companies need to put most of their support in shared support utilities under top managers who are managed separately from the backbone line structure, except for carefully defined interfaces (that is, dedicated and distributed executives). But the relationship between line and functional staff is more complex than that.

The functional staff plays three different roles: servicing, advising, and safeguarding. We've already described the role support functions can play in serving the line through shared utilities. We will describe later in the book how talent marketplaces can be used to more effectively deploy and manage functional staff. Both servicing and advising are true support roles. Having support units serve the line with a customer service role makes sense. The safeguarding role is different; in this role the job of the function is to serve as police officer. In our judgment, this role should be exercised by different people rather than by the functional executives providing support to the line. Why? Because combining a client services support role with a policing role is to introduce conflicts of interest. We would rather, instead, see these roles come together only at the corporate center, through having C-level functional executives held accountable as general managers for their effectiveness in providing support, advice, and safeguarding holistically.

Make no mistake: These C-level functional executives, far from being second-class citizens, should be powerful, but their power should be in defined arenas that do not conflict with the authority of backbone line managers in producing operating earnings day to day. Indeed, throughout this book, we will be describing several approaches to enable nonbackbone line managers to exercise power constructively within their defined arenas. As we describe both in this chapter and throughout the book, C-level executives in fields like finance, HR, IT, and marketing in our model would be able to exercise considerable power to impact the enterprise. They would do this mostly by participating in enterprisewide governance and by chairing appropriate enterprisewide committees, and then leading these groups to establish and enforce appropriate standards and protocols, within their respective professional fields.

We would also foresee these same executives exercising their power by overseeing appropriate strategic initiatives, leading formal enterprisewide networks of professionals in relevant disciplines, controlling pools of talent in these disciplines deployed through relevant talent marketplaces, and "owning" relevant knowledge domains of the knowledge marketplace.

Much of their influence, though, will come from their direct oversight of the enterprise's shared functional support utilities.

Parallel Organization, Consistent Definition of Roles

In order to provide frontline managers with the autonomy to act while still preserving the legitimate interests of leaders who are not part of that chain of command, you need to provide clear, consistent definitions of similar roles and similar units at parallel levels of the organization across the enterprise. Otherwise, left on their own, people will define roles very differently. This usually leads to unproductive complexity and dysfunctional behavior, as people use ambiguity to compete for power.

Indeed, a good portion of the confusion in the structures in large organizational units results from inconsistent definition of roles, structures, and authorities throughout the organization. In one part of the organization, for instance, marketing may be responsible for branding and distribution but not pricing; while in another it may include pricing, market segmentation, and branding but not distribution. Such differences make coordination of work and workers unnecessarily difficult.

Likewise, the country manager may be a powerful backbone line manager in one organization but in another silo may be more of an office manager responsible for running a shared geographic utility. Often roles and authorities are constructed around personalities. Hybrid roles are given to people for several possible reasons: Sometimes they ask for them, sometimes they want to ensure that the role is being played by someone who is personally loyal to the line manager, or sometimes a particular line manager wants to offload a particular responsibility. Whatever the reason, the inconsistent definition of roles, responsibilities, and authorities across a firm is one of the most common causes of unnecessary complexity and organizational dysfunction.

One of the great strengths of military organizations lies in their use of clearly defined roles and authorities, reinforced by management protocols, to enable people in different organizational units to work together. When people are assigned to a new role (such as platoon leader), they know immediately how they relate to their boss (that is, the company commander), to their subordinates (that is, staff sergeant and squad leaders), and to their staff support (for example, the signal officers). When they need to coordinate work with another unit, in other words, they know with whom to talk.

Military Secrets

One of the secrets to the success of this system is the designation of Military Occupation Specialties (that is, MOS) labels that clearly define roles. There are defined MOS roles (and rank expectations), for example, for contracting officers, battalion engineers, and infantry riflemen. There are training programs, meanwhile, that qualify individuals with slotted occupational skills (for example, basic infantry and helicopter maintenance).

Yet despite these standard definitions, military organizations can assemble a variety of very complex yet very tailored fighting forces to accomplish diverse objectives. The principle behind the standardization of such roles is not that different from Toyota, which designs automobile parts made in different factories in different countries that can be used in a wide variety of different model cars.

While companies are certainly not military organizations, they can use similar approaches. If the company chooses to organize its top-level line management hierarchy by customer group (for example, retail, small business, midmarket, or large institutions), and the next level down by business, the roles and responsibilities of the group executives and the business executives can be defined consistently across the firm, as can be the support functions (for example, finance or marketing). This is in contrast to simply letting each group executive organize these matters however he or she wants.

As you go down the hierarchy, of course, the roles may need to become more tailored, reflective of the underlying market and industry differences. One unit may need industrial engineers, for instance, while another needs product designers. As you differentiate, however, you should still try to make role definitions and responsibilities as consistent as you can.

There are multiple advantages of this approach. As a starter, it eliminates much of the politics that comes with overlapping roles, responsibilities, and authorities. Since the responsibilities and authorities for each kind of role are bounded enterprisewide, the problem is far less severe. It also serves to make it easier for people to coordinate work with one another, since the roles help define how individuals should relate to one another.

Boundaries Define Territories, Not Silo Walls

Boundary lines between roles are clear; therefore, and furthermore, they serve to define territories, not to construct silo walls. People assigned to these roles from other units know immediately what they are accountable for and how they are to relate to other people. People forming new organizational units or commissioning formal projects can specify the roles and skills they need. Meanwhile, people in one unit know with whom they should talk when they want to work with other units. And leaders, concerned with different specific issues (for example, litigation risks), usually know to whom they can target their communications (for example, managers responsible for operating risk management and compliance).

The use of consistent definitions of roles and responsibilities, in other words, can dramatically reduce the costs of searching and coordination across the enterprise. They can thereby directly attack unproductive complexity and streamline the work of both line managers and professionals. Doing so is also essential in helping to create the conditions for formal networks and talent marketplaces (as described later in the book).

While defining roles and responsibilities can help reduce coordination costs, much more is needed to overcome selfish, silo-based behavior. As we will describe in the next chapter, to break this behavior it will be necessary to move toward a one-company governance model. Changing the financial measurement and performance measurement systems to motivate collaborative and more economic behaviors is also required.

We don't want to underemphasize how much work is involved in harmonizing the definitions of so many roles. We only want to stress the importance of doing so if you want to reduce unnecessary complexity.

Backbone Line Decision Making

This chapter, then, argues for a replacement of the ambiguous decision-making processes with a backbone line structure.

As we have noted, military leaders know that they cannot anticipate the specific challenges that will face them on the battlefield, given the fluidity and complexity of combat. On the other hand, they are also aware that "ambiguity of purpose is the enemy of success." To deal with this, military leaders designate frontline field commanders. These leaders know the objectives of the mission, as stated by high command, but they are also allowed tactical freedom to achieve those objectives. Likewise, placing responsibility for the management of the marketplace at the front line allows for a simple, clear, chain-of-command backbone line structure.

No matter how you structure the organization, however, some issues naturally fall between structural roles. Some require both functional knowledge and product knowledge, or perhaps they need to reflect both client and geographic perspectives. Some of these issues are far-reaching. This is due to the magnitude of the decisions, which, after all, involve large investments and significant risks. These are the issues that should go up the hierarchical chain to be resolved by top management. But many other decisions are more routine. How can they be distributed without relying on matrix structures?

Decision making will occur at each of the three layers of leadership that we have discussed. At the front line, the answer often is in the use of a decision forum: an ad hoc organizational group that is brought together to make a single decision and then disbanded. Should the decision forum at the front line not reach a consensus, the issue will travel up the chain of command to the senior leadership layer and even to the top leadership.

Say the backbone frontline manager running the New Jersey/Long Island unit wants to launch a bundle of products in her territory. However, the marketing campaign she wants to use may conflict in the marketplace with a different program being launched by the Manhattan/Brooklyn manager in his market. Since some customers may work in one territory and live in another territory, there is a risk of customer confusion.

In this case, the first manager invites her counterpart overseeing Manhattan, as well as the manager overseeing Westchester (as a neutral party), to a meeting, along with their respective marketing executives. The intent would be to use the decision forum to make the appropriate decisions. If that proved impossible, however, then the decision would be bucked up to the senior leader (that is, the East Division executive) along with the viewpoints of the respective parties. In most cases, the decision would be made by the decision forum.

The important point of such an approach is to use, wherever possible, flexible, temporary structures to resolve specific issues rather than hardwiring these structures into the organization through matrices. To make decision forums work, however, managers who behave unilaterally when they should be collaborating will need to be held accountable for their unproductive behavior. In the case just cited, for example, if the New Jersey/Long Island manager had simply gone forward (by making the decision unilaterally herself), the Manhattan/Brooklyn manager would have had every right to call her out to the East Division executive for her behavior (which, if it happened frequently enough, could severely affect her performance evaluations or cause her to be taken out of her role—that is, "relieved of her command"). This approach assumes some well-established, enterprise-level behavioral standards, as well as senior and top leaders who hold managers mutually and individually accountable.

In fact, holding the entire organization accountable—as a single entity—is exactly the paradigm that we will discuss in the next chapter.

4

ONE-COMPANY
GOVERNANCE

WHAT CAN BE DONE for a company that is bound into a "siloed" structure? We recommend that it make a fundamental organizational change to a one-company governance structure.

After all, creating a "backbone line management structure" and making "frontline managers" into "field commanders" (as we described in the last chapter) work well only when the corporation is operating as a single economic entity. If the company is subdivided into business silos, each behaving selfishly, its frontline commanders will act more like competitors than collaborators.

Operating without corporate silos might seem extreme, but some of the best megainstitutions—companies such as GE, ExxonMobil, Toyota, Goldman Sachs, Microsoft, and Wal-Mart—already do so.

In the previous chapter we focused on the front line. Let's now turn our attention to top management, senior management, and the corporate center, since that is where a company determines whether it will operate as independent silos or as one company.

Front Line versus Corporate Center

In the previous chapter we described the need to provide backbone frontline managers with the tactical freedom to deploy the company's capabilities and mind power to produce its earnings. But to do so, these managers must be able to collaborate with people who do not report to them and to draw on support capabilities they do not personally control.

It is up to top management and the corporate center to put in place the structural capabilities needed to support the front line, to motivate and enable enterprisewide collaboration, and to undertake essential "off-line work" (such as the development of new, winning strategies). In other words, while the front line is the locus of driving the short-term performance of the enterprise, the corporate center is the natural locus for driving the long-term health of the enterprise.[1] This involves such activities as managing the company's portfolio of new wealth-creating initiatives and managing its portfolio of talented people.

The corporate center is also where goals should be set, where the balance between short-term earnings and long-term wealth creation should be managed, and where scarce resources should be wisely allocated. It is also where relationships with most of the company's external stakeholders, particularly its shareholders, need to be managed. Most important for the purpose of our discussion, the corporate center is where the creation of the one-company culture must be set in place, with conditions that enable large-scale collaboration throughout the company. For example, this is the logical place to locate responsibility for establishing the standards and protocols for the company, all of which also serve to help enable cross-enterprise collaboration (by reducing unproductive complexity). It is also the natural location for the establishment of most shared utilities (for example, technology infrastructure) and the place to sponsor the infrastructure needed to support formal networks, knowledge marketplaces, and talent marketplaces (as we will describe later in the book).

The enterprise level is also the natural locus of the performance management and performance measurement processes—processes required to drive both individual and mutual accountability for managers and professionals. While many of the actual metrics will need to be tailored to specific work activities, the overall governing approach to performance metrics needs to be devised at the enterprise level—particularly to ensure appropriate behaviors from significantly self-directed, self-organizing workers in thinking-intensive jobs. Similarly, the center is the appropriate place to locate internal controls, compliance capabilities, and consequence management. Finally, the enterprise is where the firm needs to establish the values it expects the entire firm to live by.

While we believe that most day-to-day operating decisions of most of the people in the organization should be distributed to the front line, we also see that a great many decisions, processes, and capabilities should be driven by the corporate center.

Once you accept the premise that the future profitability of winning firms relies on extensive enterprisewide collaboration, the corollary is that the enterprise needs to be led as one company—and that the corporate center is where governing the firm in such a manner must reside. We are not relying solely on our own judgment for this conclusion: In an electronic survey we administered through the *McKinsey Quarterly* in June 2005, some 84 percent of the respondents agreed with the statement, "My company's growth opportunities require extensive coordination across functional, product, and geographic boundaries."

One-Company Leadership

The starting point for one-company governance is one-company leadership. By "one-company leadership" we mean enterprise leadership that holds all employees both individually and mutually accountable for performing in the interests of shareholders and coworkers (rather than in the interests of maximizing the results of their own units at the expense of others). In short, a one-company organization is the antithesis of the silo-based organization.

The starting point for the one-company organization is the CEO. If the CEO insists on holding senior people only individually accountable, rather than both individually and mutually accountable, the company will almost always default to a multifirm approach. Historically, CEOs had three models of one-company organization to choose from:

1. One-firm CEO-driven model

2. One-firm culture model

3. One-firm partnership model

One-Firm CEO-Driven Model

In the CEO-driven model of the one-company organization, the CEO is sufficiently powerful that he or she can hold everyone in the firm both individually and mutually accountable for results. All of the employees are expected to advance the interests of the entire firm rather than their individual interests.

The CEO-driven model usually arises when the firm is still being led by the entrepreneur-founder. Under the leadership of Bill Gates and Steve Ballmer, for instance, Microsoft is run as "one firm"; in such firms, the CEO thinks from the perspective of an owner rather than that of a manager simply because the CEO is the owner. This avoids the "agency" issues Adam Smith so greatly feared.[2]

A founder-owner naturally holds all managers mutually accountable for results. When this model works, the CEO often has distinctive talents and organizes the entire firm to leverage those talents to their greatest effect. A driven CEO, furthermore, with such a mentality and personal power, is more than willing to fire people who further the interests of their own silos at the expense of the firm.

While a line management hierarchy is used to delegate authority in this model, individuals in the hierarchy are still expected to be mutually accountable to the CEO for acting in the interests of the entire firm.

Under this model, the CEO has complete discretion in appointing all the senior people in the firm. Over time, this enables the CEO to place people in senior roles whose personalities and working styles are complementary. As a result, the senior people intuitively learn over time which decisions they can make on their own and which they need to discuss with the CEO. As the CEO becomes comfortable with these informal decision protocols, he or she needn't supervise the work of these people very closely to get the behavior and performance he or she wants. The efficiency and effectiveness of these interpersonal collaborations with compatible, senior people enable the CEO to lead the entire firm as a single economic entity.

But what happens to the company when the founder retires? Will the senior people—who were willing to be subordinate to a dominant CEO—accept the leadership of a former peer? That is the big challenge of this model.

One-Firm Culture Model

A few firms have been able to institutionalize a one-company approach that persists even after the retirement of the founding CEO. In this model, the founding CEO who managed with a one-company approach leaves behind a legacy of a one-company culture that continues to be reinforced with management protocols, standards, and values. And one common reason the one-company culture persisted was that the dominant CEO had hand-picked a successor who embodied that culture.

GE, for instance, has been able to institutionalize its approach to one-company governance through a wide variety of mechanisms. For example, at GE the CEO is teamed with a chief financial officer and a human resources manager. This three-person team works together to hold people reporting to the CEO both individually and mutually accountable. While people are expected to perform as individuals, selfish behavior at the expense of the corporation is simply not tolerated. In turn, GE has often used vice chairs, also teamed with financial officers and human resources counterparts, to hold GE's diverse business activities together.

These vice chairs, and their financial officers and human resources counterparts, are individually and mutually accountable. In turn, these vice chairs hold their direct reports individually and mutually account-able, and so on down the chain of command.

At GE, a worker's failure to collaborate across the organization when asked to do so is a mortal sin. For instance, workers are expected to quickly and completely respond to any legitimate requests for informa-tion and knowledge from other parts of GE. When GE acquires a com-pany, which it does nearly every day of the year, it rapidly converts that firm to the GE culture; within a few months all the new employees have become part of the one company.

Unfortunately, it is hard to create such a culture, especially if man-agement didn't create it when the entire company was small. Many ex-ecutives have left GE for other companies only to discover that they can't bring the GE culture with them, much as they would like to.

One-Firm Partnership Model

There is another, quite different approach to forging a one-company culture and that is to set up a one-firm partnership. Goldman Sachs, Accenture, McKinsey, and similar professional services firms are exam-ples (even though most of these firms are no longer "partnerships" in a legal sense, and some of them, such as Goldman Sachs and Accenture, are now public companies).[3]

In a one-firm private partnership, a group of senior partners is usu-ally formed into a top management committee. These people are respon-sible for running the firm, for dividing up the returns among partners, and for serving as the board of directors. Since the senior partners pro-vide much of both the capital and talent that drive the firm's perform-ance, there are no agency issues separating the interests of managers from the interests of owners.

Often the "managing partner" of such one-firm partnerships is elected for a three- to five-year period, either by the entire partnership body or by the senior partnership committee. Such elections give the managing partner the authority to make decisions but also make that decision authority dependent on the consent of the governed. Much of the managing partner's power comes from the ability to make appointments, establish agendas, launch initiatives, and shape performance evaluations. Moreover, the managing partner's impact comes from speaking out on issues, setting aspirations, culling out "unpartnerlike behavior," and reenforcing values.

One of the most attractive aspects of a partnership is its ability to develop and retain large numbers of very senior, very talented professionals. Unlike managers in a top-down line hierarchy, partners view each other—including the managing partner—as peers. This social dynamic enables large numbers of very talented senior partners to feel that they have "made it"—even if they never become the managing partner or even a member of the governance committee. Within a partnership, every senior partner has status and clout. When they seek help, even in parts of the firm where they know few people, senior partners get quick responses—particularly if client service is involved.

Working in professional services firms has historically resembled working in craft-based "job shops" in many respects. In the language of the previous chapter, these "partners" are high-status, empowered, "frontline managers."

Successful professional work requires many years of experience in a senior capacity; this is less true for successful managerial work, which involves production labor and "factory" processes. This makes the growth of a professional services firm a function of how many senior partners it has who can serve as "master craftspersons." Hence the need for a model that provides senior status to master craftspersons.

One challenge to governing such master craftspersons is that senior practitioners thrive on personal independence. Managing such autonomous senior partners, therefore, is no easier than herding cats, which is why it is natural to form senior management committees. Such committees force the senior partners to come to grips with issues of managing the partnership, which in turn causes them to support the common decisions because of their personal involvement in how those decisions were made.

Governance for the 21st Century

Although all three models of one-firm leadership organizations offer advantages, we believe that none of them fully meets the needs of the 21st-century public company. Rather, we advocate a new one-company governance model, one that combines a powerful CEO, a one-firm culture, and a "partnership at the top."

A Powerful CEO

The first element in the 21st-century model is a CEO who leads rather than manages. CEOs of the 21st-century firm will need to be very powerful. But unlike the founders of these firms who exercised their power principally through management, the 21st-century CEO will generally exercise his or her power through leadership.

That means that the board of directors, which generally selects the CEO, will have to look for different qualities in candidates for this top job. The new CEO should not only deliver a strong sense of direction, make major decisions fast, and drive current earnings (by holding people accountable for results), he or she should also be able to manage the pace of initiatives, which includes determining the priorities and the sequencing of initiatives.

The 20th-century CEO was a visionary who told people what to do and ensured that they followed through. The 21st-century CEO, however, uses inspiration and aspiration, the elements of persuasion, to increase his or her power to mobilize the organization.

The 20th-century CEO held people individually accountable, while the 21st-century CEO holds people both individually and mutually accountable. The 20th-century CEO managed portfolios of businesses. The 21st-century CEO manages portfolios of initiatives and personalities. While great CEOs have to be good at both management and leadership, then, we believe the scale has tipped toward the increased importance of leadership.

Why has leadership become more important than management?

The answer is that a talented person can *lead* far more activities over a much larger scale and scope than he or she can *manage*. Today's mega-institutions are truly enormous and extremely diverse. Because of that, they are, in a sense, "unmanageable."

To manage an activity successfully, you must be immersed in the details of the activity you are managing. A CEO who is managing company activities must determine whether to trust only his or her own judgment or to accept the judgments of the people reporting to him or her. (Many CEOs have made the mistake of overriding a senior manager who has superior knowledge.) The time needed to supervise work is why the classic 20th-century model had rules requiring "span breakers"—that is, rules limiting the number of direct reports to equaling no more than five to seven people.

Leadership, in contrast, involves setting aspirations and defining tasks and roles. But it lets the CEO assign the details to others. The CEO provides ideas but does not demand that they be put into action if the down-the-line manager has a better one. While a talented person can usually manage most effectively only 5 to 7 people, the same person may be able to lead 20 or more.

Leadership by a modern CEO is also about exercising power. This power is often wielded not by telling people what to do but rather by capturing the hearts and minds of self-directed people. This encourages them to reach the aspirations set for them using the tools of their unique personal skills and judgment. In this way, the CEO of today's talent-driven megainstitution is really a more powerful version of the managing partner of a professional services firm. Like the managing partner, the CEO wields the power to make appointments, define roles and tasks, establish agendas, time initiatives, and shape performance evaluations. The CEO must make the tough decisions after full debate, however, even if many senior people disagree. This is what differentiates leadership from partnership, because the latter allows for a decision to be tabled. A CEO must represent the interests of the board of directors and the shareholders, not just the interests of other top managers. A CEO must be able to speak out forcefully on issues that would be perhaps too divisive in a partnership. Furthermore, a CEO can fire top people, which is very hard and sometimes impossible for partners to do.

Many 20th-century CEOs, although powerful, often tended to be patriarchs who kept power partly by rewarding people who loyally followed their orders. The 21st-century CEO needs to be a much tougher-minded leader—an individual who picks people for leadership roles more for their talents and their values than for their past personal loyalty to the CEO.

One-Firm Culture

Whether a firm operates as one company or not is as much about mindsets and behaviors as it is about a governance structure. In a silo-based firm, people use the term "we" to refer to people who are part of the silo and "them" to refer to people in the firm who work in other units. In a one-company culture, "we" refers to all employees enterprisewide, and "them" refers to everyone else.

Thus the second element in the one-company model is a commonly adhered to set of management protocols, standards, and values that define how the work is conducted. For example, in a one-company culture, people should be expected to exchange knowledge and information freely. But there should also be either an explicit or implicit set of management protocols to make that collaboration efficient and effective. In a one-company culture, for example, overall standards for compensating senior talent need to be established rather than being allowed to evolve in each business as it develops its own compensation approach. In a one-company culture, values also need to be distributed across the entire firm. In particular, if you want people to build enough trust to collaborate, you need a companywide standard to protect confidences.

One-company protocols, standards, and values, of course, limit the freedoms of individuals and businesses to make up their own rules. If these protocols, standards, and values are sensible, however, reasonable, fair-minded people will embrace them. If some individuals find them too difficult, they should be asked to leave.

Once the protocols, standards, and values are established, in fact, they can actually liberate talented people. Behavioral psychologists tell us that most people are inherently risk averse.[4] The ambiguity over what rules to follow not only causes them to waste time but also causes them to behave in ways that inhibit their potential to grow. If people don't realize that they can disagree with decisions from above, for instance, they'll just keep their mouths shut. Similarly, if they don't realize that they can change out their jobs for better ones in other divisions, they will never try to do that. If they do stay in their less-than-optimal positions, they may very will limit their opportunities for personal growth as well as deny other divisions the benefits of their talents.

With the percentage of significantly self-directed professionals and managers in a large company's workforce increasing, there is a growing need to have the same protocols, standards, and values apply throughout a company. Consistency in operating methods and standards will enable these people to act with greater autonomy. In turn, this autonomy will enable them to work more efficiently and effectively on their own, without continually having to go to the hierarchical leaders for permission. Furthermore, as they exercise this autonomy and learn how to take appropriate risks, they will grow their talents.

Senior Partnership at the Top

A third element of the one-company model we advocate is the organization of a "senior partnership at the top." In a large public megainstitution, this may involve 10, 20, or even 30 senior people.

The notion of a "team at the top" is not new. Many firms have "executive committees" or "managing committees" or "operating committees." A partnership at the top is different from those in that its explicit purpose is to ensure the integrated leadership and cohesive management of the "one company."

Specifically, we propose that the top 20 or so top leaders and managers be organized into enterprisewide governance committees. Many firms have senior management forums, but these most often serve as places to exchange senior management information and knowledge; the decision making takes place through normal line structures. We propose a different kind of committee, one in which its individual members, both individually and collectively, become partners who are accountable for both earnings performance and the establishment of the firm's direction.

This partnership at the top is different from the "senior partners' management committee" that runs professional services firms. First, in our one-company model, the CEO will have far more direct, personal power than most managing partners have (since CEOs are selected by the board, not elected by the partners). For example, few CEOs will need to ask for formal votes to make decisions. The CEO will have more direct, personal accountability to more stakeholders than does a managing partner, and with that accountability comes ultimate decision authority.

Second, unlike a partnership, a firmwide governance committee for a public company can never be the ultimate decision body. The need for a strong personal decision-making role for the CEO is rooted in the public ownership of the company. The board of directors, not the partnership at the top, is the top governance structure, and it is ultimately responsible for protecting the shareholders' interests.

There's another way in which a large public company is very different from a professional services firm. In a typical large professional firm, there is usually one dominant profession, and since the community of interests is often self-evident, it is relatively easy for workers to collaborate. In contrast, a typical large public company, such as Citigroup or Samsung or Pfizer, employs diverse professionals, including software engineers, brand managers, research scientists, product managers, industrial engineers, accountants, lawyers, risk managers, and strategic planners.

Most large public companies, furthermore, have a far greater number of people in managerial roles given not just their size but also the number of workers they employ in labor-intensive (rather than thinking-intensive) jobs. Even among those large private professional firms that have been organized as partnerships, there is growing recognition that they must become somewhat more line managed as they grow their scale and scope and as the number of "partners" runs into the thousands.

The biggest megainstitutions not only have far more professionals than even the biggest professional firms, they are usually bigger in every other sense as well (that is, more revenues, more employees, more capital invested, and so on) and are far more diverse. They thereby require far greater top-down, hierarchical direction than do professional firms. As a result, most members of a partnership at the top in a public megainstitution will have more direct, hierarchical, personal control over their respective areas of responsibility than would partners on a management committee in a professional firm.

Recognizing these differences, though, we still believe that a partnership-at-the-top approach, modeled on the best practices of professional firms, can yield powerful advantages in the organization of large public companies.

Need for Large Top Management Group

A governance structure that includes a partnership at the top is vastly different from the existing governance structures in most of today's big public companies. People accustomed to a line management organization may find it strange to have a group of people in top management making firmwide decisions. Why would you need to involve as many as 10, 20, or 30 people in top management?

To answer that, let's first explain what we mean by "top management."

We define "top management" as the people who are held accountable by the board of directors for the performance of the entire firm. Under this definition, top management has the perspective, the information, and the knowledge to represent the firm's interests with stakeholders. Senior management, in contrast, consists of the direct reports to top management, and it is usually responsible solely for the business arenas and support functions it leads.

In the typical 20th-century model, top management generally consisted of 1 to 5 people that might include, in addition to the CEO, a president (or chief operating officer), a chief financial officer, and a couple of vice chairs. Senior management might include 10 to 30 people.

Our design would place these senior people into top management as well, increasing top management from fewer than 5 people to 20 or more.[5] Why this increase? A 20-member-plus top management group allows the integration of a far greater scope of activities. A 20-person group also can bring to the table deep competence and expertise in almost all aspects of even the biggest megainstitution's operations. Discussions within the group can reflect a much greater diversity of knowledge and perspective, and these discussions can spread this knowledge among the entire group. As shared perspectives emerge and decisions are made, all participants in the room can explain to their direct reports the context for their decisions (as opposed to passing on the rationales from secondhand information).

Some companies may choose to divide the top committee into two committees in order to keep the number of people in the room to a smaller number. For example, you could have one committee focus on operations and the other on strategy under the leadership of the CEO. To make such a dual-committee approach work, the key backbone line top executives and the CEO and president usually will need to be on both committees to ensure integration at the top.

Such an approach does not mean that all members of the committee will have an equal say in every issue. While it may be necessary to have 20 or more senior managers on a firmwide governance committee (to receive adequate representation from the specialized interests of the firm), 20 or more is an unwieldy number to have engaged in every debate. Instead, the CEO can select the key group members who are in the best position to address the issue—and then make them mutually accountable for undertaking the more extensive debate, fact gathering, and development of alternatives outside the meetings. The CEO may choose to be a member of this offline group, but in any case the intent should be to develop a recommendation that is reviewed by the entire leadership group before the CEO makes a final decision.

Although members of the partnership at the top will not have an equal say on every issue, their participation in the decision-making process will give them the knowledge and confidence to speak with external and internal stakeholders on behalf of the entire firm. This is important: All the major stakeholders of a large public company would ideally like to interact with the CEO personally, but the CEO's time is a small quantity in relation to a very large number of stakeholders.

The CEO must interact with some of these stakeholders, such as board members, who have become far more active following the corporate scandals in recent years, the lawsuits targeted to directors, and the passage of Sarbanes-Oxley. Large institutional investors also require extensive contact with top management; for example, there may be 50 or more very large institutional stockholders in a typical large public megainstitution who expect access to top management.

Beyond the board and institutional investors, many of the firm's senior managers and professionals (perhaps numbering in the hundreds), whose personal talents drive the firm's performance, will expect to have personal relationships with the top managers. Large clients too will expect personal access to the CEO or at least to one member of top management. We know of one CEO who is leading a financial megainstitution whose staff schedules him each year to make personal contact with the CEOs of the firms' 200 largest clients through leveraging such forums as the CEO Roundtable. Since many of a firm's clients are also megainstitutions, there may be a dozen other individuals at each client, beyond the CEO, who make important decisions and hence are deserving of top management attention. Top managers of major suppliers and alliance partners are likely to expect even greater personal interaction with top managers. And let's not forget the media and disaffected parties, groups that are willing to use publicity and even litigation to force meetings with top management to discuss issues.

Fortunately, a partnership at the top expands the capacity for more people to build deeper relationships with more stakeholders. With the exception of board members and critical employees, much of this burden of managing stakeholder relations can be borne by members of top management other than the CEO, providing they have the knowledge, confidence, and responsibility to do so. Constructing a large top management group expands the company's capacity to develop deeper relationships with far more people.

A large top management group can also accelerate the development of all the people who belong to it. By participating in top management governance, these people will develop the top management perspective. As their confidence to speak out on behalf of the firm grows, so will their executive talents and abilities, which will make them excellent future candidates for the most important jobs in the firm.

By creating more room at the top, promoting a manager to a job with increased responsibility no longer means that two or three peers will leave. More room at the top also provides more roles for talented, junior people. And, over time, the one-company perspective will widen from being the perspective of only the current CEO to being the perspective of the entire institution.

Value of Partnership

The notion of "partnership" is more than a word, however. Partnership is a mindset, one that changes the way that people at the top work with one another. It is hard to overemphasize how important such mindsets are, since it is our mindsets that shape our behaviors.

As humans, we are keenly aware of which of our relationships are based on hierarchy and which are based on collaboration. By setting up a group of leaders with a partnership mindset, the foundation is set to bring the firm's intangibles to bear on opportunities in creating a culture of collaboration and mutual accountability and in providing the collective capacity needed to run a megainstitution.

In earlier chapters we described the need for frontline professionals and managers to collaborate with one another to create and exchange knowledge and information. It is even more important, however, to get such collaboration among top and senior people. Not only do the top and senior people have their own personal knowledge, relationships, and reputations to bring to bear to a collaboration, their behavior can also encourage the people who report to them to collaborate as well. It doesn't take much signaling from the top for people to understand the level of collaboration across organizational barriers that is expected of them.

Working together, 20 top leaders can deliver far more of the firm's knowledge, reputation, relationships, and talent than can a single CEO—no matter how talented the CEO is. It is much easier to get people who are involved and in the room for the discussion to collaborate in supporting that decision with "their minds and their hearts" than if they were asked to support the decision without having been involved in it. If a CEO can personally mobilize the 20 or so top people in the firm to support decisions, that group can, in turn, mobilize the entire firm.

This gets us to the final reason for the partnership-at-the-top approach. It is not enough to urge people to adopt a one-company perspective. Like it or not, most megainstitutions today resemble a confederation of "baronies" more than a single firm.

In our experience, the greatest single barrier to moving to a one-company governance approach and creating a one-company culture is getting the barons running the silos to accept the mutual accountability required to enable one-company collaboration. If the CEO doesn't involve the barons in the top management governance process, he or she will have no hope of creating a one-company culture.

In theory, it shouldn't be so hard. While different personality types may like giving orders more than collaborating with peers, or vice versa, most talented, successful people play the roles of subordinate, manager, or collaborator many different times during their careers. In truth, while most of us naturally prefer to give orders, we will accept a subordinate role when it is assigned by someone with clear authority over us.

We will also collaborate with someone whose help we need but over whom we have no ability to exercise hierarchical authority.

In real life, however, personalities and egos do get in the way. As people get more senior, for instance, they tend to choose authority rather than collaboration. This is particularly true of people promoted to the senior ranks just below top management. At that level, while they will accept subordination to top management, they are accustomed to being in control. Therefore, they increasingly resent any other person's authority—particularly when that authority is being exercised by a peer in an activity that intrudes on their perceived arena of responsibility. To be sure, given the prize (in terms of pay and power) of making it into top management, senior managers can be quite competitive with one another.

The problem arises as a direct consequence of using the 20th-century model: Most highly talented people gravitate to line management roles. When these people are held individually accountable for performance, they often become selfish. After all, they need to keep climbing the hierarchy vertically to succeed. And so they become effective infighters. They aspire to become the "king of every hill" they occupy.

As junior managers, they often become particularly effective at neutralizing or eliminating rivals (often by aligning with more senior managers who are themselves "rising stars") or by making temporary alliances of convenience with peers, whom they may later eliminate. As they climb the ladder, they pull along their loyal subordinates. When they finally get to the top of their silo, they sit on a power base anchored with the personal loyalty of people who owe their positions in the hierarchy to the baron above.

Of course, not all managers behave this way. The top people in many firms get to the top not only because they are skilled at infighting but also because they are skilled in leading and collaborating. Many of these best performers are people who are adept at creating one-company behaviors within their own silos. Boards of directors can usually tell the difference between great leaders and "selfish" barons. But even if they pick a great leader to be the next CEO—a leader who is inclined to adopt a one-company model—the challenge of moving a megainstitution (composed of multiple baronies) to a one-company approach can seem insurmountable.

Creating a Magna Carta

In 1215, King John of England was forced by his barons to write the Magna Carta, which diluted the power of the king and gave much more of it to the barons. The barons, in effect, were defining the power they could exercise within their silos. This laid the foundation for the modern English nation.

What we are proposing is also a sharing of power, but with a different twist. First, in our model the CEO still has the ultimate power over the barons (King John couldn't fire a baron, but a CEO can). Moreover, in return for accepting limits over their own power, the barons (that is, the silo leaders) get to increase their voices over the entire enterprise.

To make such an approach effective, the people at the top must contract with one another to determine just how such a partnership at the top is to work. In most firms where we've worked, ambiguity over the roles and decision-making authorities eventually evolves into unproductive complexity (for example, corporate politics) that permeates the entire firm. When individual leaders pursue their own, different approaches to organizing work, there are no enterprisewide protocols for "how we work around here," nor common standards, nor shared common values.

Most people who grew up in a 20th-century firm have no experience operating in a partnership-at-the-top organization. So if this approach is badly implemented or used without a very clear, detailed mental model of how a collaborative organization should work, the attempt to create one can make an already dysfunctional organization worse. Without clarity of purpose, and without descriptions of the behaviors expected, the establishment of a group governance system can result in a loss of accountability. In this scenario, decisions become "made by committee," and no one takes ownership for the results, which brings about chaos as different managers exercise personal power to undercut the one-firm governance decisions. In fact, confusion over decision-making roles and accountabilities can cause enormous amounts of wasted time, often in endless meetings with no resolution of issues. Ambiguity over how the organization is to work creates ample room for everyone to make up his or her own rules, which breaks down trust.

Another problem is that the president, the vice chair, and other top members may not like the notion of expanding the size of the top management group. In our experience, senior leaders who are not a part of top management generally like the idea of a partnership at the top—because it will increase their own say in how the firm is run. Existing top managers, other than the CEO, however, may not. They may even try to undermine the effectiveness of a partnership at the top—simply by "backdooring" decisions through the normal line structure rather than through the newly formed governance committee.

Shared Mental Model

To make a partnership-at-the-top governance model work, the devil is in the details. You need to first draw a "blueprint." Specifically, you need a detailed design of the governance committees, the roles of senior people, the processes of corporate management, and the related protocols and standards of operation. All participants will need to understand the rules of the game, and all of them must expect to be held accountable to those rules. This design will be the shared mental model that must be learned until it becomes second nature to everyone.

Most of today's managers have little patience for detailed organizational design work. Such work requires leaders to deal with personality issues, personal power issues, and interpersonal rivalries, not to mention the desires of individuals for personal autonomy and freedom from some of their peers. Given the pressures of the digital age, who has the time to do so? In the past, it was easier to let executives "figure it out" for themselves in the course of dealing with the complex interrelationships that dominated their work lives. In the past, most organizational thinking began and ended with "picking the right person" to do the job.

In the final chapter of this book, we will further discuss how to design and install a new organization. Let's simply say for now that creating a detailed design and getting everyone to buy in to it, is the most important requirement for a successful partnership at the top. Before we move on, however, we need to put one stake in the ground concerning the establishment of a one-company governance approach.

We believe that setting up a one-firm governance committee is an essential requirement for success. However, the approach we are advocating will fail unless limits are placed on how much time any one person can spend in firmwide governance meetings. Almost all members of a senior governance committee will have other significant management or leadership responsibilities.

As a rule of thumb, we believe that no more than 20 percent of any leader's time should be spent in firmwide governance meetings (excepting the CEO and other individuals who must also participate in board meetings). This leaves 80 percent of each leader's time to be spent on his or her "day job." The good news is, based on calendar analysis we've done in actual firms, 20 percent may actually represent a reduction in the time spent by many senior people in cross-firm committee meetings. Since committees have the potential to be time sinks, keeping to a 20 percent rule requires careful designing of how time is spent, who is in the room, and how decisions are made.

Governance Committees

A partnership at the top starts with a parent governance committee. This group, chaired by the CEO, is responsible for all the decisions that cross over the organizational responsibilities of the individual managers. This committee is accountable, furthermore, for the continuous delivery of current and future earnings, the sponsorship of corporatewide strategic initiatives, and the allocation of resources. We call this set of activities the "dynamic management process" (described further in Chapter 5). The parent committee should also approve any major decisions made by subcommittees.

In our experience, subcommittees will be essential (if one follows the rule of spending no more than 20 percent of one's time, as we proposed earlier). If every decision is attempted in the committee as a whole, the volume of cross-organizational decisions in a megainstitution will overwhelm the very finite time the leaders have to spend on them. We believe the parent committee will, by itself, consume about 2 days a month. And assuming two, semiannual, 3-day off-sites, the time spent in parent committee meetings will total about 30 days a year, or about half of the 20 percent limit (assuming a 240-day work year).

Appropriate subcommittees will vary by firm, of course, but could include committees that focus on different, shared intangibles (for example, knowledge, talent, brand, or client relationships) and shared support functions (for example, technology or risk/reward management). Subcommittees, meanwhile, would allow their members to focus deeply on specific areas requiring a firmwide perspective. These subcommittees would make decisions (within the power delegated to them by the parent committee) and recommendations on the appropriate firmwide management protocols and standards. Subcommittees may also require as much as a day or more a month (particularly for the chairperson).

Let's return to our friends at Global Bank to illustrate how the parent committee and the subcommittees could be organized. As shown in Figure 4-1, the new parent governance committee would have the 14 people reporting to the CEO as members, plus the CEO, who would serve as chair. In addition, as also shown in the figure, there would be 11 subcommittees. These would require a cross-organizational focus, one that would not be under the responsibility of the backbone line structure (for example, the European Council would embrace all senior leaders of the backbone organization and other senior leaders based in Europe). Each of these subcommittees would be chaired by the most appropri-

FIGURE 4-1

Global Bank Governance Committee

Global Bank Governance Committee
CEO - Chair

Global Consumer EVP	Chief Financial Officer	General Counsel
Global Wealth Management EVP	Chief Technology Officer (IT)	Strategic Planning
Global Securities Services EVP	Chief Marketing Officer	Chief Knowledge
Global Capital Markets &	Chief Talent Officer (HR)	Officer
Investment Banking EVP	Chief Risk Officer	
Europe Chair		
Asia Chair		
North America Chair		

Subcommittees*

Strategy	Finance	Talent	Marketing	Knowledge	Technology
Chair CEO	Chief Financial Officer	Chief Talent Officer	Chief Marketing Officer	Chief Knowledge Officer	Chief Technology Officer

European Council	Asian Council	North American Council	Risk	Regulatory & Compliance
Chair Europe Chair	Asia Chair	North America Chair	Chief Risk Officer	General Counsel

* Chief auditor reports to the board audit committee and does not sit on the governance committee.

ate leader. In this structure, every member of the parent governance committee, except the four backbone line executive vice presidents and the strategic planning officer, would also chair a subcommittee.

Once subcommittees are formed, it becomes impossible, of course, for any one person to attend all of the subcommittee meetings (if you stick to a 20 percent limit of any one person's time). Subcommittee members also need to spend some time on committee activities outside of the meetings themselves. This means that most people will be able to sit on only one subcommittee, in addition to the parent committee. This also means that everyone in the partnership at the top, including the CEO, has to trust the others to act in the best interests of the firm, without sitting in at every meeting.

One element of design that requires particular attention is the development of a detailed corporate calendar (perhaps on a rolling 18-month basis) to ensure that the time of this top management group is well spent. Most large, well-run firms usually have some form of corporate calendar, particularly for the budgeting and strategic planning processes. But we are advocating something different. We propose that a detailed corporate calendar be prepared not just for the parent governance committee but for subcommittees as well. This will ensure that the membership of the committees and the frequency and duration of the meetings are designed so that no one person spends more than 20 percent of his or her time on cross-firm governance and that, moreover, the meetings drive an organized, cohesive process for running the firm.

A related issue, given the geographic diversity of most megainstitutions, is the need to develop calendar protocols to determine which meetings require in-person attendance versus attendance by teleconference or videoconference. In turn, this also requires careful timing. For example, 8 a.m. New York time is generally a reasonable time for meetings involving most global participants in Europe or Asia (although people living on the West Coast in the United States may view 5 a.m. as a bit early).

Expanding Governance Capacity

Once you determine that no one should spend more than 20 percent of his or her time in governance meetings; that no one can be on more than one subcommittee in addition to the parent committee; and that you need at least 5 to 10 subcommittees, each with a dozen or so members to represent the diversity of the firm, you quickly discover that you need some 60 to 90 people to be involved in subcommittee governance. Since you only have at most 20 or so members of the parent committee, this means that you will need to draw more people into the governance process.

Rather than being a problem, this provides an opportunity to involve more talented people in the one-company leadership process. While you probably will always want the chairperson of each of the subcommittees to be a C-level executive and member of the parent governance committee, many of the other members of each subcommittee should be drawn from the ranks of the up-and-coming generation of leaders. Many of these people will be involved because of their roles (that is, the person overseeing the enterprisewide talent marketplace may be a natural member of the talent committee).

Picking the people on each subcommittee should be a prerogative of the CEO (after consultation with the entire parent governance committee). Each subcommittee should be selected so that it can express representative views of the entire enterprise and not just of the committee chair.

Let's look again at Global Bank to see how the marketing subcommittees could be composed. The chair of the subcommittee would be the chief marketing officer (CMO). The committee would include the four marketing officers reporting to the backbone line executive vice presidents (EVPs). This would enable the chair to influence the thinking of these people, and, in turn, to be influenced by how they think, given their line focus (even though none of the four actually reports to the CMO—that is, there is no matrix).

Other people should be on the committee as well. In this case, it was decided to include two people who reported to the CMO—the person responsible for the corporate brand and the person responsible for market research—as well as three up-and-coming representative executives drawn from line organizational units (for example, senior managers with no direct marketing roles drawn from Global Consumer, Global Wealth Management, and Global Capital Markets & Investment Banking).

Involving this next generation would greatly accelerate their career opportunities. By including them in firmwide governance, such "up-and-comers" would also expand their personal access to firmwide knowledge and firmwide talent. Their problem-solving capabilities and leadership capacities would be enhanced by their exposure to a greater variety of senior people. In short, they would learn faster by seeing the company from the top.

Making Committees Effective

While subcommittees can greatly increase collaboration, the danger is that they will wallow in issues rather than resolve them. To prevent this, committees also need a strong infusion of hierarchy, which is where the chairperson of the committee comes in.

The CEO, of course, would play the chairperson's role in the parent committee and perhaps in the strategy committee, but other very senior leaders would be expected to lead the other subcommittees. The board of directors of the company would hold the CEO personally accountable, and it would hold all members of the parent committee mutually accountable, for the effectiveness of this governance structure. In turn, the CEO would hold the chairperson of each subcommittee personally accountable, and all members of each subcommittee mutually accountable, for the effectiveness of each subcommittee. This would include making sure the CEO was kept abreast of the issues being debated and that the perspectives developed by the committee were aligned with the CEO's own thinking.

The appointment of subcommittee governance chairs would enable the CEO to make some of the most powerful people, such as the COO (if there is one), vice chair, or the CFO, appropriately "more equal" than others (if that is what the CEO desires). It would also build and test the subcommittee chair's ability to manage meetings with a one-firm perspective—a prerequisite for anyone aspiring to eventually succeed the CEO.

In Global Bank's case, given that it has no chief operating officer or vice chair, the natural person to play the role for each subcommittee would do so (for example, the chief financial officer would chair the finance committee), thereby signaling that everyone on the parent committee is an "equal" and that no one is being singled out as a potential successor.

By spreading the top leadership group among all the subcommittees, the parent committee would have at least one member who is knowledgeable about each subcommittee's activities. In turn, this would enable the parent committee as a whole to serve as a one-firm integrative body even though no one person on the parent committee would have participated in every meeting.

In composing the subcommittees, care should be taken to ensure that they are large enough to represent the diversity of the entire firm. Why? Because the intent is to be able to reflect firmwide perspectives and to mobilize firmwide intangibles within each subcommittee. On the other hand, if you have more than a dozen or so members, you may dilute the intensity of the interactions required for the work of each subcommittee.

Protocols

Protocols should be part of the detailed design process. By "protocols," we mean the explicit definition of how people are to behave with one another as they work together. Establishing appropriate enterprisewide "rules of the game" for behavior serves to improve both the efficiency and effectiveness of the time spent in meetings. It also ensures a balance between hierarchy and collaboration.

These protocols might include basic housekeeping items such as rules that require sending agendas and documents out in advance, limits on the duration and frequency of meetings, and expectations for attendance. But they can also include such protocols as the obligation to dissent before decisions are made but with an equal obligation to support decisions once they are made.

They might also define who can be in the room, and when. For example, advocates of a point of view who are not members of the committee may be allowed in the room to present their ideas, but they may be expected to leave during the ensuing debate. Protocols can also include whether points of view expressed by individuals remain private within the committee and whether it is fair game for people to tell nonmembers the personal viewpoints of different individuals.

Such protocols will drive behavior, so it is important to design them for the behaviors you want. Similarly, protocols need to be designed to ensure that decision making is effective, with an appropriate balance between hierarchy and collaboration. Should a majority vote rule? Should the chairperson of the committee always have the final say? Should votes be by a show of hands or by secret ballot? Is the chairperson required to solicit the viewpoints of every member, or just let the most passionate members speak? Do the major decisions of each subcommittee need approval from the parent governance committee, and, if so, what constitutes "major"? Who appoints the members of each committee? Without defining detailed protocols, time will be wasted and the effectiveness of the committees will be compromised.

By the way, we strongly believe that the chairperson should have the final say, because otherwise committees are prone to compromise rather than to make the tough decisions. A wise chairperson can usually gain an understanding of the views of every person on the committee without having to call for a vote and will adjust his or her decision to reflect the different views.

Once the protocols are established, the inherently cumbersome process of collaboration in these governance committees can be more efficient and effective. Given the ease with which senior people can waste time in any large firm, it is essential that the firm clarify its rules to determine how the committees are supposed to work.

Broad Partnership

Beyond establishing a senior partnership at the top, we believe that some megainstitutions may also want to organize all of the firm's senior leaders into a broader partnership, one involving several hundred people. Many of the firms with a one-company culture, including such players as IBM, Microsoft, and GE, have already set up such groups (although for most companies, the meaning of being included in the group means merely that you will be better informed and that your career will be more carefully managed). We have something different in mind, however: We feel that firms should involve their talented senior leaders in a "partnership of corporate citizens" in order to better unleash their talents.

The advantage in having a larger senior partnership is that it can greatly expand the number of people who feel mutually accountable for the firm's performance and, additionally, who have the confidence to lead it. It can greatly enable a megainstitution to become more manageable. In contrast to other employees, partners are expected to be corporate citizens who work for the benefit of the entire enterprise, not just for themselves.

Another big advantage of a broader partnership is that it greatly expands the number of talented senior people who feel that they have "made it." One of the great tyrannies of the 20th-century model was that it generated relatively few jobs to aspire to. In the 20th-century model, when one member of a peer group was promoted to become the "boss," many former peers often left the firm either because they didn't want to report to a former peer or because they viewed their opportunities for advancement as blocked. In contrast, instead of a peak at the top, a partnership puts in place a broad plateau that provides room for many people. Growth adds senior people laterally rather than in layers.

Once again, though, the devil is in the details. For starters, how many people should be considered partners? Some of the larger professional services firms already have thousands of "partners." So it is possible to conceive of "partnerships" in large firms that number in the thousands. We would err, however, on the side of creating smaller partnerships.

Remember, creating large numbers of partners, particularly when there is little discipline to the process of "electing" them, can quickly devalue the concept. Partnership depends on the partners being peers. So if the dispersion of relative talents among the partnership is too great, the best people feel no pride or accountability in being a "partner." Furthermore, once the group's size rises beyond 250 to 350 people, it becomes very difficult to have more than a nodding acquaintance with more than half of them. For all but the largest companies, a senior partnership group of 300 or so would be sufficient to ensure that all frontline managers reported to partners (that is, 300 partners with 10 direct reports each, as suggested in the last chapter, would accommodate 3,000 frontline units).

In smaller firms, partnerships could include many, if not all, of the frontline managers. Since real partnership arises from the need to collaborate, the ability of partners to have personal relationships with one another is critical. Some companies might start with a smaller partnership and then gradually enlarge it as new partners emerge with talents that equal, or are greater than, those of existing partners.

Other issues include these:

- How often, if ever, should the partners meet as a group? If they do meet, how is the time used?

- What range of compensation should exist among partners? What role should performance play versus tenure versus their job responsibilities?

- What benefits beyond compensation should a partner receive?

- How should partners be designated?

- How should they be evaluated?

- How should they be terminated?

We believe that however those issues are resolved, establishing some form of partnership of senior leaders at the top of a megainstitution provides great opportunities. As we said earlier, it helps unleash the power of talented people while simultaneously creating a culture of mutual accountability, one that pervades the entire enterprise. Having a firmwide partnership also greatly expands the number of people who can connect with and serve as role models to talented people throughout an enterprise. And it greatly expands the number of people who can be trusted to pursue enterprisewide initiatives for the mutual benefit of other employees and shareholders.

Indeed, if designed well, a partnership-based top management structure can overcome many of the agency issues inherent in the 20th-century model by greatly expanding the number of employees who think like the owners rather than merely like agents of the owners.

Foundation for a 21st-Century Model

Making a transition from a 20th-century multifirm model to a 21st-century one-company model will be difficult. It will require the full support of both a powerful CEO and the board of directors—and a great deal of time. And the personalities of some of the talented senior people will often place limits on how much the CEO and the board can actually change.

In our experience, any change in top management governance, such as changing a CEO, nearly always leads to some senior people leaving. Switching to a one-company governance model may well result in even greater turnover at the top. But such change is essential. Turf-oriented managers, who insist on personal control over every activity for which they are being held accountable, need to be either converted to collaborative behavior or replaced. Some loss of talent should be expected. The good news is that within a few months, talent lost in the transition will usually be more than replaced by new talent stepping up.

Importantly, the installation of a one-firm model will enable the implementation of many of the ideas in the following chapters. In particular, it will help eliminate the need for many of the matrix management structures, ad hoc committees, and task forces that now complicate most large organizations. Underlying the proliferation of such structures is ambiguity over protocols of how decisions are to be made and a lack of clarity over responsibilities and accountabilities. With a partnership at the top, you have the conditions in place to allow a streamlining of the line structure without giving up essential collaboration.

Another benefit is that it provides a means to define the management protocols and standards required to establish an enterprisewide culture. A partnership at the top can create not only enterprisewide management protocols but also enterprisewide standards—on issues ranging from performance measurement, to capital budgeting methodologies, to technology standards, to transfer pricing, to the protocols and standards needed to create talent and knowledge marketplaces. Indeed, focusing on establishing such one-company protocols and standards is an appropriate starting point for many of the specific subcommittees (for example, a technology committee on technology protocols and standards).

It is hard to overstate the importance of establishing management protocols and standards in enabling companies to capture the possibilities of the digital age. Protocols and standards establish the specifications for work activities where there are multiple alternatives available. Establishing a one-company protocol or standard generates far more value than allowing multiple protocols and standards to proliferate. A global company will usually be far better off picking a single language for enterprisewide communications (usually English) as a global standard, for instance, than allowing multiple "official" languages to flourish. That said, some companies headquartered in non-English-speaking countries may need to allow two languages for practical reasons—for example, a Chinese company may decide on both Mandarin and English.

Standards can be beneficial for an enormous range of work activities. They include not only "hard standards" (for example, in technology and manufacturing) but also "soft standards" (for example, in the look and feel of advertising, the definition of jobs and roles, the definition of markets, and the definition of knowledge domains).

For companies with a long history of siloed behavior, for those with highly diverse multinational operations, and for those that have resulted from mergers and/or acquisitions of other organizations, it can take decades to move fully to applying protocols and standards globally. Having said that, it is a journey well worth taking. Every step toward establishing more uniform protocols and standards will help the organization perform better.

Values

A one-company governance structure also helps establish firmwide shared values. Values define how people are supposed to behave. They include not just ethics but also how to behave with customers (that is, do customers' interests come first?) and with each other (that is, do you have to treat other people with respect?). The very idea of "one company" is a value. Many large companies espouse values, but, when employees who flout them are still given generous pay packages and promotions, the values seem hollow.

The list of casualties of firms in the last few years that fell victim to straying from values (such as Enron, WorldCom, Adelphi, and Andersen) is long, as is the list of companies whose reputations (and market prices) have been seriously damaged by scandals. Values are not just promulgated; they are instilled by people who live them every day. If you can create an effective one-company partnership and can get that partnership to live by values, the entire enterprise will comply—and one-company values will flourish and be expressed in the behaviors of the workforce.

The proper home for owning the values of the company is the parent committee. But having the CEO and the parent committee espouse values is not enough. Values must be reinforced with actions. A one-company partnership can improve both the performance measurement and performance orientation of people. It can improve the enforcement of values. Peer pressure leads to both individual and mutual accountability, and thus it can supplement the use of hierarchy to create performance pressure. Partnerships are usually far more ruthless in how they treat underperformance and behaviors that go against values than are patriarchal line managers, who sometimes may care more about personal loyalty to themselves than how particular employees are performing. Peer pressure can be reflected in the performance measurement of people who violate the firm's protocols, standards, and values by behaving in unpartnerlike ways. And peer pressure can put powerful pressure on hierarchical leaders to reenforce violations of the one-firm culture. For all these reasons, one-company governance is the critical first step in redesigning the firm for the digital age.

5

DYNAMIC MANAGEMENT

IN THE 20TH-CENTURY organizing model, as Professor Chandler famously observed, "Structure follows strategy."[1] You designed your strategy, and then you built an organization to implement it. Traditional strategy frameworks were always deterministic, based on making "reasonable" assumptions about markets, competitors, changes in technology, and so forth.

At the core of that philosophy was the 19th-century conception of the closed thermodynamic equilibrium model. This concept maintained that equilibrium is the norm, except when disrupted by shocks to the system.

The oil crisis of the 1970s, and the related rapid increase in inflation rates, was a shock that demonstrated the fallacy of this approach. Companies began to realize that they couldn't plan for the long term as they had in the stable environment that had existed since World War II. But the lesson was not well learned. Even though corporate executives realized that the model no longer worked, they still managed their companies, in terms of planning and budgeting, much as they had in the 1960s. They were stuck in the 20th-century model.

As we have noted earlier, no one can ignore the continuing changes in the world today. Even the most recalcitrant CEO now understands that change is here, and it's not going away. Physicist Stuart Kauffman was one of the first thinkers to popularize the idea that life itself is a matter of disequilibrium rather than balance. More than 10 years ago in his pioneering book *At Home in the Universe: The Search for the Laws of Self-Organization and Complexity*, he stated that life continues to evolve not through balance but by being "poised on the edge of chaos."[2]

Eric Beinhocker in the *Origin of Wealth* has picked up on that theme.[3] He states that evolution functions as a profoundly successful problem-solving algorithm that is capable of genuine innovation. The evolutionary process comprises three steps: differentiation, selection, and replication. Differentiation within a species is nature's attempt, via multiple experiments, to respond to a problem presented by an evolving environment. Selection sifts through these possible responses to the changing environment to find the ones that work—the others die off. Replication consists of the organic implementation of more of the ideas that work, leading to the growth of a population of "adaptive" organisms (Figure 5-1).

The idea of natural selection is not applicable to nature alone. As noted in a number of recent academic and business publications, business itself can be seen as a complex adaptive system. In such a system, "agents" compete against one another within a common environment. Those with a "good fit" with their environment prosper and grow; those with a "poor fit" struggle and disappear.

Kauffman says it succinctly: "In this precarious world, avalanches, big and small, sweep the system, relentlessly." In the business world this is true as well. A few years ago, Dick Foster and Sarah Kaplan's *Creative Destruction* noted that, between 1917 and 1987, 61 of the original Fortune 100 companies ceased to exist, 21 survived but dropped out of the top 100, and 18 remained on the list. Foster and Kaplan also demonstrated that evolution in the market has been accelerating by showing that, over the past several decades, the expected life span of the average S&P 500 company has been declining steadily.[4]

FIGURE 5-1

Evolution: A Three-Step Process

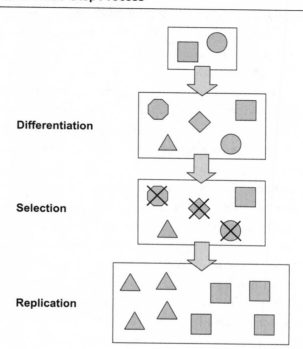

Differentiation

Selection

Replication

Source: *Eric Beinhocker's* The Origin of Wealth.

Challenges to Forecasting

The reality is that in the modern world, shocks *are* the system, and they never stop: Unexpected competition, unforeseen developments, and changing customer preferences continuously roil the waters. The traditional strategic notion that you can make assumptions about the future and optimize no longer holds. It is simply not possible to predict outcomes, because of the uncertain, interdependent variables—including each agent's action and random exogenous events—that affect success.

This also holds true for business models. You can always identify success stories after the fact, but you have no idea how many others

COMPLEX, ADAPTIVE SYSTEMS

In a complex, adaptive system, agents (that is, individual competitors) compete against one another within a common environment. Agents with a good fit with their environment relative to other competitors prosper and grow (and replicate) while agents with a poor fit struggle and disappear. The complication is that as agents compete against one another, and as some prosper and some fail, the environment is itself affected, and these changes affect the "rules of the game." And random events occur—sometimes occasionally, sometimes frequently—that change the environment unexpectedly.

In a complex, adaptive system, it is not possible to predict which agents will win over time. This is so because there are numerous interdependent variables that affect success, including random chance, and also because some agents adapt to other agents' successes in ways that are different depending on such issues as the timing of events and which particular agents "win" which particular "battles."

A simple example from evolution that was described in *The Economist* illustrates the challenge of predicting outcomes in a complex, adaptive system. Scientists undertook an experiment in which they injected the same virus strain into two identical bacteria cultures, which were being maintained at identical temperatures for identical periods of time. Since all the mutations possible for the virus under such conditions were already known, the assumption was that the winning mutation strain would also be identical (that is, the fittest would prosper at the expense of the less successful mutations). To the scientists' amazement, different strains of the virus won the battle. Why? Because despite the identical conditions, the sequence of the mutations was different, and this timing difference led to quite different outcomes. The point here is that even in this very simple system, the complexity of the adaptive process creates unknowable outcomes even when conditions are identical.

In contrast to this simple environmental system, any business environment is almost immeasurably complex.

tried similar ideas but failed.[5] The global business economy is too confusing, complex, and uncertain. Change is too rapid, and there are too many choices to be made for any leader to have confidence that he or she can set a direction and stay the course. There is no clear path to future success—particularly if it involves significant investments in intangible assets.

Forget setting the sails and tying down the tiller. Life now is a matter of constantly testing the currents, assessing the ebb and flow of the tides, making one's soundings with a line and a lead weight—constantly searching for the best course and being willing to change course in an instant when the fog unexpectedly rolls in or the alarming bump of the centerboard indicates that you are about to run aground.

Or as Kauffman says, "At this poised state between order and chaos, the players cannot foretell the unfolding consequences of their actions. . . . In such a poised world, we must give up the pretense of long-term prediction."

And so the leadership of the enterprise is on a voyage of exploration and discovery of the future. But how is it to be done?

Dynamic Management

Dynamic management is an idea that is aimed at enabling companies to mobilize the enterprisewide intangibles needed to discover new, wealth-creating strategies as the companies navigate the complexity, confusion, and uncertainty of today's world. It presumes you can build an organization that enables the company to prosper no matter how the external world changes. As we said in the Introduction, the theory is that you can't control the weather but you can design a ship and equip it with a crew that can navigate the ocean under all weather conditions.

One of the challenges of managing today is that the process of discovering new wealth-creating initiatives is a fundamentally different challenge than running the business day to day. Running the business is about using the existing capabilities of the company to full advantage—to win in the current competitive marketplace. In contrast, discovering new ways to create wealth involves lots of fact gathering, analyses, problem solving, "deductive tinkering," and trial and error.[6]

What's the answer? We believe it is in designing the processes for discovering new wealth such that they are independent of the processes for managing the company day to day. Using an urban planning analogy, it is akin to designing walkways and parks for pedestrians in such a way that they can wander at a leisurely rate safely separated from roadways designed for high-speed traffic.

Even well-managed "superclass" companies that operate as one company may have real problems in growing organically and building new organizational capabilities. After all, they can't mobilize the talent, discretionary spending, and focus to do so without taking the line's focus off of operating earnings. This is the reason why we believe the backbone frontline management should be focused only on tactics.

Developing successful wealth-creating initiatives is about managing the inevitable risks that arise from our inability to see the future. You want managing these risks to occupy the full attention of those involved. This, of course, is an impossible task for frontline people because they are preoccupied with delivering current earnings. It is another technique that can be used to keep the complexity in the outside world from seeping into the organization where it would result in unproductive internal complexity.

Traditional planning exercises typically permit strategists to assume away most risks and focus only on very specific ones—that is, the risks that are easiest to predict rather than those that are the most hazardous. At the other extreme, CEOs and their companies may simply toss the dice, taking leaps of faith to develop new businesses, enter new markets, or adapt to new technologies.

We believe that overly cautious and wildly courageous approaches to future planning are equally dangerous. Rather, we suggest that decisions on pursuing future opportunities must be made through something unfamiliar to most companies—a process akin to natural selection, in which many initiatives are launched, each with the potential to deliver rewards disproportionate to the risk involved. As these initiatives succeed and fail and are expanded or shut down, the strategy evolves, with no presumption that the path followed will necessarily resemble the starting hypothesis.

Dynamic management, then, involves the pursuit of a "portfolio of initiatives" (POI). The pursuit of these initiatives will help reveal "favorable outcomes" by managing the related investment risks through the use of "staged gate investment processes." In turn, through committee structures and a corporate calendar, the management of this portfolio of initiatives is integrated with the processes of budgeting and operating earnings management.

This process has never been more important because, unlike investments in existing business models (with returns on capital and labor that are somewhat predictable), the ability to predict which investments in intangibles will create wealth is limited. Yet, to explore new ways to make money, whether it be to find a better way to produce oil synthetically, to design a new strategy for the small business segment, or to adapt a product offering for new technology, one must always begin by mobilizing such intangibles as talent and knowledge. Making these investments always involves the very significant risk that such investments will be a complete write-off.

Strategy as a Portfolio of Initiatives

Using a POI is a survival-of-the-fittest approach, but with a number of important differences. First, companies can consciously adapt (that is, they can design their own mutations) through a process of "deductive tinkering."[7] Second, companies can develop a familiarity advantage—that is, they can acquire superior intangible assets through a staged investment process.

In a POI approach, initiatives are continuously launched as a kind of ongoing business-plan competition, one that comes from across the whole company, drawing from seed capital and from the discretionary

FIGURE 5-2

A 21st-Century Approach to Corporate Strategy

From 20th-Century Mindset	To 21st-Century Mindset
Determining the Future	**Portfolio of Initiatives**
• "Build it and they will come"	• Establishing the conditions for favorable outcomes of strategic initiatives
• Assuming away strategic risk	• Disciplined search for high-reward, low-risk opportunities (i.e., opportunities for which you enjoy familiarity advantages)
• Periodic strategic planning	• Dynamic, continuous management of portfolio of initiatives (use of time and portfolio theory to overcome residual risks)
• Visionary (predetermining where and how to compete)	• Flexible and evolutionary (natural selection of where, how, and when to compete)

budgets of senior managers. As a new initiative shows promise, it is nurtured. And when and if it becomes clear that it is going to be a moneymaker, the enterprise can decide whether to invest in it and scale it up in size. Through the staged investment process, one can continue to invest in initiatives that appear likely to work, simultaneously acquiring the familiarity necessary to make them successful, and to withdraw resources from those that don't look promising.

By "familiarity" we mean the advantages a company gains from mobilizing its intangibles—that is, its talent, its knowledge, its relationships, and its reputation—to pursue opportunities. The particular challenge is to use those familiarities as they are acquired, to make and remake those decisions in a continuously changing environment. And to frame those decisions, the transformation shown in Figure 5-2 needs to take place in the minds of top management in the 21st century.

The differences between familiarity and unfamiliarity can be appreciated if seen in the context of two runners: One is significantly

FIGURE 5-3

The Rising Value of Familiarity

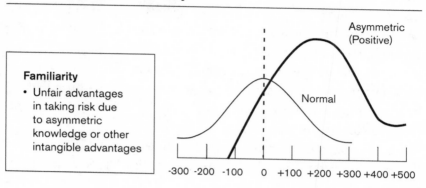

Familiarity
- Unfair advantages in taking risk due to asymmetric knowledge or other intangible advantages

faster than the other and should win every time when the two are racing on a level track. But what if the two runners compete at night, on a narrow path marked by trees, strewn with rocks, and crossed by streams? Suppose the slower runner practices both in the daytime and at night and becomes more familiar with the course, while the faster one is allowed no practice time and is prevented even from seeing the course in advance? Who will win now?

With respect to any particular opportunity, a company will enjoy either familiarity advantages or unfamiliarity disadvantages relative to competition. Or it will face uncertainty over whether any competitor has familiarity that will confer advantages (often because the situation is subject to events whose outcomes are fundamentally unpredictable). A familiarity advantage enables one to "load the dice" and to take advantage of unfolding events as the passage of time reveals what previously was uncertain (Figure 5-3). The intent is to gain unfair advantage in taking risk due to asymmetric knowledge or other intangible advantages. The strategic objective then becomes either to acquire further familiarity advantages or to avoid competing altogether.

In a perfect world, a company would enjoy both an abundance of familiar, high-return, near-term opportunities and a pipeline of familiar, long-term growth opportunities. But the world is usually imperfect.

So the most promising new product ideas may well be either unfamiliar, uncertain, or both unfamiliar *and* uncertain, and they may not materialize until years later. The company needs to invest in acquiring familiarity, testing the idea's validity as it goes forward, while knowing that future returns are years away and often highly uncertain.

Understanding where the company has familiarity and where it does not can be extraordinarily useful, because in today's turbulent environment many companies retreat when confronted with opportunities involving unfamiliar risks.

A POI approach, in contrast, leads you to an exploration of areas that your competitors may be avoiding, especially if it seems that a relatively small investment in an exploration project might bring more familiarity with the opportunity. In doing so, you can develop proprietary knowledge through the talented people you assign to the effort. Even if no immediate opportunity materializes, this familiarity will allow you to recognize complex patterns and identify new opportunities as they emerge over time.

Let's return to the ship analogy: A corporate strategist in today's global economy has no more ability to control the forces at work than a ship's captain has control over the weather. However, with a well-built ship, with a well-trained crew, and by taking advantage of weather patterns, charts, maps, and other navigational aids, the captain can with reasonable certainty sail from one port to another on a predictable schedule.

So far, so good. But a strategist must also deal with competitors that possess unknown capabilities and plans. Consider, instead, the problem of trying to move supplies and troops by ship during World War II, when crossing the ocean meant avoiding not only bad weather but also enemy submarines, ships, and airpower. The answer was to not send single ships but instead to deploy a convoy comprising a mix of superior aircraft carriers, battleships, destroyers, and escort, troop, and supply ships.

In applying this analogy to strategic initiatives, superiority comes from enjoying familiarity advantages. A portfolio increases the ability of each individual vessel to cross the ocean, which increases the likelihood that sufficient supplies will make it across. You cannot determine where the battle will occur or which ships will be lost in enemy action. But you can increase the probability of success for the mission as a whole.

The analogy can be taken one step further: Initiatives in the portfolio should be organized around multiple themes—convoys, if you will, focused on achieving a particular aspiration—such as increasing the global reach of the enterprise, entering a related industry, achieving the lowest marginal cost of production in the industry, and so on. Thematic ideas are necessary to organize the portfolio of initiatives, which might otherwise theoretically be infinite.

Many business leaders intuitively grasp the POI concept—although they refer to it in different terms. Jack Welch reportedly liked to quote Carl von Clausewitz on effective military strategy—that is, that strategy is not a long and detailed plan of action but rather the evolution of a central idea through continually changing circumstances.

The Three Elements of Dynamic Management

Dynamic management, then, has three distinct elements:

1. A disciplined search designed to enable a company to discover and—through a staged investment process—create initiatives that provide disproportionately high rewards for the risks taken

2. A one-firm management of the resulting portfolio

3. An integrated process of managing the pursuit of current operating earnings against future earnings and making the necessary resource allocation trade-offs

As we describe this process, we will again use Global Bank as an example.

Disciplined Search and a Staged Investment Process

We have spoken of the challenge inherent in today's era of rapid change, confusion, and uncertainty. The good news is that the same global forces creating this uncertainty are generating opportunities to innovate either in or close to the corporation's core businesses. To harvest these opportunities, a company could set up a day-long brainstorming session for its strategic thinkers. This type of conference could easily generate dozens of good ideas. Similar results can be achieved by asking the top several hundred people to submit their best, single ideas for how to increase long-term earnings. Thus the challenge is not usually in identifying raw ideas but in converting them into high-return, proportionately low-risk investment opportunities.

The problem is that making this conversion, particularly with ideas that require combining intangibles with tangibles into a successful business model, is inherently difficult and carries very considerable investment risk. The answer to this challenge is a staged investment process, one that matches investment levels to a company's level of familiarity. As practiced by venture capital firms, by oil exploration companies, and by companies engaging in R&D, the process typically has four stages (Figure 5-4).

- **Stage 1. Diagnostic and Directional Strategy.** At this stage, a modest amount of money is invested in a diagnostic of the new idea. It identifies what is familiar and what is unfamiliar and what is uncertain (what can be known versus what is unknowable). The goal here is to begin to acquire as much familiarity as possible, to identify what familiarities others enjoy that you do not, to map the complexities, to identify the uncertainties, to size the opportunity, and to develop a pro forma directional strategy.

- **Stage 2. Design and Operational Strategy.** Assuming the results of Stage 1 are positive, a bet is laid: Real money is spent to develop a design for the new product or process, using the (still modest) level

FIGURE 5-4

A Staged Investment Process as Mitigating Execution Risks

Stage 1. Diagnostic & Directional Strategy	Stage 2. Design & Operational Strategy	Stage 3. Prototype	Stage 4. Scale
Seed Capital	**Small Bet**	**Medium Bet**	**Large Bet**
• External and internal diagnostic to acquire knowledge.	• Develop best possible design, given familiarity, to fit with environment.	• Build prototype and test for fit.	• Invest in opportunities with loaded-dice (i.e., asymmetric) expected returns.
• Define confusion, complexity, and uncertainty.	• Mobilize management focus, talent, and expense dollars to pursue attractive opportunities.	• Test opportunities to place bets.	• Commit capital and take residual risks.
• Define familiarities.		• Acquire new familiarities.	OR
• Identify unfamiliarities.	• Estimate risks/rewards.	• Determine residual risks from complexity and uncertainty.	• Put on hold/retain familiarity.
• Size the opportunity.	• Define residual risks.	• Estimate residual risks/rewards.	OR
OR	OR	• Abandon flawed design.	• Let option expire.
• Stop the search if opportunity is too small.	• Abandon failed design.		

Example Initiatives

	Stage 1	Stage 2	Stage 3	Stage 4
Adapt	• Outsource	• Select 1,000-person unit (e.g., HR administrative staff and design off-shoring model).	• Experiment with putting 500 employees in Poland and 500 employees in India.	• Replicate process with 10,000 similar jobs.
Build	• New business idea	• Design new business model.	• Test new business model with 2 customers groups.	• Roll out new business across geography and customer base.

Reduces Confusion	Mitigates Complexity	Mitigates Complexity and Uncertainty

of familiarity to achieve a best fit with the internal and external environments. At this stage, management focus and talent are expended on the project, and an estimate is made of the risk/reward trade-off that moving forward may entail. If the risks seem too high for the rewards, it may be appropriate to stop or delay the effort. But if the rewards seem to outweigh the risks, the end of this stage is an operational (that is, blueprint-level) plan for going forward.

- **Stage 3. Prototype.** Provided the opportunity appears sufficiently attractive, real investment risk must now be taken. If the first two stages have been appropriately managed, however, some of the complexity and confusion have resolved themselves, and the company is becoming familiar with the nature of the opportunity. Prototyping helps test the proposed business model for fit with the environmental complexity and allows for refinement of the earlier risk/reward analysis. Prototyping also tests the nascent organization being established to "own" the initiative, and determines how to get it to fit with the existing line organization. If it reveals a significantly flawed design, the initiative may be abandoned or the prototyping period extended. Oftentimes, the prototyping calls for significant tinkering with the value proposition, the business model, and the organization being built for it.

- **Stage 4. Scale (Commit or Abandon).** Here is where the very significant irrevocable investment of labor and capital is made that, if successful, leads to the capture of the opportunity and competitive advantage. This is where the initiative is brought out of the hothouse and into the day-to-day line structure. Unless the company now has what we would call a "loaded-dice" opportunity—one in which its level of familiarity advantage is significantly higher than its competitors—the right response is the abandonment or reformulation of the idea.

Important initiatives, even those with a perceived low investment risk, should be part of this process. For example, a CEO might launch an apparent "no-regrets" initiative to revamp the company's core operating system to a changing technology, the goal being to reduce the firm's marginal unit costs to the industry's lowest level. But new technology might compromise this effort, or the company may, in fact, lack the skills to execute the initiative, or global industry standards may emerge that work against it, and then, the decision should be reexamined.

Chipping away at the edges of uncertainty will set the odds in your favor, but you can still be unlucky. The challenge is to pursue enough loaded-dice initiatives with sufficiently attractive returns so as to reasonably ensure that the company will have enough successes to outperform the market's expectations.

Establishing the backbone line structure and one-company governance described earlier in the book is essential for making such an approach work effectively and efficiently. For starters, a large proportion of the most attractive opportunities will cross organizational units. For that reason, a one-firm mindset is essential to capturing them. Streamlining the organization by focusing frontline managers on familiar, current opportunities is also essential. The "wander-in-the-woods" method of discovery, after all, needs to be handled offline.

Furthermore, to make the POI process work, a company must have created the capacity to manage such disciplined, formal projects under the sponsorship of a senior leader, an individual who can devote real time to overseeing the project. Such additional organizational capacities (described later in the book) as formal networks, knowledge marketplaces, and talent marketplaces can be of enormous help to the senior sponsor and the project leader to quickly and effectively be able to mobilize the firm's existing familiarities against the opportunity, and to build a team capable of acquiring any new familiarities that are required.

One-Firm Management of the Portfolio

Even if a firm enjoys familiarity advantages, it might be unlucky in pursuing them, or it will discover a competitor with significant familiarity advantages relative to its own. Sometimes, an initiative that seems promising at first doesn't meet the tests of the staged investment process.

That's why pursuing a portfolio of initiatives is better than "placing all of the eggs in one basket."

It follows that the POI approach calls for companies to keep initiatives up and running in all stages of development. In the case of Global Bank, we use a nine-cell grid to depict its portfolio of initiatives, one that maps the initiatives along time and familiarity (Figure 5-5).

The time axis of this grid conforms to the "three horizons" of strategy: short, medium, and long terms. The familiarity axis, on the other hand, needs some explanation.

- **Familiar.** By this we mean that the company possesses relevant, distinctive intangibles superior to that of competitors—giving it a familiarity advantage. This should apply to all initiatives in which the client is making a major commitment of resources. For example, Global Bank feels it has a familiarity advantage in acquiring U.S. regional banks.

- **Unfamiliar.** The company possesses fewer of the needed intangibles to pursue this initiative than its competitors. Here, if the company wishes to compete, it may attempt small to midsize investments in order to acquire familiarity more quickly. For example, Global Bank feels it is very unfamiliar with how to lend money safely to midsized private companies outside the United States.

- **Uncertain.** Neither the company nor its competitors possesses familiarity. Alternatively, the situation is subject to events whose outcomes are fundamentally unpredictable. Until the uncertainty is resolved enough to allow a reasonable assessment of risks and rewards, only modest investments in acquiring familiarity should be made. For example, Global Bank is uncertain whether it will ever be allowed to acquire a majority stake in an Indian or a Chinese bank.

Another element is also represented here: The size of the circles suggests the estimated market capitalization at stake if the initiative proves to be successful.

FIGURE 5-5

A Portfolio of Initiatives for Global Bank

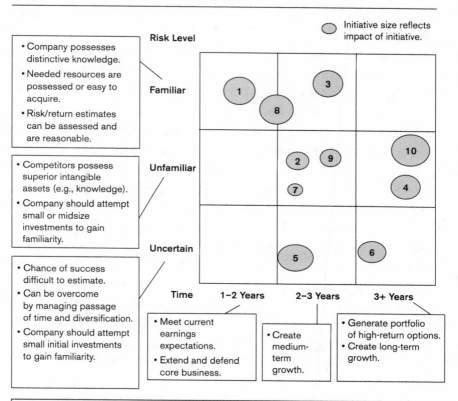

Initiative size reflects impact of initiative.

Risk Level

• Company possesses distinctive knowledge.
• Needed resources are possessed or easy to acquire.
• Risk/return estimates can be assessed and are reasonable.

Familiar

• Competitors possess superior intangible assets (e.g., knowledge).
• Company should attempt small or midsize investments to gain familiarity.

Unfamiliar

• Chance of success difficult to estimate.
• Can be overcome by managing passage of time and diversification.
• Company should attempt small initial investments to gain familiarity.

Uncertain

Time   **1–2 Years**   **2–3 Years**   **3+ Years**

• Meet current earnings expectations.
• Extend and defend core business.

• Create medium-term growth.

• Generate portfolio of high-return options.
• Create long-term growth.

Strategic Initiatives in Global Bank's Enterprisewide Portfolio of Initiatives

Adapt core capabilities:
1. Global Consumer Bank sales stimulation program.
2. Explore creation of an ultra-high-net-worth private banking offering.
3. Explore acquisition of regional bank in Midwest.

Build new business:
4. Expand midsized corporate business outside the United States.

5. Explore investment banking opportunities in real estate outside the United States.

Shape the corporate business portfolio:
6. Explore acquisition of a minority stake in banks in China and India.
7. Explore option to divest trust services.
8. Explore acquisition of major broker-dealer.

Build institutional capabilities:
9. Build a knowledge marketplace.
10. Build a talent marketplace.

Clearly, it is always essential to have some familiar opportunities in play in the upper-left corner of the grid. Under the organizing model we propose, these near-term, familiar opportunities are the province of frontline management.

Opportunities that are further out in time, however, or that involve overcoming unfamiliarity and/or uncertainty, should be handled off-line by formal project teams (with oversight from the parent governance committee, described in Chapter 4).

In our experience, there are four kinds of major initiatives that would fall within a POI review. The first is initiatives that will involve making investments to adapt current value propositions and business models to changing circumstances (for example, changes in technology). A second category is initiatives that will involve building new value propositions and businesses. A third category will involve making acquisitions or divestitures. Finally, many will involve building new, enterprisewide organization capabilities such as we describe in this book (for example, a knowledge or talent marketplace).

This last category, aimed at building organizational capabilities, is a special category that applies to all the organizational design ideas that we describe throughout this book (in our last chapter, we will explain how you can use a portfolio-of-initiatives approach to design and implement organizational change).

The longer-term, familiar opportunities (that is, the middle and right-hand boxes on the first row) represent future profit opportunities that the firm can count on. Even these initiatives, however, often have considerable execution risks and may also require allocation of significant resources to scale them. Thus they will often involve top management participation, staged investments, and decisions to be made after weighing the investments today against their impact on current earnings.

We believe that most companies will need to set up a strategy committee (one that operates as a subcommittee of the parent governance committee) to closely track the progress of the various initiatives.

In Global Bank's case, this strategy subcommittee would be considerably smaller than the partnership-at-the-top committee, but it would certainly need to include the CEO, the four top backbone line managers, and several up-and-coming senior managers (drawn on a best-available-talent basis from across the firm). Keeping the strategy committee small gives each member ample "airtime."

The strategy committee would be charged with converting potential opportunities into winning value propositions. For most companies, finding winners through such a process will usually be essential for meeting growth targets (since the market's expectations of earnings usually exceed the earnings growth that management can foresee today). The risks of pursuing such strategic initiatives are considerable, however.

Most of the unfamiliar or uncertain initiatives require small "bets" to nurture them along from Stage 1 to Stage 2. Such small bets are probably too small to occupy the time of the strategy committee. They should be under the purview of senior managers. If, during Stage 2, the potential investments and returns become sufficiently sizable, the initiative should be elevated to the corporate grid and come under the oversight of the strategy committee.

In the model we are proposing, each initiative placed on the corporate grid would have a member of the strategy committee serve as a sponsor. In addition to the senior sponsor, you would add a full-time project leader, usually someone with frontline experience picked because of his or her ability to manage the initiative on to implementation. Many of the team members involved in the early stages would also be expected to continue with the initiative.

Such initiatives will therefore give high-potential individuals the time, the room, and the resources to grow both the firm's capabilities and their own skills. Even "dry holes" will still grow the firm's talent and knowledge.

As time passes, interim results for some initiatives will be positive, and some will be negative. As the market evolves, you must manage

FIGURE 5-6

Management of a Portfolio of Initiatives

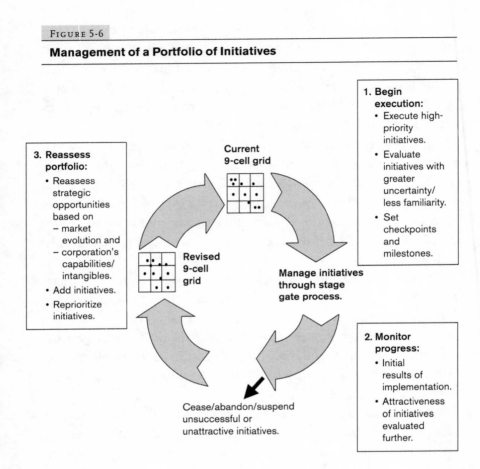

1. **Begin execution:**
   - Execute high-priority initiatives.
   - Evaluate initiatives with greater uncertainty/less familiarity.
   - Set checkpoints and milestones.

3. **Reassess portfolio:**
   - Reassess strategic opportunities based on
     – market evolution and
     – corporation's capabilities/intangibles.
   - Add initiatives.
   - Reprioritize initiatives.

Current 9-cell grid

Revised 9-cell grid

Manage initiatives through stage gate process.

Cease/abandon/suspend unsuccessful or unattractive initiatives.

2. **Monitor progress:**
   - Initial results of implementation.
   - Attractiveness of initiatives evaluated further.

your entire portfolio of initiatives dynamically so that you are constantly scaling up or cutting back your investments (Figure 5-6). Individual initiatives must constantly be reviewed against all others. They must be reprioritized and, if necessary, terminated accordingly. The idea is to make the passage of time your ally: Checkpoints, milestones, and staged investments enable you to make the most progress with the least risk. Prototypes can resolve much of the unfamiliarity and uncertainty of most investments, even before they need to be "scaled up." As time passes, the risks brought by residual complexity and uncertainty will begin to resolve themselves.

Using the POI approach, you are effectively planning on being lucky in the sense that, as Louis Pasteur said, "Fortune favors the prepared mind." And when you are lucky enough to produce a winning initiative, you will be able to put real muscle behind it (while your competitors are still figuring out what you are doing).

How many initiatives should you have in your portfolio? We have found that if you go much above 15 or 20, you have too little time for the group to review and debate each one sufficiently. The enterprisewide strategy committee should review only those initiatives that are consequential to the company (we suggest that initiatives bearing a 3 percent or more impact on earnings or market capitalization, or which reflect significant enterprisewide benefit or risk, deserve corporate level oversight). Only the company's top management team can balance the risks, rewards, and timing of investments in such important initiatives. Only they can decide which initiatives to start, cultivate, scale up, or terminate. And only they can manage the internal politics and organizational capabilities that too often doom initiatives undertaken in more traditional ways.

Large companies may need to use a similar approach for smaller initiatives; those that are below the enterprisewide size threshold (and which are under the responsibility of a single top manager). At a superclass megainstitution, after all, some "groups" earn several billion dollars a year. These smaller initiatives can be pursued by organizing a similar process, under the oversight of the relevant senior line executives (for example, group executives). In Global Bank's case, the Global Consumer Bank executive would probably have a strategy committee focused on retail initiatives that were too small for the enterprisewide committee (for example, less than 3 percent impact on market capitalization or earnings).

Such processes are essential for stimulating smaller "seed" capital initiatives—those ventures that can later develop into major corporatewide investment opportunities.

Managing Current Earnings versus Future Earnings

Deciding where and when to make trade-offs in the management of current earnings versus future earnings is a constant challenge. This has been especially true in the 20th-century model, because such trade-offs usually have been evaluated in separate budgeting and long-term planning processes that are unconnected to resource allocation. How many times have managers devised winning strategies only to get their discretionary spending cut in the budgeting process—because "we can't afford it"?

In our June 2005 *McKinsey Quarterly* management survey, 65 percent of the respondents said that a focus on short-term growth sometimes or often prevents the correct long-term investments from being made.

We've seen many situations in which no-brainer discretionary spending (to respond, for example, to a competitor's new product launch or to launch a sales stimulation program with a threefold payback within a year) has been cut from budgets because of the need to make next quarter's earnings expectations. In such an environment, where even short-term earnings improvement initiatives are cut, initiatives that could really "move the needle" in two or three years have no chance at all. When we describe such situations to top management, they usually feign being horrified, but they are also unwilling to make exceptions to budget guidance. Why? Because they are afraid to lessen the pressure on line managers to make budget.

Like many of the issues described in this book, the ambiguity over the decision rules in making short- versus long-term trade-offs leads to unintended consequences down the line. We recommend, instead, that companies establish an integrated dynamic management process that integrates the portfolio-of-initiatives approach with budgeting and resource allocation. Rather than having these critical trade-off decisions made down the line through the budgeting processes, they need to be pushed up to senior and top managers who have the perspective to make the trade-offs.

We believe that the specific decisions involving these trade-offs need debate, often because funding for some of these initiatives will come at the expense of other initiatives (or must be cut from line budgets). The debate, then, will be affected by the immediate circumstances surrounding *when* the decision is made. How important is lead time? How fast are our competitors moving? What is the earnings outlook? Are we ahead or behind projections? How exciting are the prospects for the various initiatives in the portfolio?

The traditional budgeting process often causes these trade-offs to be made a year in advance—and by down-the-line managers, with insufficient context, who are being held individually accountable for their unit's results. Instead, we recommend instituting a process that makes these trade-off decisions "just in time"—and by top and senior managers who are being held not just individually accountable but mutually accountable (as in a partnership at the top, described in the previous chapter). This approach frees the frontline managers to focus on current earnings, while senior and top managers are freed to focus on strategic and short-term performance versus long-term-health trade-offs.

As with most of the approaches recommended in this book, the devil is in the design details. For example, are POI initiatives included in the line managers' budgets? Or are they funded through an enterprisewide offline pool? If so, how big should such a pool be, and how should it be funded? What changes are being made to the process if the initiatives affect current earnings or medium- to long-term earnings? What changes are made to the process if the initiatives are familiar, unfamiliar, or uncertain? How are the initiatives sequenced and prioritized? What do we do if the firm is having an unusually good quarter or two? What if we are having tough times and our immediate earnings prospects are poor?

To illustrate this, let's describe a hypothetical dynamic management process built around a rolling, 18-month projection of earnings. Let's assume that a partnership-at-the-top parent strategy subcommittee has been created to oversee the process. In this example, 18 months forward is the time period designated as the current-earnings outlook of line management. At the end of each quarter, the next 12 months out becomes the budget, and a new quarter of projections is added to get the outlook back to 18 months. Let's assume that, as described in Chapter 4, all of the necessary calendaring and meeting protocols have been established so that the meetings are effective and efficient.

In this process, we would recommend establishing a separate pool to fund initiatives that will not be maturing into earnings opportunities until after 18 months or more and another for all initiatives that are unfamiliar and/or uncertain. These initiatives, by our definition, would be "offline." Funding for them would come either from discretionary budgets controlled by senior or top managers or, if large enough, through the corporate pool. This pool would be used to fund the first three stages of the staged investment processes. Whenever initiatives reach Stage 4 and are ready to be scaled, however, both the revenues and expenses for these initiatives would go back into backbone line management budgets (freeing up the discretionary spending for other initiatives). While the exact amount will vary by company, this pool for strategic staged gate investments could amount to 2 to 3 percent of a company's total spending (which in Global Bank's case could be $350 million to $500 million annually). The decision on which initiatives to fund would be made by the strategy committee on a quarterly basis, depending on the circumstances at the time.

Similarly, 18-month-out operating budgets and results against budget would be reviewed by the entire partnership at the top governance committee (including the strategic initiatives carve-out) with the going-forward budget adjusted quarterly.

It would be important to keep the calendars of the committees closely coordinated. For example, those people who served on both the partnership-at-the-top committee and the strategy subcommittee might want to alternate, say, every two weeks between reviews of operating performance and reviews of the portfolio of initiatives. In Global Bank's case, probably the CEO, the four top backbone line managers, and the head of strategic planning would serve on both committees. Along with any other executives selected by the CEO, this group of executives would compose the strategy committee that would be accountable for integrating short-term performance versus long-term-health perspectives.

Every six months or so, it would be wise to have the entire parent governance committee (that is, not just the strategy committee) engage in a multiday, off-site, holistic evaluation of the corporation's performance and health. This holistic evaluation would both review performance since the last off-site meeting and examine the critical variables affecting performance over the next 18 months. It would also include a review of the competitors, industry trends, and other global forces at work (including macroeconomic trends).

This off-site would include a review of the entire portfolio of initiatives as a portfolio (in contrast to the initiative-by-initiative review performed in the monthly strategy committee meetings). These off-sites could also be used to develop new themes (such as "stake out our territory in India and China" or "new business opportunities exploiting nanotechnology"); brainstorm new initiatives; and establish and reaffirm near-term and longer-term aspirations for performance (that is, profit per employee, growth in employment, return on invested capital, market capitalization, and so on).

The process we are describing uses the off-sites to create a common context for the partnership at the top as it grapples with these kinds of issues. Meanwhile the monthly strategy committee meetings serve to provide focus on in-depth reviews of the circumstances of different line units and initiatives. The reason we call this approach "dynamic management" is that it involves management's continual decision making over a long-term time frame in addition to its usual decision making on where and how to compete. It is in sharp contrast to focusing on a single time period (that is, next year's earnings). While "where and how to compete" are often thought of as the issues of strategy, we believe *when* to compete is often the real issue. After all, it involves the central, continuing trade-offs of allocation not just of discretionary spending but also of talent and of the inherently limited capacity of any organization to focus. Really important decisions often involve establishing priorities—and the sequencing of actions often are dependent on just-in-time information and the knowledge of customers and competition.

The purpose of dynamic management is to make the passage of time your friend rather than your enemy.

A Flexible, Evolutionary Approach

As we have suggested, strategic decisions organized around a portfolio of initiatives are made just in time by a kind of conscious natural selection. As efforts develop, companies invest more in initiatives that offer potential high rewards relative to the risks. And they withdraw from less-promising efforts. Under this approach, the company discovers where and how it will compete, as opposed to setting a course and sticking to it, even as conditions change. The portfolio's success is measured by its ability to create enough high-return initiatives to outperform the market's expectations for earnings and returns on talent and capital.

In one example, a company using this approach aspired to triple its share price in six years. "Business-as-usual" earnings growth expectations, however, made it clear that the company would do well enough to double its share price over this period. After undertaking the POI approach, the company was able to identify a sufficient number of low-regrets initiatives to be confident that it could close about half the earnings gap. The challenge then became to find enough additional initiatives that would justify small bets to overcome unfamiliarity, thus allowing the company to launch new efforts that would potentially close the rest of the gap. A new corporatewide process, involving the top 20 executives, was established to oversee the identification, enhancement, and nurturing of both existing and newly created initiatives.

The returns are not yet in, but the company intends to develop its strategy continuously, as individual initiatives proceed through the staged investment process and into a future not seen as being prede-termined. At any point, it may choose to continue in its current direc-tion, make a major shift, or even put itself up for sale. The goal is always to be optimally placed to make the ideal decision. It is a matter of be-coming as flexible and adaptive as the markets themselves; the acid test will be whether this kind of conscious creative-destruction process can be managed sufficiently to keep ahead of the competition. The broader point is that while traditional deterministic approaches to strategy craft-ing aren't up to the task, the alternative is not simply—as it seems to so many—to put your fate entirely in the hands of the gods.

Making the Mindset Shift

As discussed earlier, moving a company to a POI mindset is not easy. But the biggest issue is resource allocation and the related short- versus long-term trade-offs.

Almost all companies do this in one of two ways. Either the corpo-rate center controls the allocation of resources through the traditional budgeting process (using this approach to constrain investments by down-the-line managers). Or the company is thoroughly decentralized, with investments being made at the business-unit level and the corpo-rate center having visibility into the results of the process rather than into the process itself. Either of these approaches will limit the ability to take a POI approach to strategy.

The first, centralized approach, with its enormous pressure to "make budget," generally squeezes the ability of down-the-line management to focus on much beyond existing operations. Down-the-line managers have little or no money to explore new possibilities, nor are they typi-cally rewarded much for doing so. Such new investments (if they exist at all) are usually top-down initiatives created by members of top leader-ship on their own without much syndication. Given the sponsorship, it is often impossible to discuss such initiatives in an objective, fact-based manner. In practice, most investment actually ends up going to familiar, high-return, near-term operating improvements.

So promising new initiatives may not get timely, stepped-up investments, and initiatives going nowhere may well not be stopped promptly and may even be declared successes. These make-budget companies deliver results for a while, but then they stop growing. Eventually, top management is either driven to make leap-of-faith investments (which usually fail spectacularly) or sell to the highest bidder.

A different, subtler challenge often confronts the decentralized company that operates as a portfolio of business silos. Companies pursuing this approach allow units to hold on to their financial resources as long as performance is sound. This model, which makes the company a portfolio of self-contained businesses, often produces real growth, as resources are moved toward businesses that are succeeding and away from businesses doing less well, in line with the POI approach.

But that model has an enormous bias toward the status quo, because the monitoring mechanism is the quality of short-term performance. As a result, initiatives sponsored by smaller businesses with limited resources that need large Stage 3 or Stage 4 investments may not receive funding in a timely manner no matter how attractive they are. Large units may be able to afford to invest in modestly attractive opportunities, while smaller units, with better opportunities, are starved for resources. Meanwhile, cross-business opportunities—those that might capture new economies of scope—cannot get funded at all due to the siloed nature of the business-unit-focused approach.

As we worked with our clients to introduce portfolio-of-initiatives approaches to strategy, we realized just how extensively the 20th-century approach (managing companies through silos and budgets) drives the behavior of most large firms today. In our experience, unless you are willing to adopt some version of a one-firm governance approach described in Chapter 4, you can't move to a POI strategy model. While you don't necessarily have to go to a partnership-at-the-top model, you at least need to have some member of top management—be it the CEO, the chief operating officer, or the CFO—driving the necessary resource allocations across the enterprise with a one-firm perspective.

Moving to a POI approach, therefore, involves major organizational change, including revisions in the roles of top management and in the company's core management processes. Incorporating a POI approach, then, requires the right conditions. In particular, what is needed is a CEO whose desire for long-term wealth creation is sufficient to drive the transformation. Reluctance to make such changes will cause many companies to stick to the traditional approach, and they will eventually succumb to the whirlwind of creative destruction. Companies willing to change themselves so that they can adapt as fast as the marketplace is evolving, however, have the potential to use today's rapidly changing, confusing, uncertain environment to their own advantage and, as a result, outperform their competitors.

Unleashing Talent as Corporate Strategy

At a very high level of abstraction, we are advocating this: that all large companies begin to think of their strategies in terms of unleashing talent. This will increase returns by using the unique intangibles they create to earn "rents" (as measured by profit per employee and return on capital).

The POI and dynamic management approach described in this chapter is designed to facilitate the creation of rents from talent. Some of these will be opportunities to adapt existing value propositions, increasing and leveraging the value of talent and intangibles in the evolving global marketplace. Some will involve creating unique value propositions and business models built from talent and other intangibles. Others will involve making acquisitions (particularly of talent-rich firms) that create new intangible-based economies of scale or scope. Some will involve building new organizational capabilities, such as formal networks and knowledge and talent marketplaces.

The POI and dynamic management approach should itself unleash talent: Each initiative, whether it succeeds or fails, will build the knowledge and skills of everyone involved. To a huge extent, a portfolio of initiatives is also a portfolio of talent: Behind every initiative are the talented people driving it who grow their knowledge, skills, and capabilities as they pursue it. Through the POI process, then, the company can grow entrepreneurs. And these will be the individuals who can create new wealth in the 21st century.

PART III

IDEAS TO IMPROVE THE FLOW OF INTANGIBLES

6

FORMAL
NETWORKS

WE BELIEVE THERE is an opportunity to design new organizing structures that will promote the effectiveness of horizontal networking across the enterprise. We call these new structures, which use a combination of hierarchy and collaboration, "formal networks." Unlike "informal networks" that simply evolve, formal networks are designed to bring natural professional communities together. And just as "backbone hierarchy" legitimizes the authority of management, formal networks legitimize the role of networks as organizing structures for professional, collaborative work.

We think that such formal networks can help replace cumbersome matrix structures, facilitate the creation and sharing of proprietary information and knowledge, and enable the building of more, and better, personal relationships among the members of a community. We also believe they can enable the establishment and reinforcement of one-enterprise standards, protocols, and values. Most important, we believe they can help enable leaders to harness the energy of diverse groups of professionals and managers around common aspirations.

Social and Informal Networks

People with mutual self-interest have long created their personal social networks of relationships, of course, both within and outside of their firms. But in the digital age, technology has enabled these personal networks to be larger, more widespread, and far easier to build and maintain. We are all familiar with the impact of the Internet, of cell phones, of Blackberries, of instant text messaging, of Google, of MySpace, and of Facebook.

But the sharing of information is more than the story of electronic devices and Internet innovations. In order to understand how communication works across a sprawling, global company, for instance, one must understand the nature of communications and human contacts.

Social networks increase the opportunities for collaboration, as well as the effectiveness and value of that collaboration, by connecting parties with related knowledge and interests while reducing the search and coordination costs to both parties. In a professional setting, each of us develops personal social networks that range from fewer than a dozen to hundreds of people. These networks enable individuals and the teams they work with to mobilize knowledge and talent.

Such networks are self-organizing in most companies today. They arise from the mergers of personal social networks into larger shared networks. As more people join the shared network, sprawling communities of friends often form, and the amount of communication builds exponentially.

We call this organizational form an "informal network." In an informal network, people start working together because they have self-interests in common, not because they are being forced by someone to work together. In other words, they work with each other because they find it beneficial to do so. People join an informal network because of the value of the knowledge they receive and the personal relationships they build.

The benefits of informal networks are so great that most large corporations now have dozens, if not hundreds, of flourishing informal networks. These enable wide-scale collaboration. In fact, their existence may help explain why some of the intangible-rich large companies— GE, ExxonMobil, and others—have performed so well from the mid-1990s through to today. These personal social and informal networks, as they have widened and deepened, have enabled these companies to gain increased scale and scope effects. This has come from better mobilizing knowledge and talent across the enterprise.

If you were to study these social and informal networks (as network practitioners Rob Cross and Leigh Weiss have), you would come to a surprising conclusion: Very little information and knowledge among thinking-intensive people actually flows through the official hierarchical and matrix structures of the company.[1] If you were to ask people, in fact, about their valuable interactions (that is, creating and exchanging information and knowledge), they would tell you that the formal structure of the company, as manifest in the organizational chart, is not really how the work gets done.

It is often the case that one particular person—such as "Cole" in Figure 6-1—who is relatively low down in the formal structure acts as the hub in the informal network because he or she has knowledge that others find valuable. Today it is the informal networks that are crossing the lines of geography, product, customer group, and functional lines, even through the thick "silo" walls of the corporation.

Limitations of Informal Networks

But just as informal networks have helped many of the megainstitutions capture wealth during this rapidly evolving era at the beginning of the digital age, they are also causing increasingly severe headaches. Much of the overload of e-mails, voice-mails, and meetings can be traced to efforts, by tens of thousands of individuals in large companies, to find, among these vast numbers of people, productive personal social network relationships.

Part of the problem is that since informal networks are ad hoc

FIGURE 6-1

Formal Structures Do Not Reflect How Work Really Gets Done

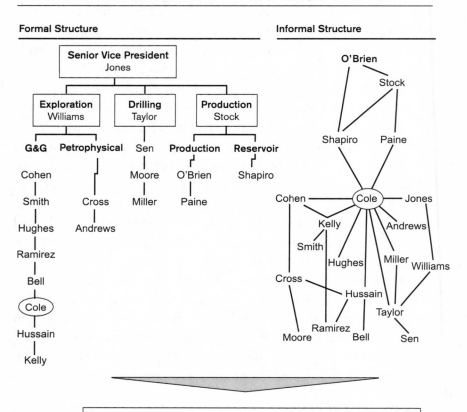

Formal Structure

Senior Vice President
Jones

Exploration — Williams
Drilling — Taylor
Production — Stock

G&G   Petrophysical   Sen   Production   Reservoir

Cohen
Smith
Hughes
Ramirez
Bell
Cole
Hussain
Kelly

Cross
Andrews

Moore
Miller

O'Brien
Paine

Shapiro

Informal Structure

O'Brien — Stock — Shapiro — Paine — Cole — Cohen — Jones — Kelly — Smith — Hughes — Miller — Williams — Cross — Hussain — Taylor — Moore — Ramirez — Bell — Sen — Andrews

The informal structure is revealed by network mapping. It shows whom people interact with to do their work, which would be difficult to discern from the organization chart:

- Cole is at the center of the information exchange network despite being relatively low down in the organization chart.
- Without Cole, the production group would be cut off from the rest of the organization.
- Jones, the SVP, is connected to only 2 people, both in Exploration.

Source: McKinsey analysis; The Hidden Power of Social Networks
by Robert Cross and Andrew Parker.

structures whose membership is dependent on individuals' discovering common interests, their effectiveness is highly variable. They rely essentially on serendipity rather than design. In large firms, multiple informal networks may form on related topics but never integrate into a single network. People who may have knowledge or skills of great value to the network may not join the network either because they are part of other informal networks or simply because they fail to discover that the network even exists.

Alternatively, some of the most talented individuals in the network may want to retain proprietary knowledge or privileged relationships for themselves. A related issue is that, without formal rules, individuals within an informal network may collaborate with outsiders and may, in the process, trade away valuable proprietary knowledge and information, which then finds its way to competitors.

Within an informal network, finding the right person to talk to may require playing telephone or e-mail tag. There is no other way to determine who within the network knows what, after all. Often, informal networks have linchpin members who serve as "hubs" through which members are connected, but the effectiveness of the network can be disrupted if the members serving as hubs become overloaded, act as gatekeepers, behave selfishly (that is, "power comes from knowledge"), or leave the company (Figure 6-2). Informal networks are limited in their effectiveness: There is usually insufficient investment in the common capabilities needed to make the network work more efficiently, effectively, and to the benefit of all network members.

The greatest limitation of self-organizing informal networks, however, is that they can't be *managed*. Most informal networks fly "under the radar" in organizations. And even when they are visible, it's hard for corporations to take full advantage of them. By not putting any investment into these networks, corporations may unintentionally frustrate their ability to flourish. Or the firm may be maintaining unintended barriers due to corporate politics—or simple neglect—that prevent natural networks from developing. Sometimes the roles and responsibilities of people in the informal networks are so ambiguous, relative to

FIGURE 6-2

Effects of Disruption on an Informal Network

Informal Network with Linchpin

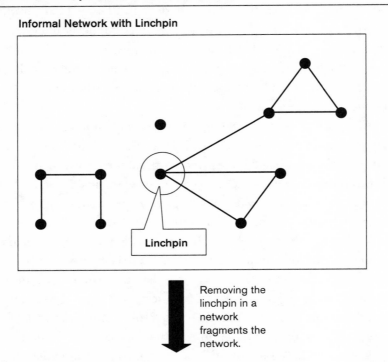

Removing the linchpin in a network fragments the network.

Informal Network If Linchpin Is Removed

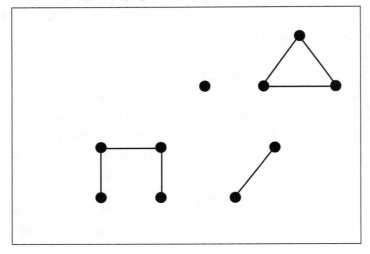

the roles and responsibilities of people with formal hierarchical responsibilities in the matrix structure, that effective control of the work done through hierarchical structures is compromised. At worst, informal networks can make dysfunctional organizations even more dysfunctional because they add to complexity or increase corporate politics.

Formal Networks

There is a solution, however, which we call "formal networks." Just as the role of the backbone hierarchy is to ensure that the company can deliver earnings, so it is the role of formal networks to increase the value and to lower the costs of collaboration among professionals. Formal networks stimulate interactions that are sponsored and encouraged by the organization and therefore are capable of being managed.

One leading petrochemical company, for example, recently designed more than 20 formal networks, ranging in size from 50 to several hundred people.[2] These networks focused on specific work areas where people could benefit from sharing best practices. This was critical because the networks had the ability to minimize downtime in these areas.

Having taken the unusual step of forming these networks, the petrochemical company wanted to assess their impact. Using network analysis, they proved that these networks were generating substantial, shareable productivity benefits. How? In one case, engineers at one oil well, through their networks, were able to find experts with the essential knowledge to help fix a problem. And they did it in two days rather than in the anticipated four.

The success of these networks came from their having been formed around focused topic areas (closely related to the way work was actually done at the wells), providing the network members with leaders and training for success, carefully identifying the members of each network (from across the geographically dispersed company), and investing in them (for example, by sponsoring a knowledge-sharing team to collect and disseminate best practices and providing resources to them such as technology).[3]

At first glance, people may mistake a formal network for a matrix. To be sure, both are organizational structures that cross line structures. But the differences are significant and start with the organizing principles that underlie each (Figure 6-3). A matrix organizes work through authority. It is therefore principally a structure based on management hierarchy. A formal network organizes work through mutual self-interest, and it is therefore principally a structure based on collaboration.

In a classic matrix organization (Figure 6-4), managers and professionals have two (or more) bosses who have authority over their work. These represent different axes of management, such as product, geography, customer, or function. Hierarchical direction is received from two different perspectives. The person in the middle of the matrix is responsible for resolving any conflicts in the directives received from different bosses. Matrix management evolved because no matter how well organized the hierarchical line structure might have been (by function, geography, customer, or product), it was felt that "secondary" axes of management were needed to horizontally cut across the enterprise, thereby managing the needed integration of other work activities.

Similar hierarchical approaches include internal joint ventures, coheads of units, and the use of cross-organizational task forces to study issues and make recommendations to appropriate hierarchical leadership.

Matrix management worked reasonably well from its advent in the 1960s until the late 1980s, particularly because it enabled some collaboration to take place across companies when it became increasingly apparent that such collaboration was required. It worked because matrix structures were used sparingly and therefore didn't confuse the vertical line structure.

Even so, matrix management was developed as an add-on to the 20th-century organizational model. It forced hierarchical managers to coordinate their work with one another. It worked well—as long as most of the success of the firm was dependent on the quality of the decisions made by top managers and as long as the number and frequency of the decisions requiring such coordination were limited.

FIGURE 6-3

Differences between Matrix Structures and Formal Networks

	Matrix Structure	Formal Network
Organizing Principle	• Organizes work through authority	• Organizes work through mutual self-interest
Mode of Influence	• Management hierarchy	• Collaboration and leadership
Number of Bosses	• Two or more representing different axes of management, e.g., product, geography, customer, function	• One manager for each person • One formal network leader for each networked community
Implications	• Proliferation of matrixed roles and complex hierarchical structure • Excessive interactions • Decision-making bottlenecks • Difficulty finding knowledge • Conflicts arising from different bosses	• Simple hierarchical structure • Streamlined interactions * Streamlined decision making • Easier and faster to find knowledge using network's resources • Number of conflicts that need to be resolved reduced by having one boss

But as more work from multiple perspectives has had to be integrated, and as the number of professionals needing to self-direct much of their work has increased, the number of matrixed roles has proliferated. Now the proliferation of such roles (in combination with the need for increased interactions and decision making) swamp the time available for matrix managers to coordinate them. Furthermore, the

FIGURE 6-4

A Classic Matrix

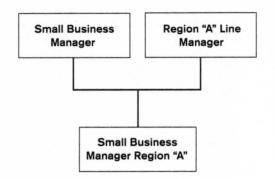

knowledge and information that needs to be absorbed and exchanged often exceeds the personal capacities of the individual.

Simultaneously, professionals who want to work horizontally across the company find themselves forced to search across poorly connected organizational silos for the knowledge and collaborators they need. And then, once they've found them, they must still gain the cooperation of their often-reluctant peers.

Worse yet are matrix structures that saddle professionals with two bosses. This forces the professionals who want to collaborate to go up the organizational hierarchy before they can go across. This contributes to a proliferation of interactions before the work can get done. As a consequence, effective collaboration often occurs only through the enlistment of senior hierarchical managers, who can resolve the conflicts that arise among competing organizational silos. Time is lost and effort is wasted on reconciling competing agendas and finding common solutions. The better answer is to get the joint managers interacting with one another directly out of mutual self-interest.

In many firms today, these matrixed and other hybrid organizations have become dysfunctional. As we described in Chapter 1, the symptoms of the dysfunction are endless meetings, phone calls, e-mail exchanges, and confused accountability for producing results.

A New Model

In the model proposed in this book, the backbone line hierarchies have broad integrative authority for running the company. They are held accountable for results. The backbone frontline manager, in particular, is responsible for delivering the entire company's existing capabilities to create earnings. This includes the capabilities of the firm's formal networks. In this role, they have clear day-to-day decision authority—not only over line activities but also over the activities of several assigned "dedicated" or "distributed" staff. We believe that all of these nonline reports, whether dedicated or distributed, should be part of designed formal network structures, each with separate network leadership.

To formalize a network, the company must define who will lead the network (that is, who will be the "network owner") and must make that leadership responsible for investing in the network so as to build common capabilities for network membership (for example, investing in knowledge that is valuable to all members). Companies can facilitate the development of formal networks by providing participation incentives (for example, providing professional development off-sites) as well as incentives for making contributions to the network (for example, boosting the reputations of people who contribute distinctive knowledge to network members).

Network owners can facilitate interactions among members, stimulate knowledge creation, maintain the community's knowledge domain, build and track a directory of network membership, and help members do their jobs more effectively and efficiently. For a formal network to work effectively, its territory must be defined (informal networks sometimes make overlapping claims on the same activities). Furthermore, standards and protocols must be established that describe how the network must work.

Let's return to Global Bank. As you recall, in the original structure the backbone frontline manager for the East Coast region had 12 either distributed or dedicated executives working with her. Of these executives, 3 were distributed to her (that is, they report to her), and 9 were dedicated to her (that is, they support her but they report elsewhere). In addition to the 3 line managers, in other words, she is expected to provide leadership to 9 people. This far exceeds the classic notion of "span of control."

How can she lead so many people? Because the dedicated and distributed people are expected to self-direct most of their work. Her role, then, is to help define their objectives and to hold them accountable for achieving them—but not to spend much time supervising their activities.

This doesn't mean that these dedicated and distributed executives are expected to work alone. Rather, under the model we are proposing, they would be part of a formal network, with a network leader, which would enable them to collaborate easily with their peers.

As we noted, the difference between a formal network and a matrix is that the network owner leading the network is not a boss but rather a "servant leader." A network owner is *not* responsible for overseeing the work or for personally evaluating the performance of individual network members (except for members who directly report up to them)— although they may play a role in leading the evaluation process through personnel committees.

Network leaders are not expected to "manage" network members or to have decision authority over them, as they would in a matrix. Instead, a formal network leader's responsibilities are primarily limited to network activities (organizing the infrastructure supporting the network, developing a knowledge agenda for maintaining the network's knowledge domain, building a training program, holding conferences, qualifying network members as professionally competent, and so on).

Despite having limited hierarchical authority, formal network leadership should be held mutually accountable with line management for the effectiveness of the network's performance. After all, they have an enormous ability to enable members of the network to perform better. Despite their lack of authority to tell people what to do, formal network leaders have the ability to shape the organization. Much of this impact comes from their control of investments and activities needed to make the members individually—and the network collectively—more effective. Much of their effectiveness, however, will come from their leadership—through their ability to inspire and persuade.

In professional firms, which have long used versions of formal networks called "practices," one can always tell the difference between a very talented practice leader and an average practice leader. Even though their decision responsibilities are the same, talented leaders create far more vibrant, exciting practices than do average leaders. It is entirely appropriate, therefore, to hold formal network leaders accountable for the performance of the network, even though they may not have any direct authority over the individual network members.

Connecting Members to the Network

In the model we are proposing, formal networks should be designed to extend the reach of professional work throughout the company, without interfering with the hierarchical decision-making processes. The idea is to achieve this extended reach by adding value to the network members rather than by exercising authority through the hierarchical leaders.

To succeed, most formal networks need to connect to two kinds of professional populations:

1. Core members of a network, whose jobs require them to be members

2. Extended members, whose membership is entirely voluntary and due only to their professional interest in the network's activities

Core Members

Core members include all of the dedicated and distributed executives, as well as any other persons who require membership in the community as a prerequisite for doing the job. One of the distributed jobs reporting to the New Jersey/Long Island manager of the Global Consumer

Bank, for instance, was in marketing (Figure 6-5). This person would automatically be a member of a formal network led by the U.S. Branch–Based Marketing leader, who, in turn, would report to the Global Marketing executive (a senior manager), who, in turn, would report to the executive vice president of Global Consumer (a top executive).

This would make the U.S. Branch–Based Marketing leader a relative peer of the frontline backbone leader (since both would be two levels down from top management). Given that each branch-based frontline manager would have a marketing person reporting to him or her, there would be about 30 core members of this network. In this role, the U.S. Branch–Based Marketing leader would be accountable for encouraging the core members of the network to work, either by themselves or in teams, for the benefit of the entire network.

The formal network leader would not take on the work personally but would normally ask core members of the network to take on discrete network tasks. For example, the U.S. Branch–Based Marketing leader could ask members to develop new branch-based promotional material for the network or find better ways to use local advertising budgets.

The network owner would have personal responsibilities as well, of course. For example, the U.S. Branch–Based Marketing executive would be responsible, when authorized by a frontline manager, for helping to mobilize marketing talent from talent pools and talent marketplaces (as will be described in the next chapter) for special projects.

In this role, this U.S. Branch–Based Marketing executive would also often work with the backbone frontline managers to identify candidates for marketing positions whenever they became available. The same executive would also be accountable for stimulating the creation of knowledge, as well as for overseeing maintenance of the knowledge in the domain of branch-based marketing (the branch signage, promotional materials, the look and feel of the branches, and so on).

FIGURE 6-5

Marketing: A Formal Network

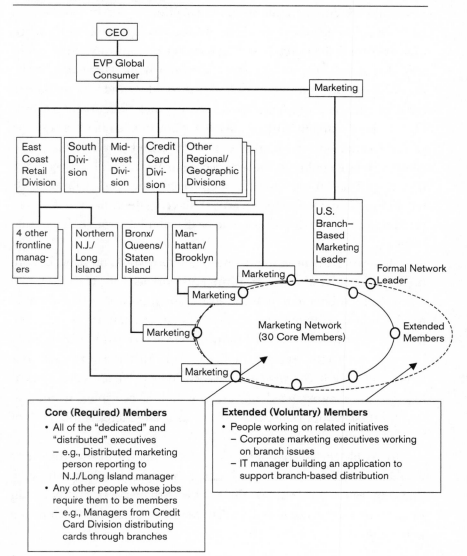

Core (Required) Members
- All of the "dedicated" and "distributed" executives
  - e.g., Distributed marketing person reporting to N.J./Long Island manager
- Any other people whose jobs require them to be members
  - e.g., Managers from Credit Card Division distributing cards through branches

Extended (Voluntary) Members
- People working on related initiatives
  - Corporate marketing executives working on branch issues
  - IT manager building an application to support branch-based distribution

Extended Network Members

This same executive, in addition to providing leadership to the core members of the formal network, would also be responsible for supporting an extended branch-based marketing community (that would include individuals in the Global Consumer Bank who wanted to be part of that community). Membership could include IT managers building a marketing application, or it could include marketing executives, as part of an enterprisewide talent pool, in such fields as pricing or advertising, who are interested in working on branch-based issues. Alternatively, it could include a project manager from IT who is building an application to support branch-based product distribution. Or it could include people working on a "staged gate initiative," focused on adding a new product offering to be distributed through the branch system.

All the individuals in the extended network would probably be core members of at least one other formal network as well. They might be extended members of one or more additional networks. The point is that beyond the core members, the extended formal network would be fluid, and it would be up to the individual to determine whether or not he or she wanted to participate in the network. All of the formal network leaders would be in competition with each other, in effect, as they worked to attract as many extended network members as possible. The motivation for the network leaders to do so would be to increase the reach of their networks.

To enable the formal network leaders to perform this role, they would be provided with discrete budgets to fund network investments. These investments would be the source of the leaders' ability to add value to their networks' members. These investments could include the following:

- Infrastructure (both human and technology based) to support network interactions

- Codified knowledge, in the form of documents, internal blogs, "net-workpedias," and so on

- Training for network members

- Social community-building activities (for example, conferences)

Some of the measures used to evaluate the performance of formal network managers would be quantitative and include the following:

- Knowledge documents produced

- Conference participation

- Standard measures from network analysis—for example, "closeness" to describe the number of steps it takes for any person in the network to reach anyone else

- Network density

And some would be tests of network effectiveness such as assessing satisfaction of network members, effectiveness of responses to inquiries, and ability to quickly find appropriate dialogue partners.

But the real measure of network success would be the qualitative assessments (made by network members and senior leaders) of the effectiveness of the network in delivering against its mission (for example, stories or case examples illustrating professional productivity improvements). In the U.S. Branch–Based Marketing executive's case, for instance, effectiveness would depend on qualitative assessments: how well that executive's formal network operated compared to others in the company, and against the expectation of the firm's senior and top leaders.

Providing Structure to Professional Work

Just as a backbone hierarchy defines the structure of management roles, then, formal networks define the structure of professional, collaborative roles. In the process, formal networks can enable large companies to overcome the problems of very large numbers by creating multiple small, focused communities of interest that are integrated within larger, wide-ranging communities of members.

Members of the U.S. Branch–Based Marketing formal network, for example, would also be part of a broader Retail Marketing network. The number of networks in which a person participated would be up to the individual, except for participation by core members as a prerequisite of being in their jobs. In other words, each person would build personal social networks within the formal networks, depending on his or her role and professional interests. Formal networks, though, serve to take much of the work out of "networking." The limits of network participation are largely a function of time and interest; members would join a network that delivered more value to them than the costs of their time, and they would leave when the network was no longer of that value.

One of the advantages of formal networks is that a person can be a member of more than one at a time. This enables a person to integrate knowledge and gain access to talent across multiple communities. A person in the U.S. Branch–Based Marketing community, for example, could also be a member of a branding community, a Premier (that is, Affluent) banking community, and a Small Business banking community. Multiple membership, therefore, also serves to integrate knowledge across professional communities. In the just-cited example, for instance, branding knowledge gained from that community would be "networked" into the other communities, as members applied knowledge gained from one network to other networks.

From the company's perspective, the number of formal networks created is limited only by how much the firm chooses to invest in them.

The number and size of individual networks could vary with the value of each network in serving its members. Effective networks would grow in membership and interactions. Ineffective networks would lose members and interactions. Formal networks are self-regulating. Indeed, rapid growth proves the value of the network, the value of the network leader, and the value of the money invested in the network.

In a megainstitution, there is room for literally thousands of formal networks. A company with 100,000 thinking-intensive workers, for example, could have 2,000 networks of 100 people per network (if each professional was a member of just two networks). Broad networks (in fields such as finance or IT) would have thousands of members, while specialized networks (such as the Turkish interest group) might have only a few dozen members. Formal networked communities could form not just along customer groups, products, geography, and functional lines but also around integrative cross-cutting themes such as risk management and global forces at work (nanotechnology, changing demographics, and so on).

Increased Clout for Nonbackbone Roles in Formal Networks

Much of the power of C-level executives will be exercised through these formal network structures. Exercising power through network structures rather than matrix structures ensures that the use of that power provides a complement to backbone line management rather than a conflict with it.

Take, for example, the chief marketing officer (CMO) for Global Bank. As shown in Figure 6-6, the CMO seems as though he or she would not be very powerful. After all, each of the top line executives (the Global Consumer Bank, Global Capital Markets & Investment Banking, and so on) would have marketing distributed to them. However, that officer would control shared corporate utilities for branding and advertising, promotion, pricing, and so on, and he or she would also share a marketing talent pool with people who have specialized skills

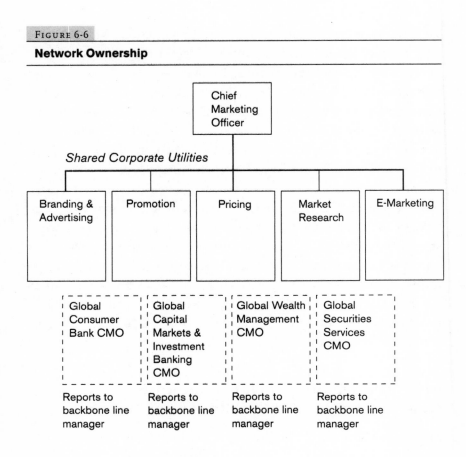

FIGURE 6-6

Network Ownership

in those disciplines that would be "loaned out" to others through the talent marketplace.

In each of these marketing disciplines, the CMO would also have a formal network owner reporting to him or her, each responsible for building a community of interest across the enterprise. For instance, anyone in the firm with a "pricing tag" on his or her designated occupational specialty would be a core member of the pricing formal network. Extended members would, of course, include anyone with interest in pricing.

These formal network structures, then, provide channels for propagating knowledge and talent throughout the enterprise. But rather than pushing knowledge and talent through hierarchical matrix structures, these formal networks provide structures that enable everyone in the firm to "pull" knowledge and talent to them.

Formal networks can truly mobilize minds. In the next chapter, we describe another such vehicle, the talent marketplace.

7

TALENT
MARKETPLACES

MOST COMPANIES UNDERSTAND the competitive value of talented people and spend considerable time identifying and recruiting high-caliber individuals wherever they can be found. The trouble is that too many companies pay too little attention to allocating their internal talent resources effectively. Few companies use talented people in a competitively advantageous way—by maximizing their visibility and mobility and creating work experiences that help them grow and develop their expertise and skills. In the *McKinsey Quarterly* survey we undertook, only 27 percent said that their companies are effective at matching talent and opportunities.[1] Many frustrated managers have searched in vain for the right person for a particular job, knowing that he or she works somewhere in the company. And many talented people have had the experience of getting stuck in a dead-end corner of a company, never finding the right experiences and challenges to grow, and, finally, bailing out.[2]

In the modern, networked, and knowledge-based business environment, intangible assets created by talented people (such as skills, reputations, and relationships) generate the highest value. Effective resource allocation means unleashing the value of talent by mobilizing talented people for the best opportunities—including, in particular, opportunities to grow their talents by finding work that creates distinctive new skills and knowledge.

As global markets become more dynamic and competitive, companies will need to deploy talent even more flexibly across broader swaths of the organization. Since management must develop and execute value-creating initiatives so quickly, talent is becoming more critical to corporate performance, specific needs for talent are more unpredictable, and companies must develop talent more rapidly than ever.

We've already shown that companies with higher proportions of thinking-intensive jobs have higher profits per employee and returns on capital than do more labor-intensive firms. But most large companies aren't set up to allocate talent easily across the traditional organizational silos that stand as their most prominent structural feature (and, even if they do, they have often allocated talent that is mismatched with the best use of that talent, given opportunities for alternative employment).

Stuck in Silos

Most talent in most firms is relatively immobile. In particular, talent often gets stuck in organizational "silos." And, to the extent that there is mobility across silos, it tends to be only for those people, designated as "corporate property," who are named as people who can move up the line management hierarchy.

Even most of the "best-practices companies" typically allocate talent through personal connections and transactions between individual bosses and individual employees or within small groups of "socially networked" people. Managers find it difficult to know who among a company's talented workers would be the best person for an available position; ditto for talented people who want to know what opportunities exist around the company and with whom they might like to work.

Some people thrive in such settings. But for many talented workers seeking personal development opportunities, this approach resembles trying to fit square pegs into round holes. They might develop more appropriately in opportunities outside the silos they work in, but companies aren't set up to allocate talent easily across broader segments.

This predicament is a common one because the majority of companies have traditionally spent most of their energy improving the quantity and quality of their line management talent as opposed to other types of professional employees. Companies focus the greater part of their efforts on helping managers move up the line management hierarchy so as to become better managers. They usually spend less time developing the people who have the talent required to cultivate distinctive client relationships, to tailor products for distribution channels, or to negotiate superior contracts with suppliers. The rewards of line management motivate talented people to seek line opportunities over professional ones.

Using this approach—one built from a paternalistic, hierarchical mindset—senior managers or human resources (HR) departments are expected to create opportunities for the most talented people through formal job rotations, job posting programs, and career development policies. These approaches may foster talent management within a particular silo, but when resources and synergies across silos are required, the conventional company is hamstrung. Some of its people may have specific knowledge but lack breadth. Others may have the requisite knowledge but lack project management skills (or vice versa). Since the company's employees were hired for conventional work, they may not have sufficient intrinsic skills—personal leadership, creativity, or even raw intellect—to do the job. Frustration runs high because employees who don't want an assignment may get it, while those who might want it are either unaware of the opportunity or not invited to apply.

Some companies have tried to use the corporate HR office to hire, train, and promote talent as "corporate property." Such efforts are not only generally restricted to a few hundred people (even in large companies) but are also usually applied to developing people for specific functions, not a broad range of jobs. Employees with diverse skills (for example, project management), knowledge (such as familiarity with

China), or entrepreneurial, self-directed instincts are often neglected. Anyone handpicked for such a program must usually relocate frequently, which discourages many talented people with families and strong preferences for living in a particular geography.

And talent needs are becoming more unpredictable given the increased fluidity of the global marketplace. Today's megainstitutions face unprecedented needs to develop ever more diverse skills, in a far greater range of specialties, over a far larger range of roles, for a far wider scope of operations, for an ever larger, more diverse, population of professionals and managers. The traditional "central planning" approach of "pushing" resources to where companies deem those talents to be most needed is proving to be too ineffective and too inefficient.

Problems in Allocating Talent

Even when companies do try to allocate talent across silo boundaries, they often wind up mismatching the talent against the jobs being performed. Partly this is due to mismatching talent against the duration appropriate to the job. Partly this is due to drawing talent from too small a pool of alternative candidates. Partly this is due to inadequate focus on what is best for the person, from a development point of view, as opposed to staffing based on the "clout" of the person wanting a job filled.

Mismatched against Duration

Much of a company's most important work is task based and can be completed as project work over a relatively short period (for example, three months). In turn, many tasks need quite specialized professional skills. Yet few companies—except professional services firms such as law firms or investment banks—are organized to undertake short-term, task-based work. For example, one of the reasons why most companies have such difficulties putting together project teams to explore strategic initiatives is that they are not organized to do so. There is a mismatch between the short duration of the task and the long duration of the minimum time period for job assignments.

While it is often possible to undertake project work if team members are all within the same silo, it can be a nightmare to staff project teams across silos because the only way to do so is to make a "permanent" (that is, one year or more) transfer. Usually such transfers require extensive negotiations. Often neither the person with the needed skills nor the person seeking those skills has any interest in such a "permanent" transfer. The person with the job opportunity is reluctant to "hire" someone for a year or more for a temporary job. Similarly, the person with the skills has little interest in transferring permanently to a job that only temporarily needs those skills.

The long duration of the transfers raises the stakes to both parties, which makes it much harder to get such transactions completed. Long assignments are often not the best way to develop talent if it puts people in jobs where their personal growth opportunities are exhausted in just a few months. And from the entire company's point of view, mismatching scarce talent against "permanent" jobs that have only short-term needs for that talent is a real waste, since there will be work requiring those scarce talents that will go unstaffed.

Too Small a Pool

A related issue is that many temporary and permanent jobs are filled from very small pools of "available" talent. Frequently, managers fill available jobs from among people who already report up to them. But picking candidates out of a small pool of "the usual suspects" usually means they have to pick from among people whose skills and experience are not right for the job. Often managers are more willing to go outside the company to hire specialized, professional talent rather than hire qualified talent from within. While in some cases this may be for "control" reasons, it's often because it is easier than trying to find and obtain such talent across silo boundaries. Yet in most megainstitutions, there may be literally hundreds of better candidates for such jobs if only they could be made available.

Not Fitting a Person's Development

Finally, assignments are often made too hierarchically, where the clout of the person recruiting to fill a job is more important than the candidate's individual development needs. Many up-and-coming people wind up going off-track because they get captured by a senior manager who places them in a role that doesn't fit their interests or their skills or their development needs. Often, once captured, if they want to break free, they have to leave the company in order to continue to develop. At best, their development gets bogged down. And, to the extent that people wind up leaving the company or fail to develop their talents, the entire company loses.

Even if these people stay, bad assignments can really hurt their careers. Talent mismatch issues often have compounding effects. For example, if the wrong talent is "permanently" assigned to roles that don't fit and to senior managers with clout, not only may the jobs be badly performed but the individuals in those jobs may also have their careers ruined when their senior managers evaluate their performance.

Talent Marketplaces

We believe there is a better approach, which we call a "talent marketplace," that enables managers to "pull" talent while simultaneously giving that talent a greater choice over which assignment to take.[3] The idea is to design and build marketplaces that use market mechanisms to match the self-interest of employees seeking the best job opportunities with the self-interest of managers looking to fill their job opportunities with the best available talent.

Historically, informal talent marketplaces developed naturally in professional environments such as academia and professional services firms where several senior people all wanted to work with the best junior people. In such circumstances it was only natural to let the junior employees choose the senior people for whom they wanted to work. As those marketplaces grew up, they followed informal rules of conduct. Such informal marketplaces work best when the market numbers are fewer than 100 and the employees know one another well.

In larger professional organizations, such as global accounting firms, law firms, and consulting firms, these marketplaces have been formalized and are used to staff projects through per diem structures. In such professional firms, these marketplaces temporarily assign people to projects, and once the projects are over, the team members are reassigned.

We believe that large companies can also formalize talent marketplaces—not just for temporary assignments but for permanent assignments as well. The idea of using talent marketplaces in large, public companies is relatively new. But we believe such marketplaces can benefit all parties: the manager seeking talent, the person being assigned, and the company. Large public companies already employing a formal talent marketplace include American Express and IBM. Formal marketplaces won't come into existence naturally; a company must invest in designing and building them to make sure they provide fair value to both parties in a transaction—otherwise the market will fail.

A talent marketplace isn't for all types of employees. It is required only for "thinking-intensive" employees who possess skills and experience that differ among the individuals involved. For example, you don't need a talent marketplace to staff the jobs in a call center or the in-store jobs of a big-box retailer, because the work is designed to make the workers interchangeable, and there are large numbers of employees available if you are willing to pay appropriate wages.

Talent marketplaces are most appropriate for large, growing, complex, talent-driven companies—companies with large diverse populations of professionals and managers engaged in thinking-intensive work. These marketplaces work because they lower the intermediation costs of matching the right people with the right jobs.

Indeed, large intermediation costs are one of the principal reasons why talent in most firms is relatively immobile today. Simply stated, getting staffing from another organizational unit requires spending extensive time searching for candidates and negotiating with them and with their bosses. While those high costs may be worthwhile for filling "permanent," senior managerial positions, they are too time-consuming to be used to fill temporary or part-time needs for junior and midlevel professional staff. Yet temporary or part-time assignments for junior and midlevel staff with specific professional skills are often just what companies need to bring to bear to enable their frontline units to perform. And the diversity of work provided by a series of short-term assignments is often just what is required to enable young professional talent to grow their skills, networks, and knowledge most rapidly.

Talent marketplaces can provide the means to lower intermediation costs both for "permanent" managerial positions and temporary professional positions. But because the needs and intermediate costs are different, the marketplace for "permanent" assignments should operate differently than the market for temporary assignments.

Permanent Managerial Jobs

"Permanent" jobs (that is, over one year in length) in our model would include all the jobs that provide the structure to the organization. In our model, these include the backbone line managers and the people who report to them, the support structure managers and the people who report to them, and the formal network owners. These "permanent" jobs are the people responsible for exercising authority and for managing costs and revenues. All of these "permanent" jobs can be defined by what the military calls a "table of organization" that lays out structural reporting relationships and jobs. Such a defined table of organization is necessary because it creates the consistent definition of roles and responsibilities and boundaries, and it provides the parallel organization needed to make the backbone line structure work. It also provides the anchor points to assign economic accountability. In our model, these are the roles that provide "homes" for their own talent but are also authorized to pull from the talent marketplace people from "home bases" they do not control. Typical "permanent" assignments could last from a year to several years depending on the role and the circumstances.

Temporary Professional Assignments

In our model, all people not in a permanent job, as described above, would be organized into talent pools available for temporary assignment. Overseeing each talent pool would be a manager with a permanent job reporting to an appropriate member of the line or support hierarchy or a network owner.[4] These managers would provide a home base for each person in the talent pool. They would be responsible for the care and feeding of everyone in the pool and would, in particular, be responsible for overseeing the performance reviews and annual evaluations of each person. They would also be responsible for managing the talent marketplace day to day by assisting people seeking talent to find the skills and knowledge they need and helping people seeking work to find the right work given their individual talents and developments. "Talent pool owners" would ordinarily have at least one HR professional to help them undertake their staffing work.

Talent Markets in Action

How might talent market transactions work? First of all, any marketplace must define what is being traded, how it is priced, and the operating protocols and standards. To facilitate exchanges, a formal talent marketplace also needs "market makers": usually central HR staff in cases of managers being staffed to "permanent" jobs or HR staff assigned to help a formal network executive in the case of specialized professional talent being staffed to temporary jobs.

Market makers must be allowed to show the hiring manager any confidential information (such as performance reviews) related to an assignment. This requirement protects the interests of both the job seeker and would-be employer, facilitates "contracting" for assignments

FIGURE 7-1

Key Elements of a Talent Marketplace (Disguised example of a global company)

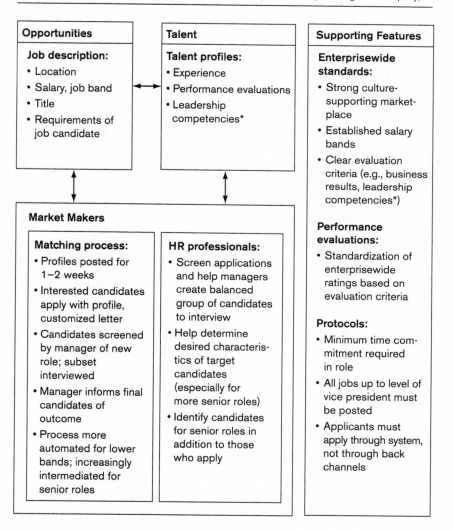

Opportunities	Talent	Supporting Features
Job description: • Location • Salary, job band • Title • Requirements of job candidate	**Talent profiles:** • Experience • Performance evaluations • Leadership competencies*	**Enterprisewide standards:** • Strong culture-supporting marketplace • Established salary bands • Clear evaluation criteria (e.g., business results, leadership competencies*)

Market Makers

Matching process:	HR professionals:
• Profiles posted for 1–2 weeks • Interested candidates apply with profile, customized letter • Candidates screened by manager of new role; subset interviewed • Manager informs final candidates of outcome • Process more automated for lower bands; increasingly intermediated for senior roles	• Screen applications and help managers create balanced group of candidates to interview • Help determine desired characteristics of target candidates (especially for more senior roles) • Identify candidates for senior roles in addition to those who apply

Performance evaluations:
• Standardization of enterprisewide ratings based on evaluation criteria

Protocols:
• Minimum time commitment required in role
• All jobs up to level of vice president must be posted
• Applicants must apply through system, not through back channels

* For example, entrepreneurial orientation, people development skills.

by the parties involved, and ensures that the terms of the "contracts" are honored after the fact.

Figure 7-1 describes the key elements of a talent marketplace.

Let's again return to the Global Bank to demonstrate how talent marketplaces could work, first for a temporary assignment, and then for a "permanent" assignment.

In Chapter 3, we described how the "backbone frontline manager" for the New Jersey/Long Island branch organization wanted to put together a marketing campaign and product bundle for the personal banking needs of the small business owners in her territory. For this campaign, she assigned one of her direct reports, in this case the Small Business executive, to direct the project and to assemble a team for the one-off project. The process began with the Small Business executive reaching out to the Branch Bank Marketing formal network leader for advice on how to structure the project and to get the names of one or two candidates to lead the project. Simultaneously, the Small Business executive posted the assignment on an internal Web site describing the nature of the assignment, the roles available, the job grade requirements, the description of the assignment, the geographic location of the work, travel requirements, and so on, and the client for the work (that is, the New Jersey/Long Island frontline manager).

In this case, there were three roles:

- A half-time senior marketing professional (that is, vice president)

- A junior role (that is, assistant vice president)

- An entry-level role

The assignment was to last three months with a follow-up project possible if the campaign was approved.

All employees in the enterprise with sufficient uncommitted time to fill the roles were eligible to apply for the roles and could apply online. The Small Business executive could also search an electronic database for candidates who had not applied. The Small Business executive had been given a budget for the project, and he was examining only those staffing possibilities whose job grades implied per diems that could be accommodated by that budget.

The Small Business executive started by searching for the part-time senior marketing executive needed to lead the project by interviewing the two candidates suggested by the Branch Bank Marketing executive. But one of the candidates had no time, and the other was not interested. Fortunately, a very qualified vice president from the Small Business Marketing talent pool applied for the role, and she had a junior marketing professional whom she wanted to bring along with her and who proved to be the best candidate. After taking an entry-level person from Branch Bank Marketing, the project staffing was complete.

In other words, even though it is internal, a talent marketplace is a real market, and as such, it has buyers and sellers, competition, and pricing.

Once the temporary project is completed, each individual's performance on the project is evaluated. For example, the Small Business executive would evaluate the senior marketing leader. The senior marketing leader would evaluate the other two members of the project team, and then, if no follow-on project were needed, the team would be disbanded and reassigned.

Let's compare how a "permanent" market transaction would differ from a temporary transaction. In this case, the head of the East Coast Bank was looking to replace the New Jersey/Long Island manager because he had just asked her to take over the role of Manhattan manager. Given the relative seniority of this role, the position attracted dozens of applicants, not just from the former manager's direct reports but also from people in similar positions nationwide. In addition, some "wild cards" from managers in Credit Card, Mortgages, and Premier also applied. In this case, a central HR professional served as a market maker to help the East Coast executive sort through the 60-odd candidates for the position and to field calls from their mentors seeking to put in a good word for them.

One difference from temporary assignments, where the price of talent is reflected in a per diem, the "price" paid for a "permanent" assignment would be salary based. Another difference is that "permanent" assignments would require much larger intermediation costs.

In this case, the HR professional would spend far more time screening candidates down to a "short list," and the process would take more time reflecting the high stakes for both parties in finding a good match. In addition to people who applied for the job, the HR market maker would also search an internal, firmwide database on potential candidates, checking it against the criteria described by the senior manager.

Let's assume that two attractive candidates express an interest in the job and that the market maker, while searching the database, identifies three more qualified and available candidates. For the candidates who are expressing interest, the market maker would interview them, answer their questions, assess their real interest, and address their concerns. For candidates found on the database, the market maker would call whichever parties "owned" the candidates to verify that the candidates are, in fact, available for reassignment. If so, the market maker would contact the potential candidates to determine their interest.

Let's further assume that both of the attractive candidates who respond to the job posting and one of those found on the database express real interest. The market maker would then show the senior manager the three candidate profiles and ask which ones the senior manager would like to interview. Often for important roles, many of the other direct reports to the senior manager would also interview candidates. Discussions would begin, leading, hopefully, to a negotiated assignment contract with one of the candidates. Once an offer is accepted, the market maker would document the resulting contract. The winning candidate would then receive a final evaluation on his or her prior contract, tie up loose ends, and begin his or her new "permanent" assignment. This matching process is more automated for lower job bands and more intermediated for senior roles (Figure 7-2).

Three important design features further support talent marketplace approaches to assigning candidates to jobs. First, performance evaluations, which are conducted across the company, must have several standardized components that permit comparisons among candidates. Second, to help keep the transaction costs reasonable, jobs

FIGURE 7-2

Fitting the Process to the Role (Example based on fictitious Global Bank)

Type of Talent Market	Open	Partly Intermediated	Fully Intermediated
Job Level	**Below Vice President**	**Vice President**	**Senior Vice President and Higher**
Job Band	• Band X	• Band Y	• Band Z
Minimum Time in Role	• 1–2 years	• 2–3 years	• 3+ years
Job Postings	• All jobs posted on Web site enterprisewide for 1–2 weeks	• All jobs posted on Web site enterprisewide for 1–2 years	• Jobs, roles identified in review meetings
Identification, Application of Candidates	• Unsolicited applications submitted online through automated system	• Unsolicited applications submitted online through automated system; (HR) helps identify additional candidates and invites them to apply	• Candidates identified by senior executives in review meetings–based on interests, talent, needs of company
HR Role	• Screens applications; ensures interviewing manager has balanced group of candidates to interview; facilitates process	• Screens applications; helps identify additional candidates; facilitates process	• Works with senior executives to identify character-istics of applicants (e.g., specific leadership competencies*) and candidates who are good fit for role; facilitates process

* For example, entrepreneurial orientation, people development skills.

should have defined minimum time commitments (no less than a month or so for project work, or no less than one year for "permanent" jobs). Finally, enterprisewide standards (such as salary bands and per diems) are defined for all jobs, from entry through senior leadership, thus facilitating comparisons across the company.

Not all jobs will be able to be staffed from the talent marketplace. If there are no sufficiently qualified internal candidates for a particular role, then it may be necessary to go outside the company to find the right person.

Breaking with Tradition

The differences between formal talent marketplaces and more traditional approaches to talent management are considerable (Figure 7-3). The existence of a formal talent marketplace makes employees (rather than line managers or HR professionals) responsible for managing the greater part of their careers. Second, it explodes the idea that senior managers "own" talent. In a talent marketplace, employees are "restricted free agents" (the restrictions define, for example, pay grades and terms of service). They are expected to find the best opportunities for themselves, and the market opens up a non-price-based competition across a range of candidates and job alternatives.

A talent marketplace for permanent assignments formalizes the terms of employment—that is, the role, its duration, the place of work, travel, job options available upon successful completion, and so forth. It does so by making the terms more durable than a mere handshake would make them and by making the protocols around the contract more explicit.

Standardized Roles

To make the market work, both parties must understand what they are trading. The skills and performance of employees should therefore be rated over time through standardized performance evaluations and job

FIGURE 7-3

Formalizing the Talent Marketplace

Elements of Talent-Assignment System	From	To
Relationship between Employer and Job Seeker	• Employee is "owned"; loyalty is expected.	• Employee manages and directs career; loyalty is earned.
Market Definition	• Silo based (i.e., within 1 organizational structure).	• Enterprisewide market.
Competition	• Job seekers have limited choices; job owners have limited number of candidates to consider for roles.	• Open competition among wide range of candidates for wide range of alternative jobs.
Terms of Employment	• Largely implicit contract between employer and employee, with limited definition of terms of employment and limited documentation of agreement.	• Explicit definition of terms of employment (i.e., role, duration, place of work, trigger points for negotiation); third-party enforcement of terms.
Protocols	• Implicit (or dependent upon negotiation).	• Explicit definition of protocols for contracting process, terms of contract, and process of ending assignment.
Exchange Mechanism	• None other than individual trust.	• HR broker to protect confidences and interests of both employer and employee.
Pricing	• One-time negotiation.	• Standard compensation per protocols; transfer of assigned person per standard terms.

brackets. Consistent definitions of roles and qualifications are also an essential requirement for making a talent marketplace work. Such definitions, long used by the U.S. military and other such organizations, make it possible to form units rapidly, consisting of individuals drawn from various parts of the world with exactly the right mix of skills and job grades (Figure 7-4). Unlike military personnel, of course, employees in a talent marketplace can reject assignments. What is common to both military and nonmilitary organizations, though, is the fact that a central database is used to provide for the categorization of each employee's qualifications, skills, and performance ratings, all of which can be divulged only if parties begin serious negotiations.

Pricing

As in any marketplace, demand ebbs and flows in a talent marketplace. The task of putting a price on talent, however, is quite different from what it is in normal markets. Talent is a resource that has alternative uses, and unlike knowledge, it must be allocated, since a talented person's time is finite, while knowledge can be shared by everyone simultaneously.

A marketplace usually employs prices to determine where resources are best allocated. The objective of a business, however, is to maximize profits per worker rather than wages per worker. It therefore makes no sense for a company to let talented employees sell their services to the highest bidder. In fact, a talent market shouldn't provide for explicit internal price competition. Rather, pay must be established through enterprisewide pay-for-performance standards, such as job or salary bands set by a central HR function. This approach bases internal competition for talent on the nature of assignments, the opportunities they provide for growth, their duration, and the personal contacts they offer, not on the money involved. This market approach also gives senior managers who have a reputation as mentors and as good people to work with an advantage in attracting talent.

FIGURE 7-4

Deployment Facilitated by Consistency (Example based on U.S. Army practices)

Standardized Categories:

Branch identifier:
- Arm or service to which soldier is assigned
- 38 branch areas defined

Functional area:
- Grouping of soldiers possessing interrelated skills that typically require significant education, training, and experience

Additional skill identifier:
- Identifies specific skills required to perform duties of a particular position
- Often used to ensure specific skills are represented in team

Projected career field:
- Indicator of future career progression
- Selected through consultation with personnel manager and senior officer within branch

For a Major in the Infantry

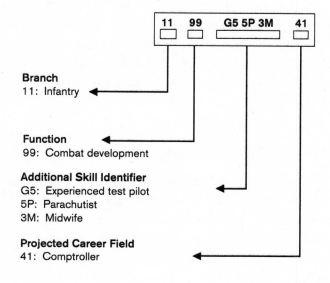

Branch
11: Infantry

Function
99: Combat development

Additional Skill Identifier
G5: Experienced test pilot
5P: Parachutist
3M: Midwife

Projected Career Field
41: Comptroller

Source: U.S. Military Academy.

We believe pricing talent for temporary assignments should borrow from the practices of professional services firms—per diems set at the estimated opportunity cost of deploying the talent elsewhere. If, for example, you pay someone $500 a day, that person's per diem could be $2,000 a day, with the difference covering days unemployed, the cost of supporting and training the professional, overhead, and margin to reflect the value of the work (that is, the value of the person's intangible assets). Executives who have work that they believe justifies paying high per diems can "buy" the talent needed to undertake it; executives who do not have such work have to find candidates they can afford (including taking risks on younger, unproven talent).

The way per diems are established needs to be governed by standards that are established enterprisewide, particularly to ensure there is no "price gouging" when critical skills are in temporary short supply. The advantage of an opportunity-based way of pricing talent is to recognize its value (or the opportunity to profit from deploying it) more than the wages paid to employees. If you take this approach, which works best for professional support services, the difference between an employee's wages and the per diem is credited to whoever is managing the talent pool from which the candidate is assigned. In turn, this provides real additional incentives for the owner of the talent pool to find and develop talent. But if the owner sets prices too high, the talent winds up going unutilized.

Benefits and Challenges

Self-directed, talented people benefit considerably from talent marketplaces. The more talented they are, the greater the demand for their services and the better their opportunities will be. Highly talented people are less likely to be blocked by less-talented bosses taking credit for their work. Better opportunities also ensure that job experiences challenge these employees, who in the process develop more quickly. Broadening their exposure within the organization also helps them to develop a more extensive network of contacts to share reputations and information. Such self-directed and talented people are the very ones an enterprise is most at risk of losing, since they are the most likely to be actively testing external talent markets to find more attractive opportunities. People not in demand in the talent marketplace also understand the need to develop more marketable skills or to risk being asked to leave.

At the same time, senior people who are pursuing important opportunities will have a greater pool of talent to draw upon, with a more diverse range of skills to tap. People who acquire reputations for developing talent will have a greater likelihood of attracting more and better job applicants, while "people eaters" will have trouble. But the real beneficiary is the company, which wins by getting far better matches between its job opportunities and its most talented people and by gaining far greater transparency into shortages and excess supplies of talent.

Of course, talent marketplaces also present challenges. In companies with well-established organizational silos, the cultural resistance to putting one in place will be enormous. Silos need to be willing to release talent. Unless companies move to a one-company governance and one-company culture as described earlier, it is difficult to envision that an enterprisewide talent marketplace would even be possible.

Most companies will need to form several submarketplaces for different skill sets (one for project managers, one for industrial engineers, and so on) and with different time horizons for assignments that then aggregate to form a total, enterprisewide talent marketplace. This is the same way that any very large marketplace works: The global capital marketplace, for example, is composed of a variety of other markets that make it up, such as the foreign exchange market, the corporate bond market, the equities market, and so on.

We do not want to minimize the difficulty of moving to a talent marketplace approach to allocating talent, since it requires not just creating the right infrastructure of brokers, standardized performance review, job definitions, per diems, compensation bands, and so on, but also reworking the entire performance measurement system, as will be described in a later chapter. Indeed, of all the ideas contained in this book, creating talent marketplaces is one of the most difficult ideas to put into practice. Yet for those large, growing, complex companies that do institute a talent marketplace, the biggest payoff of all will be when they can efficiently and effectively allocate talent to the best opportunities for that talent enterprisewide. And, in doing so, they will simultaneously be producing the conditions to enable talented people to grow and develop their skills, thus simultaneously increasing the entire company's stock of talent.

The challenges and risks of putting a talent marketplace in operation are considerable. It is a perfect example of why we believe, as we will describe in the last chapter, companies should use a portfolio-of-initiatives staged gate investing approach to designing and installing major organizational design changes.

8

KNOWLEDGE
MARKETPLACES

COMPANIES IN TODAY'S economy, just like people, find that
their primary source of competitive advantage increasingly
lies in the proprietary knowledge they possess. Companies
and individuals may have equal talent and access to public
knowledge, but the special value that comes with unique understanding provides a real edge. The bond trader who is the
first to understand an opportunity to arbitrage securities
across two different markets can earn extraordinary returns—
until other traders figure out the secret. A company thoroughly familiar with how to compete in a particular geographic market—China, say—has huge advantages over
competitors lacking that familiarity.

Simply put, there is great value in sharing, across a whole
company, proprietary insights into customers, competitors,
products, production techniques, emerging research, and
the like. In practice, of course, companies find it far more
difficult than do individuals to take advantage of all this
knowledge. An individual's knowledge is self-contained, always available. But in companies—including small ones—it
can be hard to exploit the valuable knowledge that resides in
the heads of even a few hundred employees, particularly if

KNOWLEDGE VERSUS INFORMATION

Thinking about how to mobilize knowledge begins with drawing a distinction between information and knowledge. Too often, these terms are used interchangeably when actually they refer to two different concepts. If information is the raw material—the input—used to make decisions, knowledge is what provides the context for how people think. As people approach a traffic light that has turned red, they take in that *information* and decide to stop. They do so because they understand what red, green, and yellow mean.

Companies gain a competitive advantage from information by providing the right information to the right managers at the right time. If information isnt ti mely, it is often useless. For most of the past several decades, corporate investments in IT provided employees with information useful to their jobs. These investments paid off, for the most part. Not so for knowledge management investments.

In a large company, a competitive advantage from knowledge is gained through the productive internal exchange of insights, knowledge that helps employees think differently as they make decisions and

they are scattered in different locations. In a large, diverse company, the task expands to cover thousands of highly educated professionals and managers spread across a variety of specialties, locations, and countries. But difficult as it may be to profit from this diffused knowledge, the power of mobilizing this knowledge on a large scale yields benefits that can dwarf what individuals or small teams, however brilliant or effective, can accomplish by themselves.

Many companies have long been reasonably effective at distributing knowledge, using technology no more advanced than the telephone, the mail, and the fax machine (even if they weren't terribly efficient at doing so). In the past decade, as advances in communications, software, and computers opened entirely new possibilities for sharing take actions. This is a far higher bar than the one for exchanging information. Why? Because people must be persuaded by the quality of the thought, the facts, and the logic presented that the knowledge they are being asked to acquire is superior to what they already know. Beyond personal experience, people acquire knowledge through formal training, dialogue with others, or reading, viewing, and listening to codified knowledge content.

Knowledge by nature has a much longer shelf life than information does. Knowledge about a competitor's product development pipeline, for example, can be valuable to a company for years. But even the most distinctive and proprietary knowledge, such as that held by a company's best professionals, undergoes an eventual decay curve that terminates at the point where it becomes common knowledge. A professional possessing secret information on a key business issue may initially have no incentive to dilute its value by sharing it. But as others learn what once was secret, there eventually comes a point in the half-life of distinctive knowledge when it has the greatest value to a company if its insights become easily and broadly available across the organization.

knowledge rapidly and efficiently, many leading companies, academics, and management consultants came to believe that the future belonged to large companies that could manage knowledge. The promise of bringing all of a company's proprietary knowledge to bear on every problem or issue it faced led executives to invest billions of dollars in what came to be called "knowledge management."

Of course there has been progress. But if the goal was to use a company's best proprietary knowledge to solve every problem it faced, knowledge management, as generally applied, has barely begun to fill the bill. Moreover, the unmanaged outcome of letting everyone solve the problem individually has been the unproductive complexity described in Chapter 1. In response, most companies have tried, with mixed

FIGURE 8-1

Three Common Approaches to Codified Knowledge Exchange

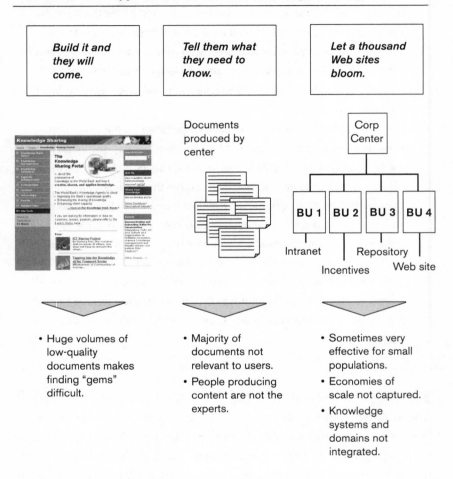

success, one of three technology-based approaches to managing knowledge to improve on self-directed knowledge exchange (Figure 8-1). Indeed, many companies have tried all three:

1. **Build It and They Will Come.** To let employees unlock knowledge, some companies relied exclusively on big investments in document management systems, shared servers, and other technology solu-

tions. Such investments are necessary but not sufficient. The sheer volume of documents at large companies today is overwhelming. Many of these documents are out of date, poorly written, or otherwise difficult to parse. We know of one large financial services firm that had over a million documents on shared hard drives and internal Web sites—in just one of their four, large organizational silos! Most of the documents were redundant, were written years ago, and had titles that revealed little of what was inside. Many of the best documents were on personal computers and not shared at all. In such situations, even a diligent search by a determined knowledge seeker is likely to produce few valuable, easy-to-access insights.

2. **Tell Them What They Need to Know.** Some companies, particularly those with large corporate staffs, have tried to push knowledge to users, often via internal Web sites. Such efforts can be worthwhile, as, for example, when the idea is to distribute top-down messages such as information about best-practice approaches or perhaps new product features. Still, the limitations of any central planning approach apply. Do the people writing the documents know what knowledge seekers really want to know, or are they just guessing? Are the real experts on the topics actually those who are producing the content? Do most corporate staffs even know who the real experts are? The typical result: Most of the knowledge pushed out in this way is simply not very valuable to most frontline employees—particularly to those who possess the most skills and existing knowledge.

3. **Let a Thousand Web Sites Bloom.** A third approach has been somewhat more successful, particularly for those companies allowing decentralized technology spending. It is to let various organizational units or informal networks solve their knowledge problems by themselves. What large company doesn't have pockets of a few hundred people who are part of an informal network with a common interest (such as employees working in a particular product group, or others working on a common design problem, or sales professionals

serving the same industry)? In these informal networks those who create knowledge and those who seek it usually know each other and exchange ideas easily. The informal networks in turn use whatever technology solution they favor to develop small, specialized approaches to managing knowledge. Authors earn recognition from peers, motivating them to produce and share more content. Usually some senior person in the group cares enough about the knowledge exchange to invest in the supporting technology and administrative staff needed to build an effective, high-quality, internal Web site or portal that makes it easy for knowledge seekers to find what they're looking for.

This decentralized approach works because it facilitates exchange among small groups of workers with common interests. Still, results are often mixed. For every example of a small organization unit with terrific success in sharing specialized knowledge among a small group, there are usually a large number of outright, often expensive, failures.

The obvious flaw is that the proliferation of approaches and technological tools, with few common protocols or standards, typically remains useful only to small groups of workers and around very specialized knowledge topics. For most companies, this approach will provide just a fraction of the potential benefit of exchanging knowledge on a companywide scale.

A Knowledge Market

The truth is that the real value comes less from managing knowledge and more—a lot more—from creating and exchanging it. And the key to achieving this goal is understanding that a company's really valuable knowledge resides largely in the heads of its most-talented employees. Moreover, they will be unlikely to exchange their knowledge without a fair return for the time and energy they expend in putting it into a form in which it can be exchanged. Then, it must also be worth the price in terms of the time and energy of the person seeking the knowledge.

The Knowledge Markets Approach

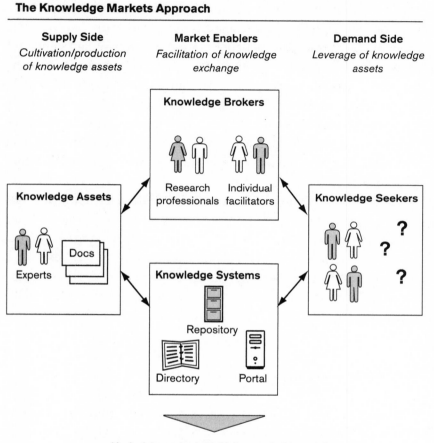

Supply Side	Market Enablers	Demand Side
Cultivation/production of knowledge assets	*Facilitation of knowledge exchange*	*Leverage of knowledge assets*

Underlying principle: Make markets work by harnessing the self-interest of participants.

In short, effectively exchanging knowledge on a companywide basis is much less a technological problem than an organizational one. That is, it is a matter of encouraging people who do not know each other to work together for their mutual self-interest. There is, of course, a well-known, well-tested solution to making it possible to exchange items of value among parties who don't know each other. We call it a "market."

We believe companies can design and put in place organizational capabilities we call "knowledge marketplaces" (Figure 8-2). The trick is to take the market inside the company. Just like any market, a knowledge market requires demand (knowledge seekers), something to trade (knowledge), suppliers (knowledge creators), market mechanisms, and infrastructure to facilitate exchange of value and to maintain standards. Large public markets for knowledge have long existed, of course, through books and articles and through public services such as libraries. More recently, Wikipedia, MySpace, and the blogosphere as a whole have joined such providers as Amazon.com, Yahoo!, and Google as external markets for public knowledge. But there are no equivalent internal markets for the valuable proprietary knowledge lodged within a company's own frontline employees.

So how does a company design and build effective internal markets when the product is something as intangible as the valuable knowledge gained from experience and personal thinking? Working markets need, among other things, valuable objects for trading, prices, exchange mechanisms, and competition among suppliers. Often, there are also standards, protocols and regulations, and market facilitators to make markets work better.

Valuable Objects to Trade

Markets will form only around items valuable enough to justify the time and effort of buyers and sellers. "Common knowledge," by definition, hardly needs trading. The opportunity lies in trading proprietary and distinctive knowledge (Figure 8-3).

"Distinctive knowledge" represents superior insights that, at the moment they are codified, are unique to the author. This is the knowledge that gives the author, and the company, competitive advantage. This is the knowledge that is most valuable to experts in a field.

"Proprietary knowledge," in contrast, represents insights that are common among "insiders" and deep experts in a particular industry or profession but are not yet common knowledge to the public at large.

FIGURE 8-3

Differences between Distinctive, Proprietary, and Common Knowledge

Types of Knowledge	Definition	Examples

Distinctive	• Knowledge that . . .
	   – Only the firm can access, through a combination of proprietary resources and experiences (previous work)
	   – Sets the firm apart from competition when directly (content) or indirectly (know-hows) delivered to a client
		• Insights on decision-making mechanisms at a given client
		 • Impact of a legal change on a given industry (before competitors come up with a point of view)
		 • Superior knowledge of how to manage complex production processes

Proprietary	• Knowledge that . . .
	   – Only the firm can access through a combination of proprietary resources and experiences
	   – Is necessary to perform everyday work and is perceived as a prerequisite by clients
		• Project management guide
		 • Basic law interpretation (before it comes to market)
		 • Database of key client sales and marketing leads

Common	• Knowledge that . . .
	   – Is directly taken from a public source
	   – Competitor can buy or replicate easily
		• Factiva
		 • Google
		 • Wikipedia

Distinctive knowledge, as it is shared, becomes proprietary. Proprietary knowledge is valuable, since it is needed to remain competitive, but it gives little advantage. This is the knowledge that is most valuable to people acquiring knowledge in an unfamiliar knowledge domain. Proprietary knowledge helps them get "up to speed," but it is not particularly valuable to experts already practicing in the field. Proprietary knowledge, as it gets more widely shared, eventually becomes available externally and becomes common knowledge (that is, it is on Wikipedia).

From a buyer's perspective, the knowledge to be acquired from the market must be more insightful and relevant—as well as easier to find, gain access to, and assimilate—than alternative sources. Usually, knowledge available through most internal knowledge management systems fails this test.

The trick is in motivating authors to produce content that meets this standard. Almost all content produced by most companies, whether short internal memos or documents packed with charts, are intended to be "oral documents"—that is, the written content needs to be backed up with some oral discussion if it is to be comprehensible to the unfamiliar reader. These oral documents often lack critical context—for example, a textual explanation of chart data—needed to help the knowledge seeker understand the author's thinking, which can be obtained only by engaging in a dialogue with the author. If companies want to provide knowledge to knowledge seekers who have no opportunity to talk with the expert, they must provide more relevant, more accessible knowledge than is available in these "oral documents."

One answer is a new, internal equivalent of a signed article, which is written out of the desire for recognition (and written well out of the fear of embarrassment for shoddy work), in which an author with distinctive knowledge is motivated to produce a high-quality document that is easily accessible to any user. Once distinctive knowledge is in this form, it can be traded in the market. This "knowledge object" allows a "buyer" of knowledge to understand an author's thinking without the parties having to talk to each other. The bad news for most companies is that most documents created today in large companies generally fail to meet this standard.

A related approach to codifying distinctive knowledge in a form that is valuable enough to "trade" is to develop "internal blogs." Like blogs on the Internet, internal blogs are electronic journals written by individual authors, continually produced as the author reflects on changing circumstances. Blogs have an advantage over other types of communication systems in that they take into account the passage of time—unlike a knowledge object, which reflects the knowledge of an author at a particular time. Blogs also have the advantage of allowing authors to wander over a whole range of topics. As with Internet-based blogs, however, the problem with internal blogs is that few of them are worth reading.

Blogs that are worth reading require authors with real writing talent, wide-ranging minds, and the persistence and drive to write regularly. Most of a company's professionals and managers lack the skill and/or the energy to produce blogs worth reading regularly. Thus, internal blogs work best when a company itself uses them to display the thinking of its true knowledge "stars" by giving them a featured forum in its internal Web sites and blogs.

In addition to motivating authors to produce knowledge objects and write internal blogs that codify their distinctive insights, another form of codifying knowledge has recently emerged: an internal version of the Internet-based Wikipedia, the online encyclopedia maintained by its users.

Companies have begun using this idea internally by creating equivalents for proprietary company knowledge. Using this approach, entries are constantly made under any topic of interest. Anyone is free to add a new entry or update an existing entry with better or more accurate information and knowledge, provided that the person "signs" his or her entries and abides by any other company policies for disseminating information. For example, a companypedia could have entries on products, customer segments, geographies, and functions. Unlike knowledge objects, which represent distinctive insights that the author wants credited to himself or herself, the motivation driving many users who update companypedias is an unselfish desire to contribute accurate, "common" knowledge to colleagues.

These internal companypedias work best if there are thousands of contributors who can provide content and some quality control of that

DESCRIPTION OF WIKIPEDIA

The Wikipedia is an online encyclopedia, accessed by users who are also—ideally—the authors of its content. A type of Web site software called a "wiki" allows its users to publish articles they wish to contribute to their fellow online wiki community. In addition, any wiki users may add to and/or edit any available wiki articles and other wiki resources on an ongoing basis. The result is that large numbers of contributions occur with minimal research, writing, and production costs to the aggregating site owner. Over time, as it is exposed to more and more critical and knowledgeable readers, the site content should become more accurate and more comprehensive. Wikipedia.org, founded in 2001, has popularized the concept and demonstrated the potential to create a large-scale reference tool from this type of user-provided content. The site today contains over 5 million articles and ranks among the 20 most-viewed sites on the Web.

Articles or documents available on a wiki Web site are almost always subject to further editing and almost never declared "complete" or "finished." They are usually allowed to be revised at will by anyone who wishes to do so. No particular user or group owns a copyright or exercises editorial control; decisions on content instead result from evolving user consensus. On the Wikipedia.org Web site, most past edits remain viewable after the fact (on separate "edit history" pages) so that users can evaluate the accuracy and relevance of individual contributions.

content. The risk is that some of the articles and their corrections will be provided by people who don't have the best knowledge or that an insufficient mass of users will be attracted either to provide the range of content needed or to control the companypedia for inaccurate content. Given the regulatory, legal, and business risks today of providing "bad" knowledge, we suspect companies will want to build such companype-

Wiki sites can be tailored with special features that make work easier for professionals. Regular users of the Wikipedia.org Web site, for example, often maintain a "watchlist" on topics of interest to them so that they can easily keep tabs on changes and updates. This kind of alert system could have applications in the corporate context as well, since employees in thinking-intensive fields will want to receive regular updates on matters of relevance in their fields.

Because vandalism and disagreement about content are common problems, the administrator of a collaborative online wiki encyclopedia must develop policies to determine which types of information qualify for inclusion. Wikipedia.org, for example, forbids the use of original research and requires that articles be written from a "neutral point of view." Of course, the policies governing an individual company's wiki Web site will be established by that company in line with its needs and circumstances.

Although Wikipedia.org has received criticism for uneven or unbalanced coverage (resulting from the work of a relatively small and unbalanced group of contributing authors), companies creating private wiki Web sites can protect against imbalance by creating incentives (enhanced reputation, for instance) for contributions to be made from across all topic areas. A well-run "companypedia" can be an effective way to disseminate formerly siloed knowledge throughout a large and complex organization.

dias, at least at first, in carefully selected knowledge arenas, using paid staff workers for quality control, under the oversight of a formal network leader who is a deep expert in the relevant knowledge arena. While such companypedias are promising (as this book is being completed in late 2006), the development of such internal companypedias is still very much on the drawing board.

Pricing Knowledge

Defining the item being traded (for example, knowledge objects or internal blogs) creates the conditions for pricing the exchange. Authors, who are the suppliers of distinctive knowledge to the market, need to receive something that justifies their "costs," or effort, in return for creating the knowledge object. In internal knowledge markets, the price that authors receive is usually the enhancement of their own personal, internal reputation. Even for internal companypedias, the signing of entries creates incentives for the contributor to make the entry accurate and of high quality. Providing knowledge that catches the eye of peers and superiors helps the author build a personal reputation and can provide plenty of incentive to codify knowledge. Buyers—those who seek knowledge—will have the motivation to go to the market, especially if they believe that they will find valuable knowledge at a price, in time and effort, that is lower than, say, making numerous phone calls to locate an expert.

Ensuring that authors are paid appropriate "prices" for their knowledge is often the hardest part of this equation. One of the characteristics that makes internal knowledge valuable is that having that knowledge can provide an employee with a performance advantage over his or her peers. But once that knowledge is codified, others can assimilate it, thereby negating the author's advantage. The trick, therefore, is to provide incentives so that individuals who contribute their distinctive, valuable knowledge receive more internal recognition and enjoy greater success than they would have had they kept their knowledge to themselves. So the company must create a culture in which smart people are expected to contribute valuable codified knowledge. Part of this culture is a reward structure, in terms of recognition, pay, and advancement, in which distinctive performers who also contribute knowledge earn more than people who perform equally well but do not make any knowledge contribution.

Ensuring that knowledge contributors are rewarded requires that the company protect individual intellectual property rights. All of the

incentives for contributing knowledge depend on providing appropriate reputational credit to the person contributing the knowledge. Those
who actually develop the knowledge—not those they report to or those
who "borrow" the knowledge to make presentations—must be identified and credited as the authors. This is important not only for equity's
sake but also to provide incentives for the best thinkers, whatever their
seniority or their position, to produce more high-value content in the
future. There is nothing more demotivating to a young person seeking
recognition than for a senior person to take credit for his or her thinking.

Who should pay the authors? Since the company is the ultimate
beneficiary of the effort to form and maintain a knowledge marketplace, it should be responsible for rewarding authors in order to ensure
that the authors receive the recognition, pay, and advancement they deserve for contributing valuable knowledge to the firm.

Exchange Mechanism

To ensure that their authors are paid requires creating an exchange
mechanism, one that permits authors and knowledge seekers to come
to the market out of mutual self-interest. Meeting this goal requires the
investment in a technological infrastructure, and in the staff to maintain it, in order to make the exchange possible.

It is important *not* to charge transfer prices from users to recapture
this investment (although some companies, particularly silos within
companies, have tried). Knowledge is by its nature a "public good." It
costs almost no more to make it available in codified, electronic form
to everyone in the firm than it does to make it available to a single person. Moreover, knowledge has a peculiar characteristic: Until it is consumed, it's impossible to assess in advance how valuable it will be to
the knowledge seeker. Therefore, most buyers are unwilling to buy it
sight unseen. After the seeker has acquired the knowledge, however,
there is no incentive to pay for it. Furthermore, the Internet has accustomed most of us to free electronic knowledge. The best solution, then,

is simply in creating a shared utility to pay for the infrastructure. It will ensure that the knowledge marketplace works, and the costs will be absorbed as corporate overhead. The beneficiaries of a knowledge marketplace are the entire company, not just individuals. But to provide accountability to the manager of the shared utility and to the formal network owners of individual knowledge domains, performance metrics should be created (documents created, volume of downloads, satisfaction surveys, and so on), and decisions must be made about how much the company can afford to invest in such public goods.

Inside companies, dialogue is the preferred method for exchanging valuable proprietary knowledge. If knowledge seekers find the right, willing expert, they can quickly pinpoint and acquire the knowledge they need. Whether meeting with them one-on-one or in a group, the knowledge provider usually has a sense that payment will come in the form of appropriate recognition from peers and superiors. But often the problem is that knowledge seekers can't find the right person to talk to because of the problem of large numbers described in Chapter 2.

One very important enhancement to a knowledge marketplace capability (that some companies have begun to develop) is an "expertise system."[1] An expertise system lets searchers enter key words, or browse a Web site, to find potential experts who can help them. In building these systems, one shouldn't rely solely on self-described expertise. Instead, searchers should qualify their findings with other data that indicate expertise, such as the experts' work experiences with the company (particularly their work on knowledge-intensive projects) and other documents the experts have produced (such as entries they have made to the companypedia).

Most of the sources needed, such as HR and intellectual property databases, already exist. Then, using search algorithms, the system can rank the people who are likely to have expertise. A person identified in this process can be linked to a personal profile that would indicate his or her position, title, work experience, documents produced, and so on, as well as contact information. Such profiles, of course, need to be created for every person in a thinking-intensive company, since the profiles are also used to provide the personal profile information needed by managers wanting to fill open jobs and job seekers wanting to learn about a person with whom they may want to work. Needless to say, because these profiles also include private or confidential information, such as performance ratings or confidential work assignments, some of the personal information they contain must be protected from public access; therefore, some parts of the profile would be open to other people in the company, and some parts would not.

Dialogue will always be an essential way of exchanging knowledge—indeed, it is the only way to exchange "tacit knowledge"—that which hasn't been codified. But a big problem with the use of dialogue alone is that it takes time, particularly on the part of the person with the knowledge. If topics generate great interest, experts in a large company simply don't have the time to both do their jobs and talk to interested parties on a one-on-one basis. Even the most willing experts may not be available to talk at all times with everyone who wants to do so. By producing a knowledge object available to everyone, however, an expert is freed from that time burden—but gets the reputational benefits nonetheless. And by focusing on the topic, the author can produce higher-quality, more rigorous knowledge than a user would receive in a normal dialogue. If a discussion is still needed, a knowledge object can at least provide a basic grounding before higher-level discussions take place.

Competition

The promise of the knowledge marketplace lies in its potential to increase vastly the reach of proprietary and distinctive knowledge for the benefit of the entire company rather than just a few individuals. However, since "knowledge buyers" can get what they need from several sources, a knowledge marketplace will work only if it can deliver a satisfying product. This requirement in turn means that authors must be kept motivated to produce high-quality content. In practice, that stimulus will take the form of competition among the authors for recognition.

All markets, including knowledge markets, thrive on competition. As with any kind of intellectual property, knowledge objects compete for attention at the levels of quality and popularity. Experience shows that companies providing recognition for those who produce the highest-quality knowledge objects (as judged by experts and senior management) or the most popular ones (as measured by download volume) ensure that the internal authors will be motivated to compete with each other for both the highest quality and the most popularity.

A Set of Standards and Regulations

The market's transaction costs—the time and effort involved in creating and seeking knowledge—must be bearable. For internal knowledge markets to pass this test, companies need to develop standards, protocols, and regulations to lower costs that act as a deterrent to both buyers and sellers. Standards can include everything from the templates used to define the content that goes into a knowledge object to the taxonomy and "metatags" used to define how documents are categorized (so that a search process will turn up relevant content). Protocols include everything from rules determining which kinds of knowledge will be traded in the marketplace to what kind of standards a document needs to meet to be qualified as a knowledge object suitable for listing in the marketplace. Regulations include whatever internal compliance mechanisms are put in place to reinforce these standards and protocols.

Market Facilitators

To date, the bulk of corporate investment in knowledge management has gone into providing the staff to build and maintain the technology platform. But that is not enough. In a true knowledge market, people are needed to apply standards and protocols and to exercise judgment in enforcing the regulations. They can operate as a shared support utility for the entire enterprise. These people in the shared utility become marketplace insiders, like brokers and specialists in a stock exchange, who facilitate the market's operation through familiarity with its mechanics. They don't have to constitute a large bureaucracy; no more than two or three dozen facilitators are needed to run and regulate an internal knowledge market at, say, a large investment bank. The alternative—relying on authors and knowledge seekers to follow protocols and standards and to regulate themselves—simply does not work; they lack the familiarity, the interest, and probably the time.

Some of the market facilitators are knowledge services employees who operate at the center of the marketplace. They can, for example, ensure that each document traded there has an attached tag, one that provides the information that enables the search process to be effective, as well as enough context to let readers preview a document before they download or read it. They can manage processes to ensure that obsolete content is removed from the marketplace. It is also helpful to have editors who, through spending a little time with the authors, are efficient at adding text to a set of figures in order to convert them into a knowledge object of sufficient quality to be listed in the marketplace.

One mistake commonly made is having this central staff actually try to "author" content themselves. The problem is that most real expertise is at the front line, and such central efforts rarely produce much distinctive content.

Knowledge Development

One unique characteristic of a knowledge marketplace is the need to establish "knowledge domain owners." Knowledge domain owners have support staff with sufficient knowledge to be able to control the quality of the knowledge in their specialties better than anyone else in the firm. In a large company, there can be hundreds of knowledge domains, each representing different subsets of users, each with common knowledge interests, who are part of informal or formal networks. In many cases, these informal networks have come into existence to support users with common knowledge interests, and they are sometimes very effective in accomplishing knowledge exchange among small populations of users. We believe the power of such efforts can be amplified by converting these informal networks into formal networks (as described in Chapter 6) and by making the people running these formal networks the owners of the relevant knowledge domain.

As knowledge domain owners, these people would determine what meets the standard as a knowledge object in their domains, or what documents, if upgraded, could meet the standard. They could also serve as owners of quality for related topics that are on the companypedia. They would also be responsible for stimulating the creation and codification of new content by experts who have an interest in their specific knowledge arenas. And they usually would maintain and update content that is still valid or remove content that is obsolete and identify any knowledge gaps that need filling.

Knowledge Markets at Work

The idea of applying market principles to knowledge management activities is relatively new. As a result, few examples exist of companies that have fully adopted the concept. Among those that have, however, the potential appears to be great.

Consider the case of J. M. Huber Corporation, a large privately owned U.S. company with three diversified business sectors. In 1995, its top management introduced an "after-action review process" to capture the lessons learned from projects and events for the purpose of enhancing its future performance. The company felt that the lessons learned, when they pertained to such areas as manufacturing processes and procedures, could be specific to a particular business sector. Other lessons—those pertaining to strategy, safety, or marketing, for instance—could be useful across all three business sectors.

At J. M. Huber, the members of a project team conduct a post-project meeting to answer three basic questions: What happened? Why did it happen? What can we do about it? At the end of the meeting, the team emerges with an action plan and a list of lessons learned. These findings are submitted to a common electronic document library accessible to all employees through a portal.

Today the process has become part of Huber's culture. The database contains more than 11,000 reports. Why is it successful? Because managers can reach knowledge seekers interested in the same subjects while simultaneously building a reputation with colleagues in other divisions—and with top management. Once the market formed, the self-interest of the knowledge creators and knowledge seekers took over. Huber's management says that this exchange of knowledge was instrumental in improving the company's performance.

Huber is an interesting case because it created a knowledge marketplace for its line management structure. But it is a relatively small company compared to a megainstitution.

Can a marketplace work for a very large firm? We are aware of three large firms, with professional staff ranging from 8,000 to 25,000 people per company, that have created enterprisewide knowledge marketplaces.

Global Bank Example

Let's illustrate how knowledge marketplaces can be powerfully effective in enabling companies to mobilize mind power, again using our Global Bank example.

Let's return to the example we used in the last chapter, in which the Small Business executive for the New Jersey/Long Island branch organization is charged with developing a marketing campaign and product bundle for the personal banking needs of small business owners.

To begin, the Small Business executive went to Global Bank's expertise system to check out the profiles of different candidates for the senior marketing team leadership position. He looked for alternative candidates by searching such terms as "personal banking needs of small business owners," "marketing to small business owners," and

"product bundles for small business owners." One of the experts identified was the same woman who had applied for the role from the Small
Business Marketing talent pool.

Once the team was formed, the senior marketing team leader gave
initial assignments to the junior marketing professional on her team
to find out what had been learned in similar projects. Upon searching
the Global Bank knowledge portal, the junior professional found eight
similar projects that had been completed, including three in just the
last year. After reading the write-ups of each project and sending them
around to the entire team, the junior professional worked with the
senior professional to identify the key open issues raised by the project
review.

In the meantime, the entry-level person on the team was busily becoming self-educated. She did this by going to the "Global Bank pedia"
to learn about different small business market segments, best practices
in marketing campaigns, product bundles, and so on. Within a week of
such a self-education, the entry-level person was able to develop a sufficient familiarity with the topic to be able to have good conversations
with the more senior members of the team.

At that point, the senior marketing professional was able to lay out
a detailed project plan for putting the campaign in place. She also
identified the key open issues raised by her review of the results of
similar projects. Why had one similar effort concluded that an appropriate product bundle should include checking accounts, personal
investment and estate planning services, and a margin-based line of
credit, while other initiatives had limited the product bundle to checking and investment services alone? Similar questions were raised over
target segments, pricing alternatives, promotional activities, and so
forth.

The team members then began to focus on finding out more about
all of these areas while simultaneously undertaking market research in
their target market. As they did so, they not only searched the knowledge marketplace, they also reached out with specific questions to targeted individuals who had either worked on similar projects or who had

authored documents that had been particularly interesting. They discovered that because their questions were targeted and reflected knowledge gleaned from their research, most individuals they contacted were quite willing to talk. For example, to the team's surprise, one of the best ideas came from a conversation with a private banking marketing person, an individual who had marketed a bundle of investment planning and estate services to wealthy individuals in the U.K. market who were not, themselves, small business owners.

After three months of such work, the project was completed—and it received rave reviews from the New Jersey/Long Island backbone executive. But the team's work was not done. Once the project was completed, the junior professional led the effort to codify the results of the project. The entry-level person provided some specific new knowledge to the Global Bank pedia about the specific service needs for one particular segment of small business owners—that is, how the coin and currency needs of cash-and-carry retailers were changing in the digital age. The senior marketing professional, meanwhile, used the campaign as one example of a new knowledge object she was writing entitled "Best Practices of Rapid-Roll-Out Marketing Campaigns." In the process, all three team members were able to build their reputations while providing Global Bank with new knowledge.

While this example is hypothetical, it serves to illustrate just how powerful this process can be in enabling people working on frontline issues to mobilize mind power enterprisewide. Such opportunities to mobilize knowledge through marketplaces are abundant in all large companies.

Unleashing Mind Power

There is enormous, unrealized potential in the minds of professionals and managers in large companies. This potential can be realized by simultaneously creating formal networks, talent marketplaces, and knowledge marketplaces. Each of these organizational capabilities makes the other capabilities more powerful. Each one builds upon the other. In combination they can enable intangibles to flow easily throughout the enterprise. Formal networks help talent marketplaces and knowledge marketplaces to be formed and to function effectively.

Without formal network owners to give temporarily assigned workers a home base, it would be hard to successfully hold them together as part of a particular professional community. Similarly, every knowledge domain needs an owner to provide quality control, maintain the currency of the knowledge, and stimulate new knowledge creation. Without formal network owners, there would be no one to play this role, at least for most knowledge domains. Furthermore, formal networks can help individuals foster social bonds with one another—which is essential to building trust that they will be treated fairly. This is particularly important in enabling individuals to trust a talent marketplace to find them their next assignments or to trust a knowledge marketplace to credit them properly for sharing their distinctive knowledge.

At the same time, knowledge marketplaces greatly enable both formal networks and talent marketplaces. For starters, firmwide knowledge marketplaces provide infrastructure and management protocols for sharing knowledge that are more efficient and effective than any one of the networks could provide on its own. Knowledge marketplaces can help provide formal network members with the reputational rewards to "pay" them for the knowledge they provide to the network. Furthermore, if this reputation can be leveraged through the talent marketplace to give the individual better job opportunities, then this access to the knowledge marketplace becomes a critical motivator of talented people, both to encourage them to participate in the formal networks and to codify their knowledge to the highest standards.

From a network owner's viewpoint, the knowledge marketplace is a place to propagate the ideas of the network, thereby influencing the thinking of the entire institution (including, in particular, the establishment of standards and protocols). To the extent that the output from the formal networks is of high quality, the knowledge marketplace also can help the entire community build its reputation throughout the firm.

The greatest value of all, however, comes from being able to tap into formal networks, knowledge marketplaces, and talent marketplaces simultaneously. The combination of formal networks with knowledge marketplaces, for example, allows talented line managers to take on tasks critical to the firm and to do so with far less risk (since they can quickly move to the state of the art in terms of knowledge).

The existence of formal networks and knowledge marketplaces also can give senior managers the confidence they need in order to assign jobs and projects to talented people who may lack certain skills or knowledge, simply because they know the people will be able to draw on the formal networks and the knowledge marketplace for help. As a result, more people can be assigned to jobs that would otherwise have been beyond their capacities. And, as they are so assigned, talented people will grow their talents much faster, and the firm will accomplish far more.

PART IV

IDEAS TO MOTIVATE BETTER BEHAVIORS

9

FINANCIAL PERFORMANCE MEASUREMENT FOR THE 21ST CENTURY

WE'D LIKE TO SUGGEST a somewhat radical idea: that companies redesign their internal financial performance measurements for the digital age.

By this we mean it's time for companies to take measure of the real engines of wealth creation in the 21st century. We're talking about the knowledge, relationships, reputations, and other intangibles created by talented people.

Companies create wealth by converting these "raw" intangibles into the institutional skills, patents, brands, software, customer bases, intellectual capital, and networks that increase profits per employee and returns on invested capital. These intangibles are true capital in the sense that they can produce real cash returns. Today, the most valuable capital that companies can use in the 21st century is not financial capital but "intangible capital."

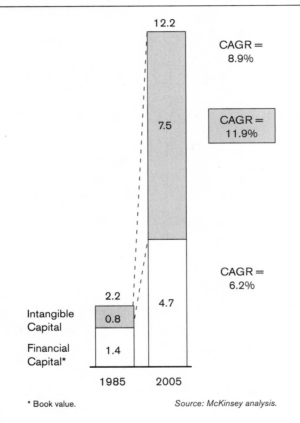

FIGURE 9-1

**Intangible Capital for Largest 150 Companies,
Measured by Total Market Capitalization**

(In trillions of constant 2005 dollars)

* Book value.   Source: McKinsey analysis.

A simple approximation of intangible capital is the market value of the firm less the invested financial capital.[1] Using book capital as a crude proxy for financial capital, the intangible capital of the largest 150 companies in the world in 2005 was $7.5 trillion versus $800 billion in 1985 (Figure 9-1).

Then why—despite the evidence that intangibles are the source of wealth in the 21st century—do companies tightly control discretionary spending on intangibles? Why are advertising, R&D, new product development, training and development, knowledge creation, software projects, and so forth, almost always expensed on a "what-we-can-afford" basis?

The problem is that our approaches to financial performance measurement are geared to the industrial age, not the digital age. The development of external financial reporting, according to generally accepted accounting principles (GAAP), is one of the foundations of our modern global capital marketplace. Financial performance, seen through balance sheets, cash flow reports, and income statements are, and will always be, the principal measure used to evaluate the success of a company and its management. But it's time to recognize that financial performance increasingly comes from intangibles and largely reflects returns on talent rather than returns from invested financial capital.

GAAP accounting currently treats investments in intangibles very conservatively compared to capital investments in tangibles. Most intangible investments, in fact, are expensed rather than capitalized. This conservatism is not necessarily bad. But it does make it attractive for top managers to cut discretionary spending on talent and other intangibles in order to deliver quick earnings. When this occurs, they may be making higher profits in the short term, but they may also be undermining the company's health in the long term.

In order to create wealth, companies first need to change their financial performance metrics so that they are focusing on returns on talent rather than on returns on capital alone. Second, they need to change how they measure performance internally in order to motivate backbone frontline managers, support managers, senior managers, and top managers to make better economic decisions (particularly in regard to spending on intangibles).

Wealth-Creating Companies

Before describing what metrics are needed, we should first reflect on the attributes that have allowed some firms, since the start of the digital age, to create great wealth.

FIGURE 9-2

Drivers of Growth for the Top 30 Companies, 1995 through 2005

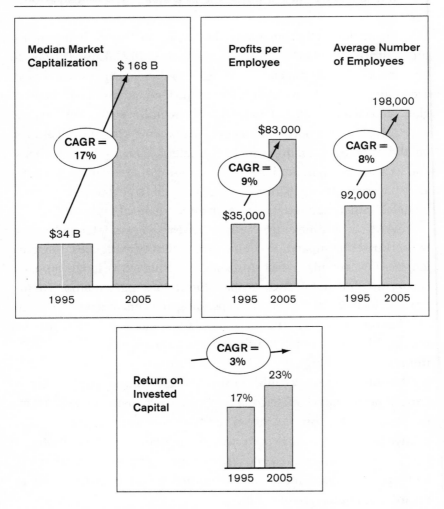

Between 1995 and 2005, the 30 winning companies identified in the Introduction have seen their profits per employee increase from $35,000 to $83,000. Their employees have grown in number from 92,000 to 198,000, and their return on invested capital (or book value, in the case of financial institutions) has increased from 17 to 23 percent (Figure 9-2). As a result, the median market capitalization of this group rose from $34 billion to $168 billion (nearly fivefold), with a compound annual growth rate (CAGR) of 17 percent per year. The driver of this increase in market capitalization was a fivefold increase in average profits—this, in turn, was driven by a more than doubling of profit per employee and a doubling in the number of employees. By comparison, returns on capital over this same period increased by only a third. What made these companies perform so well was increases in their returns from people, not from increases in returns on capital.

It is hardly news that profit growth and market capitalization growth should be closely correlated and that a fivefold increase in profits should lead to a fivefold increase in market capitalization. But it does suggest that a new approach to financial performance measurement, based on maximizing returns on people rather than on capital, is more appropriate. Total profit is the multiple of the profit per employee times the total employees, after all. So maximizing the profit per employee and the number of employees increases total profits, which drives market capitalization.

Focusing on this formula, as opposed to returns on capital, offers several advantages. For one, profit per employee is a good proxy for earnings on intangibles. Return on capital is not. Partly this is because total employees is an easy number to obtain while capital (surprisingly) is subject to the vagaries of accounting and definitional issues and such corporate finance decisions as debt-to-equity ratios, dividend policies, and liquidity preferences. And as we have said earlier, talent—not capital—is usually the scarce resource.

Clearly, then, we need a broader set of performance metrics. We believe they should include the following:

1. Profit per employee

2. Number of employees

3. Returns on capital

With these metrics, a company can set its goals for returns on intangibles (that is, profit per employee) and growth (that is, number of employees)—as well as its returns on capital (as a sanity check). Together, these three will drive its market capitalization.

1. Profit per Employee

Profit per employee is a fairly good proxy for returns on intangibles (provided capital intensity doesn't increase). As we described earlier in the book, the hallmark of the digital age is the increased ability of companies to earn "rents" from intangibles. Profit per employee is a measure of these rents, as is, of course, the return on capital. If you increase profit per employee without increasing your capital intensity, you increase your rents just as increasing your returns on capital above your costs of capital also increases your rents. The difference is that viewing profit per employee as the chief metric puts the emphasis on returns to talent. It focuses you on increasing profits relative to the number of people you employ. It argues that talented people should be used to create and use intangibles. Fortunately, the opportunities to increase profit per employee are unprecedented in the digital age. The opportunities to improve returns on capital to an equal extent, other than through employing more talented, knowledgeable people to deploy that capital, however, are not. If anything, the development of the global capital markets is commoditizing the value of investing capital unless you enjoy proprietary investment insight, particularly since capital is no longer a scarce resource.

The advantage of profit per employee is that it is readily available and easily calculable. Since intangible spending is expensed, relative to capital investments (which are usually depreciated over time), it is a conservative, output-based measure of results. And since net income is based on accounting conventions, one can easily benchmark profit per employee against that of competitors and other firms.

Profit per employee, therefore, focuses the company on intangible-intensive value propositions. In turn, the focus is on talented people, those who (with some investment) can produce valuable intangibles.

2. Number of Employees

One way to improve profit per employee is simply by shedding low-profit employees. But if the workers being shed provide profits greater than the costs of the capital used to support their activities, shedding them will reduce wealth creation rather than increase it (unless an offsetting number of workers are added that produce higher profits per employee).

You can indeed create great wealth, even if your profit per employee is modest, if you employ enough workers. The Walton family, remember, is consistently at the top of the Forbes wealth list. Why? While Wal-Mart earns relatively low profit-per-employee numbers, it has a business model that enables it to handle the complexity of managing 1.7 million employees—without incurring offsetting diseconomies.[2]

Real wealth creation, therefore, comes either from increasing profit per employee (without offsetting reductions in the numbers of employees or offsetting increases in capital intensity) or from increasing the number of employees earning such profits. Or from both.

Figure 9-3 shows this on a simple grid, one that illustrates the source of profits of the top 30 companies relative to one another using these two dimensions.[3]

The chart also shows that total employment can serve as a crude proxy for the internal complexity of a firm, particularly when comparing companies in similar industries with similar mixes of employment. From this vantage point, profit per employee becomes a proxy for how well the firm is managing that complexity, as we described in the Introduction.

To the extent that a firm can streamline its organization and can use formal networks, talent marketplaces, and knowledge marketplaces to mobilize its intangibles throughout the enterprise, profit per employee

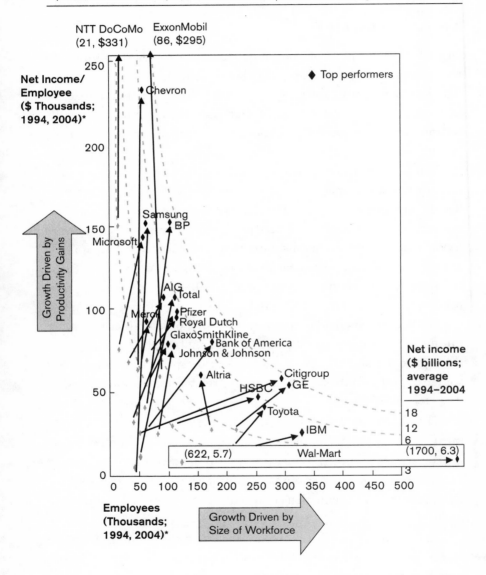

FIGURE 9-3

Drivers of Profit for Large Companies

(In constant 2004 dollars; uses first available data point for firms lacking 2004 data)

* 1994 and 2004 data points represent 3-year averages, 1992–1994 and 2002–2004, respectively.

Source: Global Vantage; McKinsey analysis.

should increase (even without discovering new, winning value propositions) simply by removing unproductive complexity.

3. Returns on Capital

By substituting capital for labor costs, profit per employee can also be improved. Of course, while capital is relatively inexpensive and readily available today, it still demands a return (and for this reason must be used carefully). But if you are using total employment to drive your growth aspirations, the amount of capital required should be a derivative of your strategies (rather than an aspiration in its own right).

We are advocating, then, that you look at your returns on capital more as a sanity check than a metric to aspire to. As long as returns on capital exceed the costs of capital, profit per employee is a better metric. Why? Because profit per employee not only represents the scarcest resource, it also reflects profits after expensing the investments needed to produce them. Capital investment, meanwhile, is depreciated or amortized and thus may overstate profits if the investment later needs to be written off.

Total employees, furthermore, is a measure that doesn't depend on subjective accounting judgments.[4] Book capital, on the other hand, is (surprisingly) relatively ambiguous. It is subject to somewhat arbitrary accounting conventions (accounting for goodwill, depreciation schedules, and how stock options are expensed, among others). Calculating return on invested capital, meanwhile, has its own limitations. This is particularly true for financial institutions (most of their assets are financial, which makes invested capital a meaningless concept for them and which also requires making some heroic assumptions).[5]

Maximizing Market Capitalization

Market capitalization is perhaps the most important single measure of a company's total size and economic relevance. It directly affects whether a company is in strategic control of its own destiny. As we've already noted, total market capitalization is highly correlated to total net income; of the top 30 companies by net income from 2002 to 2004, all but 5 are in the top 30 by market value. You can see this correlation by displaying net income as a return on equity times book value and then comparing that relationship to a strategic control map (one that displays total market capitalization disaggregated into a market-to-book ratio times book equity, as in Figure 9-4).[6]

You can see this same correlation, as well, if you disaggregate net income using profit per employee and total employees, displaying the total market capitalization as a function of market capitalization per employee and total employees (Figure 9-5). It is valid therefore to think about net income and market capitalization as either a function of returns on capital or returns on talent. What we are arguing is that while the measure of returns on capital—and the returns on talent—are both appropriate ways to think about financial performance, thinking about returns to talent is a more powerful mental model in the 21st century.

Today's annual reports are filled with information about how capital has been used, but they offer little information about the number of employees or the different kinds of employees (beyond a simple compensation-and-benefits expense item) that populate the company. Yet, as we've been arguing throughout this book, it is thinking-intensive talent, not capital, that is driving today's wealth creation.

Motivating Economic Behavior

Changing the financial metrics of the enterprise is a start. But much of the real power in changing financial performance measures is in changing the behaviors of the managers. In the model we've been describing throughout this book, the responsibility for driving financial results falls largely upon the backbone frontline managers, support managers, and senior and top managers. Let's explore, then, how one can create measurement approaches that will motivate better economic behaviors in these groups.

FIGURE 9-4

Income and Market Capitalization Shown as Returns to Capital, 2002 through 2004 (Average)

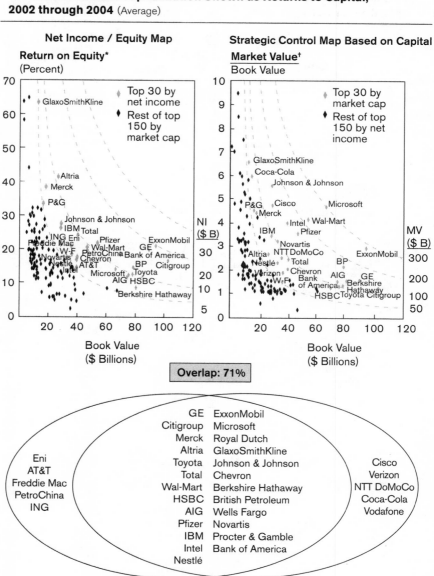

Constant 2004 dollars.

* Not pictured: Royal Dutch.

† Not pictured: Vodafone, Royal Dutch.

Source: Global Vantage; McKinsey analysis.

FIGURE 9-5

Income and Market Capitalization Shown as Returns to Talent, 2002 through 2004 (Average)

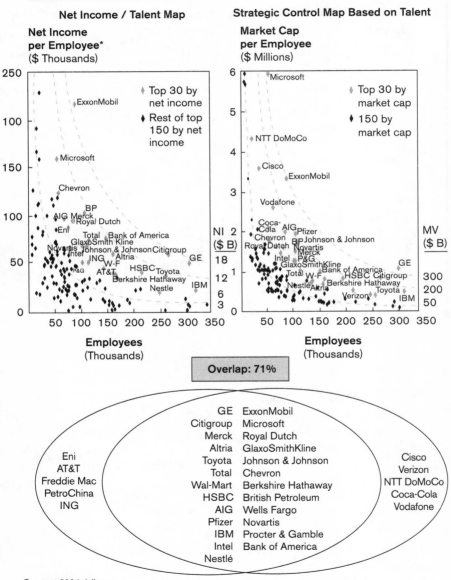

Constant 2004 dollars.

* Not pictured: Wal-Mart; Federal Home Loan Corp.; PetroChina.   *Source: Global Vantage; McKinsey analysis.*

Performance Measurement of Backbone Frontline Managers

As described in Chapter 3, the backbone frontline manager is the primary role responsible for delivering day-to-day financial results. In our model, these managers are responsible for substantially all of the enterprise's revenue producing capabilities, as well as any unique costs used to produce these revenues. Their role is to maximize, from the firm's existing capabilities, the production of current earnings and, in particular, to increase returns to talent. In this role, they can directly or indirectly control nearly 100 percent of the firm's current revenues and the lion's share of the company's costs.

These managers must be free to get the resources they need, within defined boundaries. Beyond performance measures, they must also be bounded by standards, protocols, and values, of course—these limit their ability to complicate or compete against other managers of other units or to make short-term decisions that hurt the long-term health of the enterprise.

We believe that the backbone frontline units should be "contribution centers" rather than "profit centers." Why not let frontline managers of these units focus attention on the activities they can actually control? In contrast to a profit center, which includes allocation of all the costs and revenues of the company to businesses, a contribution center includes only the unique revenues and unique costs (including the costs of capital) of the unit. The unit, then, contributes to the profits of the company. It is measured on its contributed returns versus targets—rather than by its "fully loaded" profits after all allocations. The targets for each contribution center should be set so that the sum of all contribution centers covers the indirect/overhead costs and achieves the targeted corporate profit margin. The manager of a line unit is therefore accountable for the contribution of the unit to enterprisewide profits rather than the "profits" earned by the unit. Later in this chapter, we will illustrate these concepts with a sample financial performance report that will detail how the contribution center concept (direct revenues, direct costs, stretch targets, capital charges, and so on) can be put into practice.

CONTRIBUTION CENTERS, NOT PROFIT CENTERS

The underlying assumption behind making units profit centers is that they are self-contained in their ability to drive earnings. In most cases, of course, this is not true. Businesses within large companies are not independent. They often share intangibles, distribution networks, production capabilities, and customers, not to mention shared utilities, corporate overhead functions, and balance sheets. Therefore, to produce "business profitability statements," financial officers in these units need to make heroic assumptions. They must make subjective decisions in determining how to allocate corporate overhead, transfer costs, and attribute revenue that, as a result, often seem arbitrary to the profit center manager.

The problem with making arbitrary allocations is that it often leads to bad decision making. Take the example of a large firm that served the large corporate marketplace. It produced quality products, but it had expensive overhead costs. Meanwhile, "double counting" allowed

By making this shift, the management of the line unit becomes entirely focused on improving the economic activities of what it is managing—that is, the unique revenues and unique costs of the unit. In the process, the financial measurement of the manager is also simplified, and backbone line managers are motivated to improve revenues while minimizing costs. They do not spend their time arguing or negotiating the allocations of overhead or nonfinancial charges (for example, amortization of goodwill). They do not try to game the system.

Costs that vary with volume used, of course, or are incurred for the benefits of a particular line unit by another unit (or by a shared utility) would still need to be attributed to the line unit creating the demand. This is consistent with making units responsible for the costs they control. But in this case what they control is the volume used, not unit costs.

A unit using a computer utility, for example, would be charged for its different units to get credit for the same revenues (leaving multiple units thinking that their margins were higher than they actually were). This made them more inclined to spend "whatever it takes" on support. To grow, the firm decided to enter the midsized corporate market, and it was able to do so with some success (at least by the unique revenues created relative to the unique costs of entering the market).

But because the firm allocated overhead (through formulas that used a full cost rather than a marginal cost approach), the new midsized corporate business looked unprofitable. Why? Because it was forced to absorb the costs of overhead functions designed for a different market. The faster the business grew, the more overhead it absorbed. Eventually, to stop "the bleeding," the firm decided to kill the business even though the business's marginal economics were good. The truth was that neither the support functions nor the finance functions were willing to change their allocation approaches for this one business. They didn't want to set a precedent that would change how overhead was allocated to other existing, mature businesses.

its usage of the utility at a predetermined, standard rate. Additionally, it would be charged at an opportunity rate for the time of temporary or part-time talent that was "pulled" from the talent marketplace. Line units would also be charged, at a standard rate, for the capital they used.

The intent, as we described earlier in the book, is to focus frontline managers on their tactical abilities to increase returns. In this situation, backbone frontline managers would be responsible for maximizing the returns from existing capabilities and value propositions. But they would not be responsible for creating new capabilities and new value propositions. The line managers would be focused entirely on the creation of current earnings.

This approach assumes that investments in activities with time horizons longer than 18 months—particularly intangible heavy, risky activities—would be managed offline, under the sponsorship of senior

UNDERINVESTMENT IN INTANGIBLES

It is easy for prudent business executives to conclude that investing in intangibles is not a good strategy for success. In particular, the specific contribution of each intangible is hard to assess. That is what makes intangible accounting hard.[7] Because intangibles are embedded in the value chain of production, it is generally unclear which intangibles are the source of profits—and what balance of tangibles versus intangibles should be credited for the results.

How does one place a value on a brand, for instance? There is no market that trades in brands, so we cannot value brands based on their market prices. Advertising has a short shelf life (for example, Wendy's is not still reaping all the benefits of the "Where's the beef?" campaign), so past expenditures do not count one for one in today's brand value. To be sure, past expenditures do influence the present value of the brand. For example, Coke's history of advertising over the last 60 years has contributed to its enormous brand value; a new cola producer that matched Coca-Cola's current advertising budget would not have a brand that is as valuable as Coke. Similar problems exist with other types of intangibles.

Tangibles, by comparison, are easier. Labor has a wage rate that is set in the labor market; land has a value that is set in the real estate market; capital is priced at the going interest rate and the price of equity traded in the market. For each of these tangible assets, there is a corresponding market price.

Such measurement issues are not just academic issues. They influence how companies make decisions and measure the performance of individuals. The treatment of intangible investments, for instance, causes many companies to underspend on intangibles.[8] Intangible assets pay off over the life of the asset and, in theory, should be depreciated over time. But since the value of that spending (and the duration of that value) is highly uncertain, firms following GAAP wind up expensing most intangible investments.

or top managers (with separate budgeting as described in Chapter 5). They would be added to a line manager's numbers only when future revenues and costs could be reasonably estimated.

Line managers would be continuously projecting their unique revenues and unique losses 18 months forward. These projections would be best estimates rather than implicit contracts for performance. And rather than receiving their evaluations based on their ability to achieve these projections, they would be evaluated on their ability to achieve targets for total contribution earned (net of capital charges), total contribution per employee, and the numbers of employees. These "stretch targets" would be set high enough to ensure that (if met by all the frontline backbone managers) the company could meet its aspirations for total profits, profit per employee, number of employees, and returns on capital. These targets, furthermore, would be validated by being benchmarked against both the internal financial performance of similar units within the company and whatever external benchmarks are available.

Unlike stretch budgeting, the only way line managers could reach these financial targets would be by producing unique revenues (while minimizing costs). First and foremost, the backbone frontline managers would be challenged to decide which specific intangibles to invest in to get better day-to-day returns from each employee they manage (for example, training, marketing, and relationship building).

Performance Measurement of Shared Utility Managers

Managers of shared support costs play another critical role. Throughout this book we have emphasized the advantages of shared functional utilities—those scale-effective cost centers that are operated for the benefit of multiple organizational units. We want to emphasize the words *for the benefit of multiple organizational units,* because such centers should not be created unless they can provide better support at lower costs than the units might provide for themselves.

Let's examine how a senior manager, running a shared support utility and reporting to a C-level executive, might handle this. Shared utilities would receive no revenues from customers but instead would be cost centers. They would recover costs by charging line units, or the other support functions, according to the volume of the services used.

Not all the costs of a particular shared utility would necessarily be charged back to its users (companies often get it wrong when they build overhead allocations, and even profit margins, into the transfer rates used to charge users for the utilities' services). We will describe later how a company can recover such overhead costs, thereby achieving profit targets.

Shared utilities capture scale effects rather than have multiple organizational units undertake similar, subscale activities. Their goal is not to make the utility either a contribution center or a profit center but rather to make it a well-run cost center. Shared utilities have only internal customers, after all. Booking "profits" in such centers only confuses the source of the economic value. To make a shared utility work, it must provide cost-effectiveness to users. This, in turn, means that the volume-based costs charged back to the users must be less (hopefully significantly less) than what the users would incur for equivalent services if they didn't use the utility.

All costs dedicated to a single unit would be charged to that unit. For costs that are shared significantly across units, however, a different approach would be used. Users of shared costs should be charged only the marginal costs of volume, with the utility incurring the shared fixed cost of operations as overhead (as we said earlier, we will describe later how to cover overhead costs).

In practice, many of the services and activities of shared utilities, which today involve significant investments in digital technology, do not vary with the volume of transactions processed. Rather, they vary with the number of people supported, the number of end customers serviced, the volume of inquiries, and so on. Increases in the costs of such activities usually come from frequent step functions rather than volume. This, in turn, creates the need for complex transfer-pricing algorithms. No matter how the transfer rates are set, however (even if complicated algorithms are used), it is essential that the rates charged are standardized (rather than individually negotiated) and lower than if the users did it themselves or used an outside vendor.

In measuring the financial performance of shared utilities, one of the complicating issues is their extensive use of variable cost labor. Indeed, many activities often placed in shared utilities (such as call centers, payroll services, and IT maintenance) are labor intensive (rather than talent intensive). As these shared utilities charge users for their activities, they need to charge for the variable, marginal costs of the labor used as well. The problem (or opportunity) is that using variable cost labor—if it is off-shored—can have a lower marginal cost than existing labor.

Sourcing labor in New York, for instance, can be 6 to 10 times more expensive than in India. Should the shared utility capture the difference, or should it transfer the savings from arbitraging the labor costs to the line? A practical answer is in the use of a blended labor rate, one that prices the rate above the marginal costs of the lowest-cost labor being used (say, in India) but well below the price for labor in the developed world. Such an approach motivates the manager of the shared utility to source the lowest-cost labor (of the desired quality) available.

The idea is to construct the utility's financial measurements on sound economic principles and to focus attention only on those activities that the shared utility can actually control. Thus, managers of such units would receive no overhead allocation (although they would receive volume usage charges from other shared utilities), and they would pay for the talent they pulled from other units. Since a shared utility is a cost center, however, charge-backs to users would be viewed as reductions in expenses rather than as "revenues." Later in this chapter we will illustrate this concept with a sample financial performance report.

Differences from the Traditional Approach

Moving in the direction we propose raises a number of questions. In terms of financial reporting, how would you price the talent traded in the talent marketplace? How can capital costs be recovered? How should one ensure that returns are sufficient to cover unallocated overhead costs and still meet profit objectives?

Pricing Talent

We've already discussed talent marketplaces. But how should one price talent to encourage units to contribute talent to the marketplace while also ensuring that they are paid and/or credited appropriately for that talent?

As we said in Chapter 7 on talent marketplaces, we believe the answer for permanent assignments made through the talent marketplace is to have the unit employing the talent pay the full cost of employment (for example, salaries and benefits). By becoming a full-time, longer-term employee, both the individual and the organizational unit are making mutual commitments to work together. For the individual, this is part of his or her career development; for the unit, this is a person who is "joining the team."

Much of the work performed by talent today, however, is temporary or part-time work. Formal projects, in particular, require diverse talents brought together to perform discrete tasks. In such temporary work, the people engaged in the projects are not necessarily switching their organizational units. In fact, they view these assignments as small steps in their career progression. In such situations, the people assigned to such projects have alternative opportunities. Likewise, the people who are sponsoring the hiring are not looking for permanent hires or long-term commitments.

There is, of course, a time-tested approach that law firms, accounting firms, and consulting firms use to price such work. This is by charging for the person's time not at cost but at a rate that reflects the opportunity to deploy that time elsewhere.[9] Usually such opportunity rates are significantly higher than what the person was being paid—often three or more times the person's wages. This is appropriate. It is the opportunity to price talent at a higher rate than cost that enables winning firms to increase their profit per employee.

This type of system underscores the need for standardized role descriptions (that is, consistently defined role and skill sets such as those used in the U.S. Army Military Occupation Specialties [MOS] system described in Chapter 7). Each role and skill set would have an established per diem rate and a system for charging time and transferring the resulting time charges from the organizational unit paying the wages of the talent to the organizational unit temporarily deploying the talent against a given opportunity. In effect, the unit paying the wages of the talented person receives revenues (or, if a cost center, a "negative expense") equal to the opportunity rate. The unit deploying the talent, meanwhile, receives a corresponding charge.

While many of the talented people being "time charged" out may be part of an assignment pool, the same system could be used to recover the costs of the contribution center or shared utility managers for the time their people spend on projects sponsored by other organizational units. Often, line and support organizations are reluctant to contribute the time of their best people to help other units. But they would probably be more willing to do so with this approach because it compensates them for the opportunity cost of making their people available.

The advantage of time charging is that it helps allocate supply to whoever is willing to pay the market opportunity price. In doing so, it helps establish what a particular talent is worth, using the marketplace to establish its value. After all, the pricing of talent, even in an internal marketplace, is self-correcting: If prices are too high, demand will fall, and excess supply will accrue. If prices are too low, demand will increase, and the talent will be in short supply.

Prices for different roles should be benchmarked against other internal roles, in addition to outside services. A market price for talent, based on its opportunity value, can help overcome some of the measurement issues of intangibles. Since talent is the ultimate source of all intangibles, being able to establish an internal market price helps enable a company to overcome the intangibles' valuation challenge. A company allocating talent through a marketplace that sets prices at opportunity rates will know not just the value of the labor and capital invested in different activities but the value of its invested talent as well.

Capital Costs

Capital in today's developed world, as everyone knows, is no longer a scarce resource.[10] It offers little competitive advantage. It has become just another factor cost of production. Capital costs can either be accounted for as capital charges (that is, capital employed times cost of capital equals capital charges) or incorporated into target returns (for example, return on invested capital objectives). Either approach works. We prefer charging for capital, however, since doing so eliminates the need to set targets based on return on capital. Furthermore, this enables returns to people rather than returns to capital to be the principal performance objective.

Target Returns

As we noted earlier, top managers should use stretch targets to drive financial performance.

To start, the company should understand what its profit aspirations are relative to past results as well as to the future profit expectations of the marketplace. Then it should translate those objectives into profits per employee, employment, and return-on-capital targets (Figure 9-6).

The next step is to disaggregate the firm's existing returns. What are the unique revenues and unique costs of the contribution centers, the direct unallocated costs of overhead centers (including corporate-level portfolio-of-initiative investments) including all capital charges that need to be recovered, and the net costs of shared utilities?[11]

Once these are disaggregated, the enterprise can establish stretch target returns for each unit that cover these costs and charges and that meet profit expectations. Stretch targets could be set, for instance, so

FIGURE 9-6

Setting and Meeting Target Returns

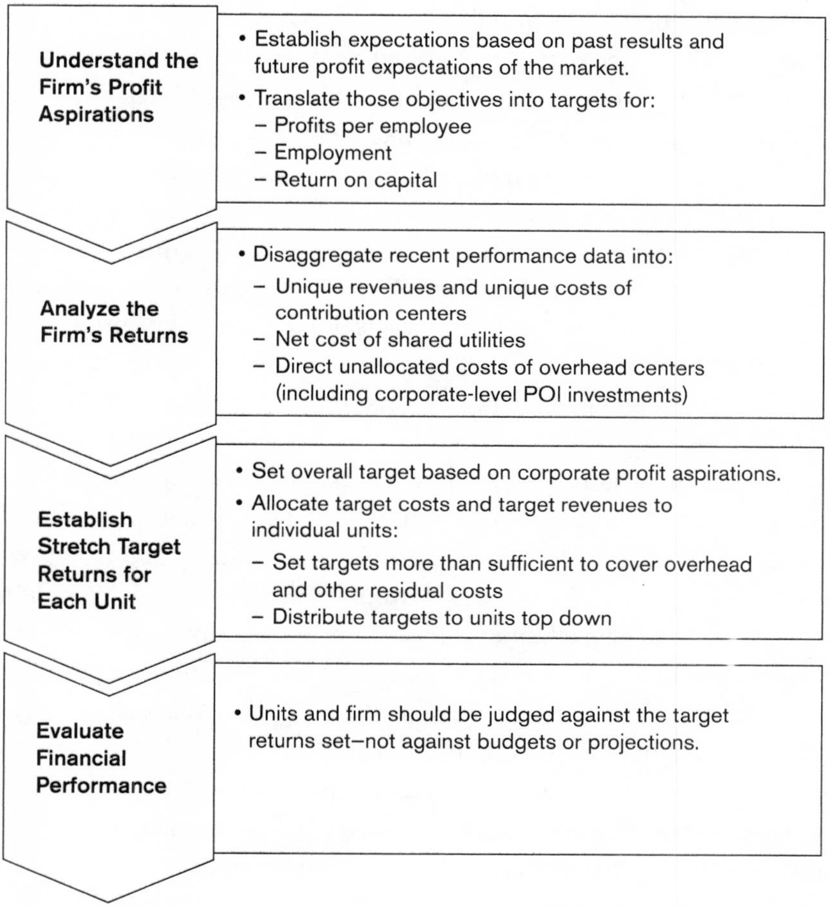

Understand the Firm's Profit Aspirations	• Establish expectations based on past results and future profit expectations of the market.
	• Translate those objectives into targets for:
	  − Profits per employee
	  − Employment
	  − Return on capital

Analyze the Firm's Returns	• Disaggregate recent performance data into:
	  − Unique revenues and unique costs of contribution centers
	  − Net cost of shared utilities
	  − Direct unallocated costs of overhead centers (including corporate-level POI investments)

Establish Stretch Target Returns for Each Unit	• Set overall target based on corporate profit aspirations.
	• Allocate target costs and target revenues to individual units:
	  − Set targets more than sufficient to cover overhead and other residual costs
	  − Distribute targets to units top down

Evaluate Financial Performance	• Units and firm should be judged against the target returns set—not against budgets or projections.

that the company would exceed its profit aspirations if all the units met them. In other words, rather than allocating out overhead and other costs that the units *can't* control, top management instead allocates out targets, which, if met, more than cover these costs.

While the target returns should be set annually, each unit should be responsible for projecting its expected economics for the next 18 months. This is not a budget but rather a best estimate. These projections would then be rolled forward every 3 months, so the company would find itself continually requesting that each unit provide its best estimate for the next 18 months. Unlike budgets, of course, these estimates would not be part of the evaluation of each unit's financial performance. Rather, the evaluation of each unit would be based on its ability to make its annually established target returns.

The target returns for a contribution center, for instance, would include objectives for total financial contribution (net of capital charges), contribution per employee, and total employees. If a unit exceeded its financial projections but fell short of its targets, it would be underperforming. A unit that exceeded its targets but fell short of its projections would still be performing well. In other words, managers would be evaluated on their ability to perform rather than on their ability to forecast results and "make budget."

A unit that dramatically improved its total financial contribution (and contribution per employee) but that still fell short of target returns might be considered to have performed well—simply because it was making progress against targets. It would also be evaluated through its contributions to help other units meet their contribution targets through "memo credits." Figure 9-7 shows the "top-page" financial performance report for the New Jersey/Long Island frontline manager example we've been using throughout the book.

Through this approach, top management can explicitly set aspirations and standards for what constitutes good performance—without resorting to negotiations around the budgeting process.

It would be up to the top management team to determine how much to tailor these targets to the individual organization unit. It is essential that the targets are set high enough to cover all overhead costs (not allocated out) and still achieve overall corporate profitability aspirations. The more targets that are made into companywide, absolute standards, the more pressure there will be to divest low returns to capital and labor-intensive activities and, in their place, invest in high return

FIGURE 9-7

Financial Report for New Jersey/Long Island Branch System

Direct contribution

N.J./Long Island 2007 Contribution Report $ Millions		Total employees = 1,300 Total branches = 100	
Net interest margin[a]	$225		
Fees/service charges[b]	75		
Less:	300		
Direct expenses[c]	($80)		
Shared utility charges[d]	(60)		
Talent market charges (net)[e]	(10)		
Gross contribution	$150	**Contribution ($)**	
		per Employee	**per Branch**
Less: capital charges[f]	$75		
Net contribution to profit[g]	$75	$57,700	$250,000
Projected contribution to profit[h]	$60	$48,100	$600,000
Target contribution to profit[i]	$85	$65,400	$850,000
Surplus/(shortfall) to target[j]	($10)	($7,700)	($100,000)

Contribution to other units

Memo credit ($ millions)	Actual	Target	Surplus/Shortfall
Contribution to credit card[k]	$30	$25	$5.0
Contribution to mortgages[l]	$25	$30	($5.0)

a   Interest income credited to deposits and earned on loans less interest paid to deposits (excludes mortgages and credit cards).

b   Fees and service charges on branch-based services and deposit accounts.

c   Expenses to operate branches and management structure.

d   Charges from service utilities such as call centers, deposit operations, IT, etc.

e   Opportunity costs of talent loaned to other units, net of talent borrowed from other units.

f   Capital charged to support loan book (excluding mortgages and credit cards) and to support branch system at 15% pretax cost of capital.

g   Contribution to profit (excludes all overhead and other non-branch-related accounts), net of capital charge.

h   Projected contribution as of 12/31/07 by N.J./Long Island frontline manager.

i   Target contribution to profit to meet 2007 profit aspirations set by Global Bank CEO.

j   Difference between contribution to profit and target.

k   Net interest income and fees earned from credit cards of N.J./Long Island branch-based customers.

l   Net interest income and fees earned on mortgages of N.J./Long Island branch-based customers.

to capital and talent-intensive activities. Most firms, by benchmarking units against each other, would probably set targets that are a mix: some tailored to the conditions of the individual units, some that are set as absolute standards, firmwide.

Under a target return system, the use of a talent marketplace and opportunity rates would encourage the deployment of talent to its greatest opportunity. Managers needing temporary infusions of talent, either to turn around a unit or to invest in opportunities, would quickly assemble teams to do so, but they would have to pay for those resources by time charges. Therefore, the "borrowing" units would reduce their contributions (or, for a cost center, increase their costs) while simultaneously increasing the returns of "lending" units.

In borrowing a talented employee, the unit would reduce its total contribution, but it would avoid having to add an employee to the denominator in the contribution-per-employee metric. A lending unit would increase its total contribution, but it would also include that employee in the denominator. Whether a particular unit would want to borrow or lend an employee would, of course, depend on the opportunity rate attached to the employee's per diem, alternative opportunities available, and the target returns that were established.

Similar approaches would be used for shared cost centers and overhead functions (except that financial targets would be based on net "cost-effectiveness" rather than on "contribution"). An illustrative top-page report for the head of the Global Consumer Bank's Marketing Shared Utility is shown in Figure 9-8.

Senior and Top Management Roles

Under a target return system, top management and the financial function would be responsible for managing external expectations of financial results (for example, profits, earnings per share, and return on equity), for using accounting conventions, and for delivering against these expectations.

This approach would enable internal units to provide their best

FIGURE 9-8

Financial Report: Cost and Effectiveness of Global Consumer Marketing Utility

Cost of marketing ($ millions)	
Direct cost of employees	$60
Talent market charges (net)	(40)
Net cost of marketing	$20

Utilities charged to users	Actual	Transferred	Unrecovered
(based on volume used)			
Advertising	$250	$227	$23
Promotion	125	120	5
Market research	50	48	2
	$425	$395	$30

User customer satisfaction index	Actual	Target	Last Year
(1 to 10; result of surveys)	7.3	8.0	7.0

Unrecovered costs (overhead)	
Marketing costs	$30
Utility charges	20
Total unrecovered costs	$50
Target unrecovered costs	80
Surplus/(shortfall)	$30

estimates of future results, as opposed to gaming their budgets. The objective, then, is to make or exceed the target rather than to make budget. The approach would also provide greater clarity to all parties, including top management and line management, concerning the real economics of different units. This should improve decision making. But most important, it would provide top management with new tools to motivate economic behaviors.

The ability to set target returns, focused on total contribution and contribution per employee, is an aspiration-based model. It puts the burden largely on the self-directed managers of the units. It is up to them to figure out how to meet these aspirations. This approach focuses managers on activities they actually can influence rather than on activities they can't—such as negotiating overhead allocations for activities over which they have absolutely no control.

At the same time, it prevents them from deciding to cut discretionary spending on future wealth-creating initiatives simply to meet their budgets. Rather, to make target returns, they will need to invest in the intangibles that can improve the day-to-day performance of the people they manage. Meanwhile, through the dynamic management processes described in Chapter 5, major short-term/long-term trade-off decisions can be firmly in the hands of senior and top management.

For the purpose of investing in portfolios of special initiatives, the use of an opportunity-based model for pricing talent is advantageous. It provides multiple advantages over the inclusion of these initiatives in line budgets. For one, it ensures that the decision to invest or not is made by people with sufficient perspective to make the short- versus long-term trade-off. Second, by pricing talent at its value, senior and top management will better understand the real costs of pursuing such initiatives (while fairly providing returns to the units that contribute talent).

Third, it keeps major investment decisions segregated from operating decisions, thus enabling better comparisons between the operating results of different frontline units. Fourth, it makes it clear how much the firm, in aggregate, is investing in the future. It also makes the trade-off decisions explicit rather than implicit.

Using this approach, top managers would have powerful tools to control earnings, but they would take a different form: Under this model, control would be exercised by putting pressure on making the target versus making the budget. This approach has the advantage of taking away the ability of managers to game a traditional budget system. To make the target, a unit would truly need to perform better.

There is one additional lever top management can use both to maintain control of enterprisewide earnings and to motivate good behaviors. As we will describe in the next chapter, companies can create a firmwide compensation pool for partners, and the size of the pool would vary directly with the company's performance (as measured by total profit and profit per employee, net of capital charges). It's still another way of redesigning the firm for the 21st century.

10

ROLE-SPECIFIC PERFORMANCE EVALUATION

THE HIERARCHICAL MANAGERS in most large firms today determine how the people under them should work together. Since different managers have different personalities, the work is often organized quite differently.

One may organize his or her particular business silo so that the people in it work quite well with one another. Another may not. When cross-silo collaboration is required, the two groups may find themselves in conflict or competition. Even when there is goodwill on both sides, the costs of coordinating their work may be extreme. Using matrix structures, co-heads, and other patchwork fixes to solve this problem often just adds to the dysfunction.

We believe there is a better way.

Earlier in the book we described several structural solutions to promote cross-silo collaboration. For the solutions to help people work together, those structures need to be reinforced by a consistent system of performance metrics and performance evaluations, standards, and protocols. The key to this system's effectiveness is what we call "role-specific performance evaluations." In these evaluations, definitions are set for what constitutes "superior," "good," "average," and "poor" performance in a specific role.

We believe that by defining how people with different roles should work with one another and holding them accountable for doing so, you can make it in their mutual self-interest to collaborate effectively. Simply by reducing the costs of coordinating work with one another, you can simultaneously reduce much of the unproductive complexity of the organization. Furthermore, "one-company governance" begins to become a "one-company culture." Indeed, by institutionalizing how people are evaluated and developed, the "partnership at the top" can be turned from words into an operating reality.

We believe that enterprisewide standard definitions should be created for all of the important roles in the organization. Through this, the roles and responsibilities of all the hierarchical managers are understood relative to one another: what it means to be a backbone frontline manager, a shared utility manager, a senior manager, or a top manager. Standard definitions should also exist for *all* the important professional roles in a company as well, not just for the hierarchical management roles.

Once you have created standardized role definitions, you can then define how people should make their roles and responsibilities complementary to those of their peers. By clearly designating both a backbone line hierarchy and a support structure, for instance, the relative roles of both "line" and "support" can be understood by both parties. By making the roles complementary, the costs of coordinating the work among these people are reduced. Such definition helps different parties delineate their rights to make certain decisions. If the decision concerns the amount of support that should be mobilized against a given revenue opportunity, for instance, the decision is clearly a backbone line decision. If the decision involves making changes in the operation of a shared utility, however, the decision is clearly a support decision.

To make this work, however, standards must be reinforced with performance metrics, reward systems, and compliance processes. These will motivate individuals to behave in a manner consistent with how the organization is designed to operate. Otherwise, some individuals may simply ignore the design and behave as they want. In this case, the organization will not work as intended.

To avoid this, the performance measures must be tailored to the specific roles people are expected to play. This means holding workers individually accountable and, moreover, mutually accountable for their performance. It also means using rewards systems and compliance processes to reinforce the measurement of their performance.

Role-Specific Performance Measurement

In the final chapter of the book, we will describe how an "overall master plan" can holistically define and standardize the major roles and responsibilities in an organization. Such an architecture provides a mental model for how the organization should work. Through it people will understand how their roles should operate relative to other roles.

Let's assume you've completed such design work. You have a good idea of how you want the people in the different roles to behave. Now you are ready to use role-specific performance measurement to drive the behaviors you want.

This measurement involves evaluating people against the expectations of their roles, as well as against the performance of other people in similar roles throughout the enterprise. In this you are not only comparing likes to likes but individuals against institutionalized standards of performance.

In the New Jersey/Long Island branch unit described in Chapter 3, for instance, every person holding a job that requires subjective judgment would receive an annual role-specific performance evaluation. The New Jersey/Long Island manager would be evaluated, as would the other 60-odd frontline managers in the Global Consumer Bank. The support executives reporting up to that manager would also be evaluated against people in equivalent roles throughout the Global Consumer Bank. All the Small Business managers reporting up to frontline managers, for example, would be evaluated as a group. All the 100 branch managers within the New Jersey/Long Island geography would be similarly evaluated.

Such approaches can work with professionals as well as with managers. One can create role-specific performance measures for investment bankers, petroleum engineers, lawyers, research scientists, or accountants, for instance. In a large company there will be dozens, if not hundreds, of roles with sufficiently large populations to make this approach workable.

In role-specific performance measurement, the art is in the design of performance metrics for each role. This design is based on a detailed understanding of the talents and behaviors that should be exhibited by outstanding practitioners in those roles. In other words, you need role models, and you want to motivate these role models to exhibit the behaviors and to develop and demonstrate their talents. Once people know what "superior" performance looks like, they can try to model it themselves.

It is particularly important to use performance metrics to motivate collaborative behaviors for roles that come in pairs. For example, managers of distribution capabilities need to work closely with product managers, investment bankers need to work closely with capital market specialists, and so forth. In such paired roles, it is essential to design performance metrics that motivate people to collaborate successfully with one another.

Evaluating Populations

The approach we are advocating is very different from the evaluation processes most commonly used. Traditionally, individuals are evaluated on their personal performance by the person they report to. We believe that individuals should be evaluated not only on their personal achievements, but also on their contributions to the success of others. Furthermore, rather than being evaluated by a single manager, we feel that they should be evaluated through personnel committees.

This process adds weight to how well an individual works with others, which in turn requires a measurement beyond the ability to please one's immediate superior. It increases the weight of the opinions of a range of others and diminishes the power of an immediate superior, who might have encouraged the subordinate into selfish actions detrimental to the institution. To be sure, the assessment by one's immediate superior still carries a great deal of weight, but the opinions of others would weigh in heavily as well.

We are proposing, then, that individuals be held both individually and mutually accountable and, furthermore, that they receive two separate performance ratings: one for how well they perform as individuals and one for how well they perform when working with others. These ratings could be displayed on a performance grid (Figure 10-1) and integrated into a single performance rating, one that would compare individuals in similar roles against each other. It would also help determine compensation.

As an example, take the evaluation of the 60-odd Small Business executives in the Global Consumer Bank. As you may recall, while these executives report to the frontline managers, they are also part of the Small Business formal network.

Individual Performance Measurement

Most evaluations would begin with a financial report, in which each person in the unit would receive a report that tracks the specific financial results appropriate to the role he or she is playing. For example, each branch manager reporting up to the New Jersey/Long Island manager would receive a branch accounting report showing the unique revenues and unique costs of his or her branch. The report would also consist of even more detailed information. It might break out, for example, the split in revenue and costs between the Small Business and Consumer segments.

In the example described in Chapter 3, the Small Business executive is not a line manager but rather a staff person whose role is to promote

Performance Evaluation Grid

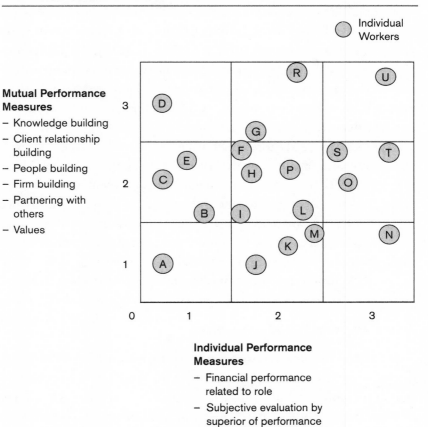

Mutual Performance Measures

- Knowledge building
- Client relationship building
- People building
- Firm building
- Partnering with others
- Values

Individual Workers

Individual Performance Measures

- Financial performance related to role
- Subjective evaluation by superior of performance versus expectations

small business across the entire geography. That person would still be judged by financial performance measures. However, in this case, you could simply add up the unique costs and unique revenues attributed to small business customers across the entire geography and, with that, compare these figures against historic results and against target returns.

Because there is no confusion about who is primarily responsible for small business economics, this is "memo accounting" rather than "double counting." In this case, it is the individual branch manager and the backbone line structure above him or her who are responsible. Other quantitative metrics, such as new account openings, product volumes cross-sold, and so on, could also be tracked in these memo reports. In memo accounting (unlike double counting), you report only on measures that a person can actually *influence*. A Small Business Marketing manager at Global Bank, for example, might receive a memo report only on volume and revenue measures for small business activities, one that doesn't show the costs of delivery at all.

The primary source for evaluating an individual's personal performance, however, would remain the subjective, personal evaluation by the person's immediate superior (in this case the backbone frontline manager). Only the person's manager understands fully what performance was expected and can therefore evaluate the individual's achievements against those expectations. The only major change we would advocate in this instance is the creation of role-specific criteria for what constitutes outstanding versus good, average, or poor performance.

Mutual Performance Measurement

What makes the approach we are advocating really different, however, is not the measurement of individual performance but rather the addition of measures that determine how well the person has contributed to the success of others and to the success of the institution at large. The Small Business executives, who are serving as staff support to the frontline managers, for example, must add value through their skills in intangibles (as well as their influence skills and project skills) rather than through sheer authority. Some corporations have 360-degree feedback tools to incorporate input from a broad group of colleagues, thereby developing an effective collaboration metric.

This raises a question: How do you determine whether a person has created intangibles and contributed to the success of others?

It takes some work to do so. For the Small Business executive in New Jersey/Long Island, that information would come from the people the executive has worked with on projects, from the people the executive has worked with in social and formal networks, and from other reports to the backbone frontline manager.

Some of the other ideas in this book can also help produce information that can be used to provide credit. For example, if you create a knowledge marketplace, it is easy to track whose contributions do well in that marketplace. However, absent taking 360-degree feedback surveys or finding new means of collecting information (for example, knowledge marketplaces), most companies lack easily quantifiable sources of information on collaboration.

In reality, often the person evaluated is the only one who really knows what he or she has contributed and who is sufficiently motivated to describe those activities in detail. The individual, then, should be asked to provide a detailed self-assessment of his or her contributions and asked for the names of the people he or she has worked most closely with.

This self-assessment serves many purposes. By designing the form to reflect what talents and behaviors constitute superior performance, it establishes standards for the role. It also establishes the range of alternatives to contribute. Completing a self-assessment causes the individual to think hard about what he or she has done well and about what he or she could have done better (including working better with others). Finally, it provides an evaluator with evidence that, if validated, lends insight into how much help the person has been able to give to others.

There is really only one way to validate a self-assessment, however, and that is to confidentially interview a reasonable sample of the people with whom the person has worked. Undertaking such confidential interviews and surveys, and interpreting the results, takes time. Who is going to do all this work?

Evaluation through Personnel Committees

When you institutionalize performance evaluations and talent development, you do not remove the person's superior from responsibility for mentoring that person and assessing his or her performance. Such responsibilities are one of the most important accountabilities a manager can exercise.

But it does mean that you need to provide processes that balance the role of the hierarchical manager to do so. Many managers have their own personal standards of performance and may evaluate their people based on their personal loyalty to them or on their willingness to obey direction at the expense of the company's larger interests. These natural human tendencies need to be counterbalanced with more processes that reflect institutional values.

The way to do this is through the use of "personnel committees." Personnel committees, which are common in many professional services companies, should be created for every significantly sized population of talent in the enterprise. In the evaluation of the Global Consumer Bank's Small Business executive's population of 60-odd people, for example, you would need to form a committee of some 6 or 7 people who would be collectively accountable for evaluating and developing everyone in this population. Generally, you would pick a committee chair with sufficient clout (and with sufficient natural interest in the group) to run a disciplined committee process with, of course, considerable help from the HR function.

How you would institutionalize the process would vary with the role. The New Jersey/Long Island frontline manager, for instance, would be the natural person to chair a committee tasked with evaluating the 100-odd branch managers operating in the committee's geography. Members of the committee would include selected direct reports to the frontline managers, including, in particular, the territorial managers to whom the branch managers report. There would be a mechanism to calibrate across reviews to ensure that the New Jersey/Long Island manager was evaluating the performance of the branch managers consistently with their peers (for example, the Mid-Atlantic manager).

Let's take a hypothetical example of the evaluation of a nonbackbone role. In this case we'll look at a committee that is reviewing the Global Consumer Bank's 60-odd population of Small Business segment staff, those who report to the various backbone frontline managers. In this situation, you would probably pick as the chair of the personnel committee for this population the formal network manager overseeing the support to this community. You would also place 6 or 7 other members on the committee, including several of the best role models you could find for the role being evaluated (either who have played the role in the past or, occasionally, an outstanding performer still playing the role).

Assuming that there are 6 members on the committee in addition to the chair, each member (except the chair) would take responsibility for evaluating 10 different individuals and for providing each of them, following the evaluation, with personalized, developmental feedback. The chairperson's time would be spent overseeing the process. Each member would be responsible for gathering and reviewing the information about each person being evaluated, including, particularly, the manager to whom the person reports.

The evaluator would recommend a rating, but a committee vote, after a debate, would determine each person's final rating. If someone actually was on the committee to be rated by the committee, it would be the chair's responsibility to serve as the evaluator. The individual would leave the room for the rating discussion and would be told the results by the chair following the meeting. We estimate that each member of the committee would spend about 10 days annually on the evaluation and development process, including interviews, committee meetings, and feedback processes (or about a day per person evaluated). This time commitment would vary by company or role being evaluated, perhaps ranging from 5 to 10 days. Generally, people would serve on only one personnel committee at a time. As people changed roles, the committee responsible for evaluating them would, or course, change as well.

We recognize that this process is both far different from and more time-intensive than traditional performance evaluation processes. It is especially so considering that the process would eventually include most of the firm's professionals and managers. But we believe that it is more than worthwhile, given that the process not only evaluates people but also promotes development and collaboration enterprisewide. If

FIGURE 10-2

Completed Performance Evaluation Grid

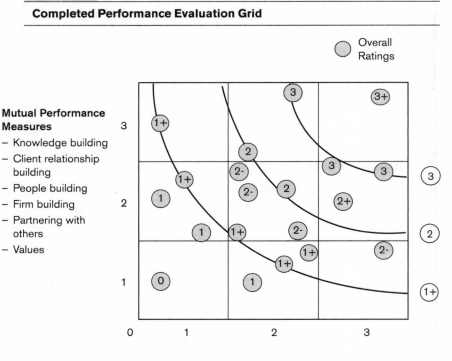

you believe that you can boost profit per employee by making such organizational changes, then investing time in evaluating, developing, and motivating talent is one of the highest-return activities a firm can undertake.

At the end of this process you would have a complete evaluation grid (Figure 10-2), tiered performance ratings for the entire population, and a development feedback note for each person. Additional benefits would include enterprisewide standards of performance for each role, a better understanding of success for individuals to follow, and increased encouragement of collaborative behaviors. Behaviors complementary to the role would be recognized, while behaviors conflicting with the role would be discouraged.

Reward Systems

Implicit in this design is the presumption that people vary enormously in their ability to perform in their jobs. Therefore, the only way to judge a person's performance is to compare it to people in similar jobs. When you consider that a single manager may have no one else to compare a subordinate's performance to and, furthermore, may not have any experience in that person's professional discipline, it is little wonder that a manager may have difficulty assessing an employee's true performance potential.

In any normal population, the performance range between the best and the worst is usually very large. In most firms today, however, performance ratings and compensation for a given role usually do not fully reflect these differences. There are some exceptions (for example, bond trading), but for the most part a very talented person's ability to be paid for outstanding performance may be unnecessarily constrained. While the job may allow great variation in performance, the classic performance evaluation range often does not accommodate this variance. Thus, if an individual wants to achieve more, he or she will need to change roles. Too often, mediocre people who can please their bosses get paid more than people who can offer real performance in a role. Moreover, there is often little visibility beyond the person's immediate superior of any one person's talents, potential to grow, or readiness to take on greater roles. Promotions, meanwhile, are often based as much on "time in grade" as on performance and potential.

All of this changes, however, when one institutionalizes the process of evaluation and development. The ability to compare similar roles across the company enables one to truly differentiate superior, good, average, and poor performance. Since they are vetted through an institutional process, the resulting performance ratings have greater value in determining compensation and promotions. Similarly, developmental feedback takes on greater weight, since it reflects not only individual but institutional norms as well. Meanwhile, both outstanding and poor performance become much more visible.

Compensation practices will vary by company, by industry, and by professional role, of course. Having said that, though, an approach like the one described in this chapter can enable sharp differentiation in the ability to reward superior performance.

Evaluating and Rewarding Senior Populations

There is one special population for which a committee-based, role-specific, performance evaluation and reward system is particularly important—the senior and top managers, those who make up the partnership at the top.

Creating a formal, enterprisewide, committee-based approach to evaluating senior and top managers enables a company to institutionalize a partnership culture that is more than just words. To make it work well, you need to create a "compensation pool," the size of which being dependent on the company's overall performance (the board needs to determine both the size of the pool and the rules for how it should be distributed). Each person's share in the pool is established not only by the role he or she occupies and his or her performance in that role but also by how good a *partner* he or she is.

As we have said before, we are advocating an approach for public companies that mimics actual partnerships. In this case, the CEO would chair the committee evaluating the top management group. Certain top executives, meanwhile, would chair the personnel committees that evaluate the senior partners. In Global Bank's case, the Global Consumer Bank executive would likely chair the committee that would evaluate the senior partners in the Global Consumer group.

Members in these committees, however, would be drawn from across the enterprise. The personnel committee evaluating the senior partners in the Global Consumer group of Global Bank, for instance, would include the senior executives not just from the consumer group but from other areas as well. Thus, the performance evaluations of even these senior populations would be institutionalized.

The evaluating process for these senior populations would be similar to those of the more junior populations, although the stakes, and the time expended per person, would be far greater. By necessity, the comparisons would be in terms of contributions as partners rather than comparisons in terms of similar jobs. Senior populations across a global megainstitution will be diverse, of course, including not only backbone line managers but also managers running support utilities, owners of formal networks, and so forth.

Taking this route, you put real teeth into one-company governance, one-company culture, and a partnership at the top. As evaluators gather information from across the enterprise (and even from clients), illustrating both good and bad behaviors, the actions of individuals suddenly have consequences. People who may be top individual performers but who behave selfishly will find themselves downgraded relative to individuals who perform similarly but who are more effective collaborators.

Said differently, the idea is to make senior people behave so that they complement rather than conflict with one another. It is the behavior at the top that determines whether the organization performs for the greater good or is driven instead by individuals with their own agendas.

Values and Consequence Management

In today's world (and more than ever before), bad behaviors can have severe consequences. Public companies live in a fishbowl. Every action is visible. A bad decision by a senior manager can lead to negative publicity that can undermine a firm's reputation with shareholders, customers, and employees. Or it can lead to lawsuits, which not only can damage the company's reputation but also lead to enormous financial losses.

Like it or not, companies are responsible for how their employees behave. The first line of defense is a company's values. Values establish the way "we do business around here." If followed, these values will support behaviors of which the company will always be proud. Values reflect a company's attitudes toward its customers, its employees, its competitors, and the public at large.

But values are not enough. Problems usually arise not when the values are wrong but when companies do not attach consequences to violating those values or when they reward not adhering to those values. If the company espouses collaboration as a value, for instance, but rewards selfish behaviors, it will get the behaviors it rewards. The same is true for standards and protocols.

What's the lesson in this? That values, standards, and protocols must be reinforced not just by performance metrics and reward systems but also by consistently applied consequence management processes. Like any punishment system, the punishment must fit the crime. For example, clear violations against values (for example, taking an illegal action) usually results in termination of employment.

Most violations against values, standards, and protocols, however, are less clear-cut. Often they are exhibited through playing corporate politics, gaming the system, or passive-aggressive behaviors such as glad-handing people while stabbing them in the back.

This is why interview-based and committee-based processes are so critical: Patterns of bad behaviors are generally hard to find through quantitative metrics. Moreover, a person's hierarchical boss often does not observe the worst behaviors. And even if the boss does see it, he or she may find it hard to depersonalize the feedback so that the offender understands it is the behavior, rather than the person, that is the problem. Besides, people are often loyal to their subordinates. They turn a blind eye to their failings. In contrast, when negative messages are delivered through a committee process, the feedback carries more weight. It reflects institutional, not individual, behavioral norms. And if the punishment is less compensation or a delayed promotion, the bad behaviors are far less likely to persist.

If individuals don't want to change their behaviors, on the other hand, they are likely to leave the company, voluntarily or involuntarily. In either event, the firm's values, standards, and protocols will be maintained.

Under the approach we are advocating, the personnel committees of the firm become the custodians of the firm's values, standards, and protocols. How they develop and evaluate people will reinforce the desired values and discourage bad behaviors.

PART V

CONCLUSION

11

ORGANIZATION DESIGN AS STRATEGY

IN THE LAST DECADE, organizational design has often amounted to little more than an afterthought, or, alternatively, a ceaseless reshuffling of players without much purpose. But today the time has come for corporate leaders to consider an optimal organizational design not only as a strategic imperative but also as a high-return opportunity for investment.

To be sure, the design of an organization cannot in and of itself mitigate all the complexity that the world generates today. But a well-thought-out intuitive design can help an organization navigate that complexity deftly. It's much like the weather and ships on the sea: You cannot prevent storms at sea, but you can design a ship that will take the brunt of a storm's fury and still make its way home to port.

But how do you undertake such a design and put it in place?

Overall Architecture

Building an organization that can navigate successfully in the digital age begins with the creation of a "master plan," one that integrates the elements of organizational design into a holistic mental model. The model describes how your organization should operate at a specific point in the future.

In designing such a plan, you probably won't have the luxury of beginning with a clean sheet of paper (unless it's a new company). Think of yourself instead as an urban planner, one who must deal with the city as it exists. The first step, then, is to understand the legacy organization surrounding you. This is best done through an in-depth "diagnostic"—that is, a study that will reveal how the company is organized today.

Enterprisewide Organizational Diagnostic

We've been struck by how *few* leaders really understand how their organizations work at the front line. Many leaders may have grown up in only one organizational "silo" or with only one dominant functional perspective or even in a different company entirely and therefore don't know how their organizations really work. They may think they know, but all you need to do is to take them down a couple of layers into various organizational silos to see that many of their assumptions about what people do and how they work together are wrong. Yes, they may have some familiarity with hierarchical roles, but usually they have very little real knowledge about how key processes work, how professionals work, how people acquire their knowledge, how talent gets assigned, how people are evaluated, and so on.

Undertaking an enterprisewide organizational diagnostic involves understanding how all the elements of the organization work—what works well and what works poorly, particularly in terms of the company's success in the external marketplace. Undertaking an organizational diagnostic, therefore, involves getting an understanding of both the internal organization and how well it matches the requirements for success externally.

An internal diagnostic requires interviewing professionals and managers in different geographies, businesses, and functions to find out what works well and what does not. In large companies such interviewing can't be comprehensive, but the overriding objectives can be met by taking "core samples"—for example, by interviewing the chain of command in two or three silos to understand how they really work. Such interviews can be supplemented by a wide variety of analytic techniques, including a number of survey approaches, for example, "social network analysis." This type of survey helps you understand how information and knowledge flow through the organization and where the congestion points and the "undoable jobs" reside. Again, such analyses can't be taken comprehensively but rather should be undertaken through representative sampling.

You also need to analyze the global forces at work in the economy and how they drive your opportunities, challenges, and requirements to adapt. Gaining this understanding will also involve extensive external interviewing—particularly of customers.

Such an internal and external diagnostic may take several months to complete. However, it can usually pay off quickly, since this process often yields immediate ways to make the organization function better (often by simply changing people and roles). But it will also reveal the fundamental structural flaws. The immediate fixes may be small ones, just as an urban planner may improve traffic generally by strategically placing a few one-way streets. Fundamental problems are different. The urban planner may be recommending mass transit—and the equivalent suggestion in an organization will take time and the creation of a master plan.

Master Plan

Just as a house can be designed in a Colonial, Tudor, or Victorian style, there are many alternatives to choose from when considering how to organize a particular company. The trick is to find the one that best fits the needs of the people who work in the company with the needs required to compete in the external world.

At the end of the diagnostic, you should be able to sketch out a number of alternative master organizational plans. Each alternative master plan should show the different ways the organization could work three to five years into the future.

Each alternative organizational architecture you develop will be composed of a number of different organizational elements. Most of these elements have been discussed in the earlier chapters of this book. Each alternative, for example, should describe how hierarchical authority is going to be used to manage the various populations of people in the company and to govern at the top. It should define the balance between "one company" and "many businesses," which, if any, shared utilities to create, and how enterprisewide processes should work. You should also draw some conclusions about the role you want standards, protocols, and values to play.

We believe an organizational architecture should also include nontraditional elements. Examples of such elements are the design of formal network structures; structures and processes to create and mobilize knowledge (for example, knowledge marketplaces); and structures and processes to develop and mobilize talent (for example, talent marketplaces). We also believe the design process should address how financial reporting works and how performance evaluation works, because these elements are critical in the organization.

Just as a city plan incorporates formal zoning districts, building codes, and inspection rules, so too can a company formalize its organizational architecture. Once formalized, moreover, these standards become business as usual. They don't have to continuously be reinvented. They're easy for anyone in the organization to follow. And they even allow for creativity, within certain bounds.

Of course, you need to shape these ideas to best fit your organization. An overall architecture requires making choices for how all of these ideas would work together. Making these choices at the enterprise level is essential for companies that want to head in the direction of one-company governance. If a company wants to continue to operate as a series of silos, then the design choices should be made silo by silo. But our point of view, of course, is that you should first design the overall architecture at the corporate level and then design the architecture of silo organizations to complement that structure.

What choices are right for any given company will depend on its own particular circumstances. The best urban plan for a Paris will be different than the best choices for a Chicago. But just as it is important to consider not just roads but also transit lines, power grids, water lines, and sewage systems in an urban plan, it is important to think about how line management hierarchical authority will be used, how corporate governance will work, how strategies will be created, how talent will be mobilized, and so on. Which of these elements should change first will also depend on the individual company's circumstances. In a poorly managed company, it may be hard to construct a master plan that accomplishes much more than simply streamlining the existing hierarchy and moving to a one-company governance model. Other companies may want to make only a few modifications to their existing models. They may want to standardize role definitions, for instance, while leaving their existing hierarchical structures intact. In this case, they may want to focus their energy on such elements as formal networks and talent marketplaces, which are dependent on standardized role definitions to work effectively. Well-managed companies may want to focus on changing financial reporting. The end product, once all the design choices are made, is an overall architecture.

Once created, the overall architecture should be viewed as a target. It is, of necessity, a paper plan at a high level of abstraction. As long as it is a paper plan, it is easy to modify as conditions change or better information or thinking becomes available. Realistically, a master plan should be viewed as a working document, one that can be adapted to changing conditions.

Once the organizational capabilities are actually built, however, they become a part of the reality of the organization (just as once a road is built, it becomes a part of the reality of a city). A badly designed road becomes an inconvenience that the occupants of a city must live with, unless it creates such havoc that it must be redesigned and rebuilt. The same is true for badly designed parts of organizations.

In addition to an overall architecture, therefore, you also need to develop a "game plan." This should describe how to put the target organization in place and how to prevent design flaws from having unintended systemwide effects. It is important, therefore, to think through the sequence: Which capabilities should we build first and how should we incorporate the lessons we are learning along the way so that we can make appropriate midcourse corrections. If you run into unexpected problems while building a road system, after all, you want to be able to fix those problems before you complete the entire system.

Game Plan

A game plan works backward from the target organization to the present day. You start with envisioning how you would like your organization to look by a certain point in the future and work back to the present. That way you can estimate what it will take to get to the desired destination on time.

Part of this game plan will include steps you can take along the way to make the existing organization better immediately and in the near future. Make sure, however, that these are not quick-fix add-ons that will have unintended consequences, but that they are instead actual first steps toward a destination you are sure you want to reach.

The first part of the game plan for a poorly managed company, for instance, may well be to streamline the hierarchy and simultaneously remove both people and organizing structures that would block the establishment of the target organization. In urban planning terms, think of it as removing blockages from roads and removing obsolete buildings. While there may be some short-term pain involved, it will usually lead to immediate benefits and will enable you to move far more quickly and effectively than you could move without those changes.

The game plan should be owned by leadership. Most leaders,

though, will need a program office to oversee its implementation. The game plan itself should include each of the major organizational initiatives required to put the target organization in place. Each initiative will require people to set the timetable, including starting dates, milestone dates (to check against progress), and decision dates to make go/no-go decisions, as well, of course, as a target end date. Because many initiatives may depend on successful completion of other initiatives, the game plan needs to define the dependencies between initiatives as well as allow for contingency planning (should a key initiative run into unexpected difficulties or delays).

Building a new financial reporting system, for instance, is a very long lead time activity, and it can take many years to complete. Yet having a new system may be essential for driving better economic behaviors by line managers or making a short-term talent marketplace practically effective. If delays develop in building such a system, then you must make other adjustments to how you implement those dependent elements. You probably want to use interim approaches until the more fundamental fix becomes available.

Designing and Building Organizational Capabilities

When you are ready to build your new organizational capability, you need to design it with all the detail of an architectural "blueprint."

Most megainstitutions are simply too big to design all at once (except the design of the firm's one-company governance). Rather, you need to develop prototype designs for parts of the whole organization. Use the prototypes to help you understand the enterprisewide implications, and then, when you are confident you know what you're doing, complete the design for the entire enterprise and roll it out.

In other words, the four stages of building an organizational capability are the same as those that are used for any portfolio-of-initiatives undertaking:

1. Diagnosis and Directional Strategy

2. Design

3. Prototype

4. Scale

This exercise is actually less perilous than similar external market-place initiatives. External initiatives, since they are exposed to uncontrollable risks, can create large losses if they don't work. Organizational initiatives involve only internal risk. The losses in the case of internal reorganization are usually opportunity costs rather than large exposures to financial losses. This makes the rewards of organizational initiatives far more attractive than most external strategic initiatives. They represent unconverted opportunities, chances to mobilize unused mind power, and areas in which to eliminate unproductive spending. These are gains that require very little new investment of labor or capital (that is, they are "rents").

To explain how a portfolio-of-initiatives approach would be used to build an organizational capability, let's look again at the Global Consumer Bank.

* **Stage 1. Diagnosis and Directional Strategy.** For each separate organizational intervention, the starting point is undertaking a "deep diagnostic dive" to understand how the existing organization actually works today. It's particularly important in such deep dives to get a perspective on the organization from people operating in different levels of the hierarchy and from people in different roles.

    In Global Bank's case, let's assume that leadership had decided to use the Global Consumer Bank as the prototype for creating a backbone line structure for the entire enterprise. Given the large size of the Global Consumer Bank, it was decided to go deep (that is, take core samples) in the East Coast region as a proxy for what was going on in the other branch-based regions. In addition, deep dives were also taken in the Mortgage and Credit Card businesses and in the Finance and Marketing support functions. Each of these deep dives would, in turn, employ a variety of diagnostic approaches including interviews, surveys, and financial analyses. The objective would be to understand and map out the roles, processes, and decision making of the entire division and to understand the economics of different organizational units. In addition, lighter-touch diagnostics would be undertaken in the regions, businesses, and support functions not undergoing deep dives in order to verify that these units did not have unique circumstances that would require closer examination.

The diagnostic would provide the very specific identification of the core organizational issues facing the division in getting its hierarchy to work more effectively. The next step would be to create alternative organizing approaches to address these issues (for example, making geography the backbone line structure versus making product the backbone line structure). At the end of this phase, management would decide from among these alternatives. These decisions would then be codified into a directional design (that is, "rough sketch") of the target organization and the game plan for putting it in place.

- **Stage 2. Design.** Assuming top management approved the directional strategy, the next step would be to take the rough-sketch design to the operating level of detail. Part of this effort would involve designing the prototype, which for Global Bank, we'll assume is the East Coast region. The detailed design would consider how to simulate working with shared utility managers, the specific roles of dedicated and distributed executives, and so on. As part of this effort, a detailed blueprint of the target new backbone line structure would be created, roles would be standardized and defined, and new management processes would be installed, including interim financial reporting and performance measurement processes. At the end of this stage, the company would decide whether the emerging design is validating the original directional strategy and, if not, what changes need to be made.

- **Stage 3. Prototype.** Next, the company would put the prototype into action to see how well it works and to reveal unexpected problems. An important part of this initiative, of course, is to develop and test approaches for changing "the hearts, the minds, and the behaviors" of the workers in the East Coast region.

    Not every design initiative will require prototyping. In some cases, the desire to move quickly may outweigh caution, or prototyping may be impracticable, such as when a company moves to a one-company governance structure. In such situations, though, "10,000-mile check-ups" come in handy. These make sure the organization is working, and they offer the opportunity to make mid-course corrections as needed. When you are trying to change the behaviors of thousands of people, however, and not just dozens, prototyping makes sense.

    The end of this stage marks the last opportunity to easily make changes to the design. Usually tinkering with the design to reflect lessons learned in the prototype can help improve it. Now you can start thinking about extending the design beyond the initial unit. In Global Bank's case, this would mean extending the rollout from the East Coast region to the South, Midwest, and West, and the rest of the world. It would also mark the time to start the detailed design work for the non-branch-based units of the Global Consumer Bank (such as the Credit Card and Mortgage groups).

- **Stage 4. Scale.** The last stage is "scaling." In organizational design, this means rolling out the organizational changes through the entire company while winning the hearts, minds, and behaviors of the company's employees.

    This would be the time to explore the introduction of a backbone line structure into Global Bank's other business areas (Global Capital Markets & Investment Banking, Global Wealth Management, and Global Securities Services). After all, a backbone line structure will have to work differently in an investment bank or in a securities services business than in a retail branch network, and therefore the design requires going through a separate stage gate process.

Hearts, Minds, and Behaviors

What do we mean by "hearts, minds, and behaviors"? Organizations are about people interacting with one another. Unless the people in an organization become better at this, the new organizational design is worthless.

Improving the quality of those interactions while reducing unproductive interactions is the goal. In fact, when an organizational design works, the people in it don't even think about the design of the organization at all—any more than people in a city think about the benefits of urban planning as they stroll around public parks or make an easy commute home.

But while most people appreciate the benefits of good design, they also hate change. Human beings in an organization adopt mindsets and behaviors that enable them to survive and prosper within that organization. Changing how any organization works, even a dysfunctional one, involves disruption. Without knowing why they need to change, what changes are expected, what the benefits and the penalties are for not changing, people are reluctant to change their behaviors. Therefore, you need more than an improved organizational design to bring your company into the digital age. You need to get your people to embrace the changes. You need to win their hearts and minds and reinforce the changes by creating mechanisms to permanently change their behaviors.[1]

Winning Hearts and Minds

How do you do that? One way is by beginning the design process with extensive interviewing. This helps you understand the shortcoming of the present organization as it is seen by the people who work in it.

Then, as you work your way through the design process, you can continue to involve the people who will be affected, by making them part of the problem-solving process. From this you not only get a better design but you also get the enthusiasm of the people who have helped create the design that emerges.

To win the hearts and minds of *all* the people requires that you first win over the people who are most respected and powerful in the organization. You need to convert the key influence leaders (who may or may not be the hierarchical leaders). One-on-one sessions are often critical to getting these key leaders onboard. They need to understand the roles you expect them to play and the behaviors you expect them to exhibit before you announce the changes you plan to make. These influential people should be part of the prototype process so that you will be able to refine the design with their input before you attempt to scale it.

While it is impractical to talk to everyone one-on-one, you do need to communicate the decisions to everyone. All employees need to understand how the new organization will affect them personally. By designing the organization this way, individuals can learn the roles they are expected to play, what behaviors they are expected to adopt, and why the change makes sense.

Our experience has shown that it is impossible for management to overcommunicate its intentions while it is in the process of making organizational changes. You need to celebrate heroes and heroines. You need to trumpet success stories. You need to explain midcourse corrections. You need to reinforce the logic of the change. You need to explain the process. And you need to manage expectations, particularly concerning when changes are coming and how long the change process will last.

While all this may seem obvious, managers often fail to spend the time and energy to win the hearts and minds of their people.

Changing Behaviors

The real benefits come when behaviors change. Some of the behavioral changes will come simply from winning the hearts and minds of the employees. But to really change behaviors, you need to make it in the self-interest of each individual to do so.

To do this, the hierarchical leaders must hold their people accountable for behaving in accordance with how the organization is designed to work. This presumes, of course, that the leaders are onboard with the change (which is why it is important to put the right people in the right roles and to remove people who won't get onboard).

But you can't rely on supervision alone. Self-directed people will exercise their own judgment. In other words, you can't just tell them how to behave, you need to motivate them. And you can do that best through performance metrics.

We believe you can use performance metrics to motivate people to work well together, and in doing so, you can also enhance the effectiveness of hierarchical authority. This is the way to drive performance while simultaneously making it in the self-interest of people to collaborate with one another. You can also reduce much of the unproductive complexity of the organization simply by reducing the costs of employees' coordinating work with one another.

Because such systems drive behaviors, an essential part of any game plan for organizational change must include changes in the way performance is measured and the way people are evaluated. Unfortunately, putting in place fundamental revisions to financial performance measurement and performance evaluations (such as described in the previous two chapters) will take years, not months. But organizational changes should not wait. The stakes are simply too high. We advocate instead that you develop interim approaches that move in the directions we describe—even if you can't change the financial systems and performance evaluation systems overnight.

Conclusion

We believe that the opportunities to create better organizations have never been greater. At stake are the opportunities to increase profit per employee and to increase the number of employees who can work profitably together. For a large company, the value of doing so can literally be in the tens of billions of dollars of increased market value.

We believe also that most companies will find it exceptionally rewarding to invest in designing and building organizations that better fit the digital age. Such an investment will usually represent the highest returns, relative to the costs and risks, as compared to almost any alternative investment. This is because high returns can be earned without making significant new investments of labor or capital. Of course, such design work will require a significant investment in the energy and focus of the company's leadership.

Huge investments have been made in designing better ways for employees to do labor-intensive work, such as engineering the design of call centers or plants. Companies have also made huge investments in such activities as designing new products. We believe the time has come for applying such levels of investment in designing how thinking-intensive work is undertaken within an organization. The challenges may be great, the journey may be long and sometimes daunting, but the profits will be even greater, and the future, brighter.

ENDNOTES

Preface and Acknowledgments

1. Harold J. Leavitt, *Top Down: Why Hierarchies Are Here to Stay and How to Manage Them More Effectively* (Boston: Harvard Business School Press, 2004), p. 63.

Introduction

1. "We" refers to Lowell Bryan's coauthors for *Race for the World: Strategies to Build a Great Global Firm*: Jane Fraser, Jeremy Oppenheim, and Wilhelm Rall (Boston: Harvard Business School Press, 1999).
2. This list of top 150 companies means the top 150 companies *each year*. Therefore, the list of companies keeps changing year to year as individual companies move on and off the list.
3. David Ricardo, *On the Principles of Political Economy and Taxation*, 3rd ed. (London: John Murray, Albemarle-Street, 1821), Chap. 2, "On Rent."

Chapter 1

1. Net Future Institute (NFI) Research, "Business Workload Too Heavy," press release September 26, 2006, and "Managers Overloaded with Communication," press release August 16, 2006, Madbury, N.H.
2. Patrick Butler, Ted W. Hall, Alistair M. Hanna, Lenny Mendonca, Byron Auguste, James Manyika, and Anupam Sahay, "A Revolution in Interaction," *McKinsey Quarterly*, no. 1 (1997): 4–23.
3. Survey of 7,827 global business executives, *McKinsey Quarterly* (June 2005).
4. W. Brian Arthur, *Increasing Returns and Path Dependence in the Economy (Economics, Cognition, and Society)* (Ann Arbor: University of Michigan Press, 1994).

Chapter 2

1. Eric D. Beinhocker, *The Origin of Wealth: Evolution, Complexity, and the Radical Remaking of Economics* (Boston: Harvard Business School Press, 2006).
2. In the interest of being brief, we have condensed the thinking of many of the world's greatest economists into a few paragraphs. John Roberts in *The Modern Firm: Organization Design for Performance and Growth* does a very good job of summarizing this thinking in a single chapter of his book. The leading economists whose thinking we drew upon in this short history include particularly Adam Smith, *An Inquiry into the Nature and Causes of the Wealth of Nations*, vol. 2 (New York: Oxford University Press USA, 1976, originally published in 1776); Roland H. Coase, "The Nature of the Firm," *Economica*, vol. 4 (November 1937): 386–405; and Kenneth Arrow, *The Limits of Organization* (New York: Norton, 1974).
3. Roland Coase is widely credited with focusing attention on the economic importance of interaction costs in his treatise "The Nature of the Firm," *Economica*, vol. 4 (November 1937): 386–405.
4. John Micklethwait and Adrian Wooldridge have written a fascinating book called *The Company: A Short History of a Revolutionary Idea* (New York: Random House/Modern Library, 2003). This book is filled with insights and interesting facts for those really interested in how companies came to exist and have evolved over time.
5. Alfred D. Chandler, Jr., *Scale and Scope: The Dynamics of Industrial Capitalism* (Cambridge: Harvard University/Belknap Press, reprint edition, 2004).
6. Again, you will find the details of these developments in *The Company* by John Micklethwait and Adrian Wooldridge.
7. See note 4.
8. The formula for the number of bilateral relationships given N number is $(N^2 - N)/2$.
9. Malcolm Gladwell, *The Tipping Point: How Little Things Can Make a Big Difference* (New York: Little, Brown, 2002).

Chapter 3

1. We use the term "distributed" to refer to a person who has a full-time job devoted to a particular support role, such as HR, who reports to a single manager but who is also responsible for being a "core" member of a formal network in his or her support specialty. In this distributed role, the person has the responsibility for "pulling" support from that formal network for the benefit of the unit he or she is supporting and for being an effective member of that network.
2. We use the term "dedicated" to refer to a person who has a full-time job in a support function devoted to serving a single organizational unit. Although the person reports to a manager in his or her respective function, a dedicated

executive is responsible for serving the organizational unit being supported with a "client services" mentality.

3. A "table of organization" defines the number of people in an organization and the roles they play. It creates the standards to reinforce the parallel definition of roles and prevents managers from simply adding people and creating their own roles. Not all organizational units need these tables, but they are essential if you want to enforce standards that limit the ability of individual managers to design their own organization (that is, if you want a backbone line hierarchy or a support function to have strictly defined roles). They are also essential for managing organizations (such as the retail bank's frontline units) of labor-intensive work for which consistent execution is critical. The ability to pull staff from a talent marketplace provides the means for line managers to get more support if they need it, if the table of organization prevents them from simply adding a support role.

4. Richard Dobbs, Keith Leslie, and Lenny Mendonca, "Building the Healthy Corporation," *McKinsey Quarterly,* no. 3 (2005): 63–71.

Chapter 4

1. Richard Dobbs, Keith Leslie, and Lenny Mendonca, "Building the Healthy Corporation," *McKinsey Quarterly,* no. 3 (2005): 63–71.

2. Adam Smith worried about "agency" issues and was concerned that hired managers would not bring the same "anxious vigilance" to their companies as owner-managers. *An Inquiry into the Nature and Causes of the Wealth of Nations,* vol. 2 (New York: Oxford University Press, 1976; originally published in 1776).

3. Large global accounting and law firms, for liability reasons, are often organized as a series of country-based partnerships overlaid with a strong one-firm governance board or committee for such processes as branding, risk management, and coordinating cross-geographic client services.

4. Daniel Bernoulli, "Exposition of a New Theory on the Measurement of Risk," *Econometrica,* vol 22 (1954): 23–36; Ralph O. Swalm, "Utility Theory: Insights into Risk Taking," *Harvard Business Review* (December 1966): 123–136; and Daniel Kahneman and Amos Tversky, "Prospect Theory: An Analysis of Decision Under Risk," *Econometrica,* vol. 47, no. 2 (1979): 263–293.

5. In turn, this also makes the next layer down senior management, which expands that 20- to 30-member group to a 200- to 300-member group.

Chapter 5

1. Alfred D. Chandler, Jr., *Strategy and Structure: Chapters in the History of the American Industrial Enterprise* (Cambridge: MIT Press, reprint edition, 1969).

2. Stuart Kauffman, *At Home in the Universe: The Search for the Laws of Self-Organization and Complexity* (New York: Oxford University Press USA, reprint edition, 1996).

3. Eric D. Beinhocker, *The Origin of Wealth: Evolution, Complexity, and the Radical Remaking of Economics* (Boston: Harvard Business School Press, 2006).
4. Richard Foster and Sarah Kaplan, *Creative Destruction: Why Companies That Are Built to Last Underperform the Market—And How to Successfully Transform Them* (New York: Doubleday/Currency, 2001).
5. This is called "survivor bias," and it is one of the reasons why it is hard to succeed by imitating others who may simply have been lucky rather than smart.
6. Beinhocker, *The Origin of Wealth*.
7. Ibid.

Chapter 6

1. Robert Cross and Andrew Parker, *The Hidden Power of Social Networks: Understanding How Work Really Gets Done in Organizations* (Boston: Harvard Business School Press, 2004); Robert Cross, Jeanne Liedtka, and Leigh Weiss, "A Practical Guide to Social Networks," *Harvard Business Review* (March 2005): 81–89; and Robert Cross, Roger Martin, and Leigh Weiss, "Mapping the Value of Employee Collaboration," *McKinsey Quarterly*, no. 3 (2006): 29–41.
2. Robert Cross, Roger Martin, and Leigh Weiss, "Mapping the Value of Employee Collaboration."
3. Etienne Wenger, Richard McDermott, and William M. Snyder, *Cultivating Communities of Practice: A Guide to Managing Knowledge* (Boston: Harvard Business School Press, 2002).

Chapter 7

1. *McKinsey Quarterly* June 2005 survey of 7,827 global business executives.
2. The 2002 Universum European MBA Survey found that students are more focused on their own professional development, seeking a diverse mix of jobs in a short time span to accelerate their learning, than were the students of the past, for whom job security was a higher priority.
3. John Hagel III has emphasized that organizations need to focus more on pulling than on pushing intangible resources, such as talent, knowledge, and brand relationships. See John Seely Brown and John Hagel III, "From Push to Pull: The Next Frontier of Innovation," *McKinsey Quarterly*, no. 3 (2005): 82–91.
4. For small talent pools of 20 or fewer employees, there may be no need to have a separate, full-time person.

Chapter 8

1. Michael Idinopulos and Lee Kempler, "Do You Know Who Your Experts Are?" *McKinsey Quarterly*, no. 4 (2003): 60–69.

Chapter 9

1. Karl Erik Sveiby, *The New Organization Wealth: Managing & Measuring Knowledge-Based Assets* (San Francisco: Berrett-Koehler Publishers, 1997).

2. In 2004, the year we did most of our analysis, Wal-Mart had 1.7 million employees at $6,200 profit per worker. By 2005, it had 1.8 million earning $6,239 profit per worker. As a point of comparison, in 1995, as measured in 2005 dollars, Wal-Mart earned $5,680 per worker. In other words, Wal-Mart's profit per employee has remained approximately the same over a decade as it has nearly tripled the size of its workforce.

3. We used an average of both profit per employee and number of employees over the years 2002 to 2004 to eliminate aberrational years for individual companies. We updated the numbers for 2005, but we found rising oil prices distorting the data somewhat. We therefore decided to use 2002 to 2004 data although adding 2005 would have shown much the same picture.

4. Some argue that some megainstitutions use large amounts of contractual, temporary workers and that these should be also counted as employees. We disagree. While these workers are dependent on the company for work, they are largely fungible labor and do not, usually, undertake the intangible-intensive work that drives the company's profits, which is why the company chooses not to make them employees.

5. In their recent article, Flexi Barber and Rainer Strack propose using economic profit per employee as a metric to gauge the true performance of "people businesses." Economic profit takes profit per employee and subtracts out the costs of capital. While economic profit per employee is in principle a useful metric, we believe net income per employee is more practical because it can be taken directly from accounting statements, and it allows for straightforward comparisons of performance across companies (calculating economic profit per employee often requires internal company data). We believe a related concept, economic contribution per employee, can be a useful internal metric. See Flexi Barber and Rainer Strack, "The Surprising Economics of a 'People Business,'" *Harvard Business Review* (June 2005): 80–90.

6. The notion of a strategic control map was introduced in *Race for the World*, authored by Lowell Bryan, Jane Fraser, Jeremy Oppenheim, and Wilhelm Rall. It looks at market capitalization as a function of market-to-book ratio and total capital deployed, and it puts a spotlight on a company's strategies over time from a capital perspective. It also highlights whether a company has the market capitalization, relative to competitors, to maintain strategic control of its own destiny or is vulnerable to being acquired.

7. Baruch Lev, *Intangibles: Management, Measurement, and Reporting* (Washington, D.C: Brookings Institution Press, 2001).

8. Baruch Lev, "Sharpening the Intangibles Edge," *Harvard Business Review* (June 2004): 109–117.

9. If a factor cost is scarce and unique (that is, it can earn rents), then its value is its alternative return from deployment elsewhere (that is, its opportunity cost).

10. Lowell Bryan and Diana Farrell, *Market Unbound: Unleashing Global Capitalism* (New York: Wiley, 1996). The development of an efficient and effective global capital market and the securitization of assets have led to universal access to capital and credit for any company (public or private) with reasonable business prospects and/or creditworthiness. In particular, the risk-adjusted law of one price increasingly applies generally throughout the global capital market (that is, financial assets of equivalent risk have equivalent prices throughout the market), eliminating advantages due to enjoying privileged access to capital. The only exceptions to this are in emerging market nations lacking well-developed capital markets and the related derivative instruments.

11. Net of volume variable, attributable marginal costs are charged out to other units. The principle of using variable, marginal costs rather than full costs to transfer price fungible factor costs was long advocated by Professor John Deardon of the Harvard Business School who was one of the people credited with inventing modern cost accounting in the 1940s.

Chapter 11

1. Our colleagues in McKinsey & Company's Organizational Practice, including in particular Michael Rennie, have worked extensively on how companies can get mindsets and behaviors to change more broadly in an organization. They have identified the importance of role-modeling, defining for people in detail what jobs they are to perform, skill building, and designing reinforcing performance measures as the keys to getting mindsets and behaviors to become aligned with how the organization is designed to work. As readers will appreciate, we have kept these thoughts in our minds throughout the book as we have worked through our ideas for building a 21st-century organization.

BIBLIOGRAPHY

Books

Arrow, Kenneth J. *The Limits of Organization*. New York: Norton, 1974.

Arthur, W. Brian. *Increasing Returns and Path Dependence in the Economy (Economics, Cognition, and Society)*. Ann Arbor: University of Michigan Press, 1994.

Beinhocker, Eric D. *The Origin of Wealth: Evolution, Complexity, and the Radical Remaking of Economics*. Boston: Harvard Business School Press, 2006.

Bryan, Lowell L., Jane Fraser, Jeremy Oppenheim, and Wilhelm Rall. *Race for the World: Strategies to Build a Great Global Firm*. Boston: Harvard Business School Press, 1999.

Bryan, Lowell L., and Diana Farrell. *Market Unbound: Unleashing Global Capitalism*. New York: Wiley, 1996.

Chandler, Alfred D., Jr. *Strategy and Structure: Chapters in the History of the American Industrial Enterprise*. Cambridge: MIT Press, reprint edition, 1990. First published 1969.

——. *Scale and Scope: The Dynamics of Industrial Capitalism*. Cambridge: Harvard University/Belknap Press, reprint edition, 2004.

Cohen, Dan, and Laurence Prusak. *In Good Company: How Social Capital Makes Organizations Work*. Boston: Harvard Business School Press, 2001.

Collins, James C., and Jerry I. Porras. *Built to Last: Successful Habits of Visionary Companies*. New York: HarperCollins, 1994.

Cross, Robert, and Andrew Parker. *The Hidden Power of Social Networks: Understanding How Work Really Gets Done in Organizations*. Boston: Harvard Business School Press, 2004.

Davenport, Thomas H. *Thinking for a Living: How to Get Better Performances and Results from Knowledge Workers*. Boston: Harvard Business School Press, 2005.

Davenport, Thomas H., and Laurence Prusak. *Working Knowledge*. Boston: Harvard Business School Press, 2000.

Drucker, Peter F. *Management Challenges for the 21st Century*. New York: Harper-Collins, 2001.

Forty, George. *U.S. Army Handbook 1939–1945*. Gloucestershire, England: Sutton Publishing, reprint edition, 2003.

Foster, Richard, and Sarah Kaplan. *Creative Destruction: Why Companies That Are Built to Last Underperform the Market—And How to Successfully Transform Them*. New York: Doubleday/Currency, 2001.

Gladwell, Malcolm. *The Tipping Point: How Little Things Can Make a Big Difference*. New York: Little, Brown, 2002.

Hagel, John, III, and John Seely Brown. *The Only Sustainable Edge: Why Business Strategy Depends on Productive Friction and Dynamic Specialization*. Boston: Harvard Business School Press, 2005.

Hagel, John, III, and Marc Singer. *Net Worth*. Boston: Harvard Business School Press, 1999.

Handy, Charles. *Gods of Management: The Changing Work of Organizations*. New York: Oxford University Press USA, reprint edition, 1996. First published 1978.

Herbold, Robert. *The Fiefdom Syndrome: The Turf Battles That Undermine Careers and Companies—And How to Overcome Them*. New York: Doubleday/Currency, 2004.

Jay, Antony. *Management & Machiavelli: An Inquiry into the Politics of Corporate Life*. Austin, Tex.: Holt, Rinehart & Winston, 1968.

Kaplan, Robert S., and David P. Norton. *The Balanced Scorecard: Translating Strategy into Action*. Boston: Harvard Business School Press, 1996.

Kauffman, Stuart. *At Home in the Universe: The Search for the Laws of Self-Organization and Complexity*. New York: Oxford University Press USA, reprint edition, 1996.

Kim, W. Chan, and Renée Mauborgne. *Blue Ocean Strategy: How to Create Uncontested Market Space and Make Competition Irrelevant*. Boston: Harvard Business School Press, 2005.

Leavitt, Harold J. *Top Down: Why Hierarchies Are Here to Stay and How to Manage Them More Effectively*. Boston: Harvard Business School Press, 2004.

Lev, Baruch. *Intangibles: Management, Measurement, and Reporting*. Washington, D.C.: Brookings Institution Press, 2001.

Malone, Thomas W. *The Future of Work: How the New Order of Business Will Shape Your Organization, Your Management Style, and Your Life*. Boston: Harvard Business School Press, 2004.

McKinsey & Company, Inc., Tim Koller, Marc Goedhart, and David Wessels. *Valuation: Measuring and Managing the Value of Companies*, 4th ed. Hoboken, N.J.: Wiley, 2005.

Micklethwait, John, and Adrian Wooldridge. *The Company: A Short History of a Revolutionary Idea*. A Modern Library Chronicles Book. New York: Random House/Modern Library, 2003.

Ricardo, David. *On the Principles of Political Economy and Taxation*, 3rd ed. London: John Murray, Albemarle-Street, 1821.

Roberts, John. *The Modern Firm: Organizational Design for Performance and Growth*. New York: Oxford University Press USA, 2004.

Smith, Adam. *An Inquiry into the Nature and Causes of the Wealth of Nations*, vol. 2. New York: Oxford University Press, reprint edition, 1976. First published 1776.

Sveiby, Karl Erik. *The New Organizational Wealth: Managing & Measuring Knowledge-Based Assets*. San Francisco: Berrett-Koehler Publishers, 1997.

Thompson, Grahame F. *Between Hierarchies & Markets: The Logic and Limits of Network Forms of Organization*. New York: Oxford University Press USA, 2003.

Wenger, Etienne, Richard McDermott, and William M. Snyder. *Cultivating Communities of Practice: A Guide to Managing Knowledge*. Boston: Harvard Business School Press, 2002.

Newspapers

Immen, Wallace. "Where's the Best Place to Think About Work? Not at the Office." *Globe and Mail*, July 21, 2006, p. C1.

Thurm, Scott. "Theory & Practice: Teamwork Raises Everyone's Game—Having Employees Bond Benefits Companies More Than Promoting 'Stars.'" *Wall Street Journal*, November 7, 2005, p. B8.

Periodicals

Barber, Flexi, and Rainer Strack. "The Surprising Economics of a 'People Business.'" *Harvard Business Review* (June 2005): 80–90.

Beardsley, Scott C., Bradford C. Johnson, and James M. Manyika. "Competitive Advantage from Better Interactions." *McKinsey Quarterly*, no. 2 (2006): 53–63.

Bernoulli, Daniel. "Exposition of a New Theory on the Measurement of Risk." *Econometrica* 22 (1954): 23–36.

Brown, John Seely, and John Hagel III. "From Push to Pull: The Next Frontier of Innovation." *McKinsey Quarterly*, no. 3 (2005): 82–91.

Bryan, Lowell. "Just-in-Time Strategy for a Turbulent World." *McKinsey Quarterly*, special edition, *Risk and Resilience* (2002): 17–27.

———. "Making a Market in Knowledge." *McKinsey Quarterly*, no. 3 (2004): 101–111.

Bryan, Lowell, and Claudia Joyce. "The 21st Century Organization." *McKinsey Quarterly*, no. 3 (2005): 21–19.

Bryan, Lowell, and Michele Zanini. "Strategy in an Era of Global Giants." *McKinsey Quarterly*, no. 4 (2005): 47–59.

Bryan, Lowell, Claudia Joyce, and Leigh Weiss. "Making a Market in Talent." *McKinsey Quarterly*, no. 2 (2006): 99–109.

Butler, Patrick, Ted W. Hall, Alistair M. Hanna, Lenny Mendonca, Byron Auguste, James Manyika, and Anupam Sahay. "A Revolution in Interaction." *McKinsey Quarterly*, no. 1 (1997): 4–23.

Coase, Roland H. "The Nature of the Firm." *Economica* 4 (November 1937): 386–405.

Cross, Robert, Jeanne Liedtka, and Leigh Weiss. "A Practical Guide to Social Networks." *Harvard Business Review* (March 2005): 81–89.

Cross, Robert, Roger Martin, and Leigh Weiss. "Mapping the Value of Employee Collaboration." *McKinsey Quarterly*, no. 3 (2006): 29–41.

Dobbs, Richard, Keith Leslie, and Lenny Mendonca. "Building the Healthy Corporation." *McKinsey Quarterly*, no. 3 (2005): 63–71.

Drucker, Peter. "Knowledge-Worker Productivity: The Biggest Challenge." *California Management Review* 41 (January 1999): 79–87.

———. "Managing Oneself." *Harvard Business Review* (January 2005): 91–100.

Economist. "The New Organisation: A Survey of the Company." (January 2006).

Idinopulos, Michael, and Lee Kempler. "Do You Know Who Your Experts Are?" *McKinsey Quarterly*, no. 4 (2003): 60–69.

Kahneman, Daniel, and Amos Tversky. "Prospect Theory: An Analysis of Decision Under Risk." *Econometrica* 47, no. 2 (1979): 263–293.

Kaplan, Robert S., and David P. Norton. "The Balanced Scorecard: Measures That Drive Performance." *Harvard Business Review* (February 1992): 71–80.

Lev, Baruch. "Sharpening the Intangibles Edge." *Harvard Business Review* (June 2004): 109–117.

Mandel, Michael. "The Real Reasons You're Working So Hard . . . and What You Can Do about It." *BusinessWeek* (October 3, 2005).

Miller, Matt, and Jody Miller. "Get a Life!" *Fortune* (November 2005).

Swalm, Ralph O. "Utility Theory: Insights into Risk Taking." *Harvard Business Review* (December 1966): 123–136.

INDEX

ABOUT THE AUTHORS

Harvard MBA Lowell L. Bryan is a Director (Senior Partner) at McKinsey & Company. Over the past 30 years, he has spoken and written extensively on strategy, organization, and financial services. Bryan has been a frequent contributor to the *Wall Street Journal* editorial page and has had articles published in numerous periodicals, including the *Harvard Business Review* and the *McKinsey Quarterly*.

· · ·

A graduate of the Kellogg School of Management at Northwestern University (MBA) and of the University of Chicago (B.A. in Economics), Claudia I. Joyce is a Principal at McKinsey & Company and a core member of the Financial Services and Strategy Practices. Her work has been published on McKinsey's Knowledge Web and in the *McKinsey Quarterly*.